DEVELOPING
SELF-ACCEPTANCE

WILEY SERIES
in
BRIEF THERAPY AND COUNSELLING

Editor
Windy Dryden

Brief Rational Emotive Behaviour Therapy
Windy Dryden

Brief Therapeutic Consultations
An approach to systemic counselling
Eddy Street and Jim Downey

Brief Therapy with Couples
An integrative approach
Maria Gilbert and Diane Shmukler

Counselling Couples in Relationships
An introduction to the RELATE Approach
Christopher Butler and Victoria Joyce

Brief Group Counselling
Integrating individual and group cognitive–behavioural approaches
Michael J. Scott and Stephen G. Stradling

Brief Therapy for Post-traumatic Stress Disorder
Traumatic incident reduction and related techniques
Stephen Bisbey and Lori Beth Bisbey

Developing Self-acceptance
A brief, educational, small group approach
Windy Dryden

DEVELOPING SELF-ACCEPTANCE

A brief, educational, small group approach

Windy Dryden

Goldsmiths College, University of London, UK

JOHN WILEY & SONS

Chichester · New York · Weinheim · Brisbane · Singapore · Toronto

Copyright © 1998 by John Wiley & Sons Ltd,
Baffins Lane, Chichester,
West Sussex PO19 1UD, England

National   01243 779777
International (+44) 1243 779777
e-mail (for orders and customer service enquiries):
cs-books@wiley.co.uk
Visit our Home Page on http://www.wiley.co.uk
or http://www.wiley.com

Other Wiley Editorial Offices

John Wiley & Sons, Inc., 605 Third Avenue,
New York, NY 10158-0012, USA

WILEY-VCH Verlag GmbH, Pappelallee 3,
D-69469 Weinheim, Germany

Jacaranda Wiley Ltd, 33 Park Road, Milton,
Queensland 4064, Australia

John Wiley & Sons (Asia) Pte Ltd, 2 Clementi Loop #02-01,
Jin Xing Distripark, Singapore 129809

John Wiley & Sons (Canada) Ltd, 22 Worcester Road,
Rexdale, Ontario M9W 1L1, Canada

Library of Congress Cataloging-in-Publication Data

Dryden, Windy.
    Developing self-acceptance : a brief, educational, small group
approach / Windy Dryden.
        p.   cm. — (Wiley series in brief therapy and counselling)
    Includes bibliographical references and index.
    ISBN 0-471-98099-4 (pbk.)
    1. Self-acceptance.   2. Rational-emotive psychotherapy.   3. Group
psychotherapy.   I. Title.   II. Series.
    RC489.S43D79   1998
    616.89'152—dc21   97–38900
                                                                              CIP

British Library Cataloguing in Publication Data

A catalogue record for this book is available from the British Library

ISBN 0-471-98099-4

Typeset in 10/12pt Palatino from the author's disks by Dorwyn Ltd, Rowlands Castle, Hants
Printed and bound in Great Britain by Biddles Ltd, Guildford and King's Lynn
This book is printed on acid-free paper responsibly manufactured from sustainable forestry, in which at least two trees are planted for each one used for paper production.

CONTENTS

ABOUT THE AUTHOR

Windy Dryden   *Department of Psychology, Goldsmiths College, University of London, New Cross, LONDON SE14 6NW, UK*

Windy Dryden is Professor of Counselling at Goldsmiths College, University of London. He is also a practitioner with his own psychotherapy practice. He has written and edited numerous books in psychotherapy and counselling, and is general editor for several distinguished book series, including the Wiley Series in Brief Therapy and Counselling, in which this book appears.

FOREWORD

Windy Dryden has done it again. As has been his forte for the last two decades, he has taken one of the key theories of Rational Emotive Behavior Therapy (REBT), added to it considerably, and also shown in detail how it can be successfully implemented by teachers and therapists with their clients and with members of the public. That theory is the core theory of REBT dealing with unconditional self-acceptance (USA).

Although some other psychotherapies, notably the person-centered method of Carl Rogers, also teach clients the importance of unconditionally accepting themselves whether or not they perform important functions well, they tend to do so passively. The therapists fully accept clients with their human failings, and assume that they will consequently model themselves after the therapist, himself or herself, and accept themselves without conditions, just because they are human, are alive, and are unique individuals. Unfortunately, this indirect method of teaching is seriously flawed because it encourages most clients to honor and to respect their own existence largely because their therapist fully accepts them. But this is *conditional* self-acceptance, and depends on *others'* approval. Unconditional acceptance specifically means, as I pointed out in *A Guide to Rational Living* in 1961 and the first edition of *Reason and Emotion in Psychotherapy* in 1962, people's unqualifiedly accepting themselves *whether or not* they perform well and *whether or not* they are approved by others. Unlike Rogers' estimation of oneself, it depends on *no* external criteria, including *the therapist*'s unconditional positive regard. One gains it because, existentially, one *chooses* to have it and not because others give it to you.

Consequently, REBT practitioners not only *give* their clients unconditional acceptance but actively *teach them* how to give it to themselves. They realize that, preculiarly enough, it is a difficult concept for humans to solidly learn, even though its endorsement brings them exceptionally good results and its absence harms them in many ways. People, because of innate and learned modes of irrational, self-defeating thinking, easily give themselves global ratings, excoriate their *selves* for their dysfunctional or immoral *behaviors*, and almost always wind up with self-disesteem instead of USA. They have to forcefully interrupt this natural self-evaluating and often self-damning process, and unless they are actively-directively shown how to do this, they will rarely succeed and will fall back to conditional self-acceptance.

The beauty of Professor Dryden's book is that it shows specifically how unconditional self-acceptance can be taught not only to psychotherapy clients but to members of the general public. This is extremely important because, obviously most people who are afflicted with conditional self-acceptance or self-downing are not going to have even a few psychotherapy sessions, let alone intensive counseling, which will teach them the fundamental principles and methods of Rational Emotive Behavior Therapy (REBT) and its close cousin Cognitive Behavior Therapy (CBT). So it would be beneficial if children and adults learned some of their essentials in courses, seminars, and other mass educational settings. Eventually, as I have pointed out for almost 30 years, and as Martin Seligman has recently shown, REBT and CBT may be so thoroughly used in the classroom, in self-help groups, and in manuals, workbooks, and computer programs for the public, that many people who have emotional problems and who now require professional counseling will largely be helped by psychoeducational procedures.

This is where Windy Dryden has made a pioneering presentation in *Developing Self-acceptance*. He has provided a group of students with the first REBT-oriented course on self-affirmation that has been devised. He has included, in the ten lessons of this course, lectures, discussion, experiential exercises, handouts, and homework assignments that clearly and forthrightly present the REBT theory and practice of dealing with emotional and behavioral disturbance and of achieving self-acceptance. At the same time, he has included valuable material on two other methods that are an essential part of education in REBT – unconditional acceptance of other humans and the acquiring of high frustration tolerance. His book, therefore, shows readers how to benefit from acquiring and working at some of the main principles of REBT. But it specifically shows therapists and teachers how to present these principles to regular classes and how to make the practice of self-acceptance available to great numbers of people.

I am not sure of course how widely the excellent materials in this book will be adopted by readers, therapists, and educators. If they do become as popular as they deserve to become, however, I am reasonably sure that something of a revolution in the acquiring of unconditional self-acceptance by great numbers of people will be set in motion. Windy Dryden has done a great service to emotional education by providing us with this unusually sound and practical manual.

Albert Ellis, Ph.D.
President, Albert Ellis Institute for Rational Emotive Behavior Therapy
45 East 65th Street, New York, NY 10021-6508

SERIES PREFACE

In recent years, the field of counselling and psychotherapy has become preoccupied with brief forms of intervention. While some of this interest has been motivated by expediency – reducing the amount of help that is offered to clients to make the best use of diminishing resources – there has also developed the view that brief therapy may be the treatment of choice for many people seeking therapeutic help. It is with the latter view in mind that the Wiley Series in Brief Therapy and Counselling was developed.

This series of practical texts considers different forms of brief therapy and counselling as they are practised in different settings and with different client groups. While no book can substitute for rigorous training and supervision, the purpose of the books in the present series is to provide clear guides for the practice of brief therapy and counselling, which is here defined as lasting 25 sessions or less.

Windy Dryden
Series Editor

PREFACE

This book charts the work that I have done in running brief, structured, educationally oriented, self-acceptance groups. This work is based on the principles of REBT, an approach to counselling and psychotherapy that has a lot to offer clients with low self-esteem problems. First, it has a philosophical position on the self which stresses a person's uniqueness, humanity, complexity and fallibility. In this way, REBT advocates self-acceptance rather than self-esteem. Second, it argues that this position can be taught and learned in a short period of time. Third, it holds that clients can learn and practise a wide range of methods to facilitate the acquisition of a self-acceptance philosophy and its integration into the belief system of a person.

The book is divided into two parts. In the first part I present the theoretical and organizational bases for the work. Thus, in Chapters 1 and 2 I present an overview of REBT theory for those who are unfamiliar with current thinking in this therapeutic approach. In Chapter 3 I review the role that REBT therapists adopt in running self-acceptance groups, while in Chapter 4 I discuss the issues that need to be considered when setting up such groups.

The second part of the book (Chapters 5–14) is devoted to a detailed session-by-session review of the self-acceptance group curriculum. In discussing the practice of running self-acceptance groups, I illustrate the many points by referring to eight group members The people to whom I refer are not real individuals, but each is a composite of clients that have been members of one of my self-acceptance groups. I have taken this approach to preserve the confidentiality of past members of my groups. However, I have tried to make the people as lifelike and as representative of actual group members as possible.

Windy Dryden
London and East Sussex

ACKNOWLEDGEMENT

I wish to thank Jane Halfpenny for her work in the preparation of this manuscript.

Part 1

Basic Principles and Preparing the Ground

1

THE ABCDE MODEL OF REBT

My approach to helping people to achieve self-acceptance is based on Rational Emotive Behaviour Therapy (REBT), an approach to counselling originated by the famous American clinical psychologist, Albert Ellis, in 1955. REBT is one of the pioneering approaches in the cognitive-behavioural tradition. So that you are able to understand the rest of this book, in the first two chapters, I will present the basic ideas of Rational Emotive Behaviour Therapy. In this opening chapter, I will discuss a model which lies at the heart of REBT. This model, known as the ABCDE model, outlines REBT's view of human functioning and personal change. Let me consider each of the five components of this model.

A

'A' stands for a critical activating event. In an emotional/behavioural episode, a critical activating event is that part of the situation in which you find yourself that you pay most attention to and which triggers your beliefs that underpin the way you feel and the way you act. This critical activating event can be:

1. An observable part of the situation.
2. An inference which goes beyond what can be observed and which can be accurate or inaccurate. As such an inference is a hunch about reality which needs to be tested out.
3. A present event.
4. A past event.
5. A future event.
6. An external occurrence which you did not author although you may have influenced (e.g. someone else's behaviour).

7. An occurrence which you did author (e.g. dreams, thoughts, feelings, sensations and behaviour).

The important point to remember here and throughout the book is that while As may well influence the way you feel and/or act, they do not determine your emotions and/or actions. What does are your beliefs about these critical activating events. In the REBT model these beliefs are to be found at B.

B

As I have just mentioned, 'B' stands for beliefs. These beliefs are cognitions with which you appraise or evaluate the particular critical activating event in question. For this reason, beliefs in REBT are sometimes referred to as evaluative beliefs. In REBT theory, there are two sets of beliefs. These are known as healthy and unhealthy beliefs.

Characteristics of Healthy and Unhealthy Beliefs

Beliefs that are healthy have the following characteristics. They are:

1. Flexible.
2. Consistent with reality.
3. Sensible or logical.
4. Conducive to your psychological well-being.
5. Conducive to the pursuit of your basic goals and purposes.
6. Conducive to the development and maintenance of healthy relationships between yourself and others.

By contrast, beliefs that are unhealthy have the following characteristics. They are:

1. Rigid or inflexible.
2. Inconsistent with reality.
3. Illogical.
4. Detrimental to your psychological well-being.
5. Detrimental to the pursuit of your basic goals and purposes.
6. Detrimental to the development and maintenance of healthy relationships between yourself and others.

Types of Healthy and Unhealthy Beliefs

There are four types of healthy beliefs and four types of unhealthy beliefs. The four types of healthy beliefs are as follows:

1. Full preferences.
2. Anti-awfulizing beliefs.
3. High frustration tolerance beliefs.
4. Acceptance beliefs.

The four types of unhealthy beliefs are as follows:

1. Rigid demands.
2. Awfulizing beliefs.
3. Low frustration tolerance beliefs.
4. Depreciation beliefs.

In what follows I will consider each healthy belief before discussing their unhealthy alternatives.

Full Preferences

Preferences point to what you want or what you don't want in life. They come in the form of statements such as: 'I wish to join the club'; 'I want to be accepted by my reference group'; 'It would be desirable if you would treat me with respect'; and 'It would be better if I got up every morning at 8.00 a.m. to exercise for twenty minutes'.

However, for such statements to truly represent a preference, the non-dogmatic or flexible nature of that preference needs to be made explicit. Let me restate the above statements so that the non-dogmatic or flexible nature of the preference is made explicit: 'I wish to join the club, but my application doesn't have to be successful'; 'I want to be accepted by my reference group, but they don't have to accept me'; 'It would be desirable if you would treat me with respect, but you don't have to do so'; and 'It would be better if I got up every morning at 8.00 a.m. to exercise for twenty minutes, but there is no law of the universe which states that I have to do so'.

You will note from the above statements that there are two defining characteristics of a preference: a statement of what you want and an acknowledgement that your desire does not have to be fulfilled. If a person only states the first part of a preference statement, e.g. 'I want to be accepted by my reference group', then you cannot know for certain that this statement truly represents a preference. This is because the person can implicitly convert their flexible desire into a dogmatic demand as in the statement 'I want to be accepted by my reference group (and therefore they have to accept me)' – the implicit conversion of the desire into a demand is shown in brackets.

Let me summarize these points as follows: (i) A statement in which only a desire is articulated (e.g. 'I want to be accepted by my reference group') is known as a 'partial preference'. We do not know at this point whether or not this statement represents a rational belief because the person can either implicitly believe '. . . but there is no reason why they have to accept me' or 'and therefore they have to accept me'. (ii) A statement in which both the desire and the acknowledgement that one's desire does not have to be fulfilled are articulated (e.g. 'I want to be accepted by my reference group, but they do not have to accept me') is known as a 'full preference'. This full preference is a healthy belief. (iii) A statement in which a partial preference is explicitly converted into a demand (e.g. 'I want to be accepted by my reference group and therefore they have to accept me') is an unhealthy belief (see pp. 9–10).

The founder of REBT, Albert Ellis (1994), argues that full preferences are at the core of constructive responses to negative critical activating events and that the other three healthy beliefs stem from these full preferences. Other REBT theorists do not make this claim and regard the four healthy beliefs as having equal power in explaining constructive responses to negative critical activating events.

Anti-awfulizing Beliefs

Anti-awfulizing beliefs are healthy when they point to situations where you recognize that it is bad when you do not get your preferences met, but that it is not terrible, awful or the end of the world as in such statements as: 'It would be bad if I did not join the club, but it would not be terrible'; 'It would be very unfortunate if I were not accepted by my reference group, but it would not be awful'; 'It is bad that you have not treated me with respect, but it is not the end of the world'; and 'It is bad that I do not got up every morning at 8.00 a.m. to exercise for twenty minutes, but worse things happen'.

In each of these statements the person acknowledges the badness of the situation where his or her preference was not met, but does not take this to an extreme position which implies that nothing could be worse. Anti-awfulizing beliefs are succinctly and accurately encapsulated in the following statement which Smokey Robinson's mother said to the Tamla

Motown singer when he was a young boy: 'From the day you are born 'til you ride in the hearse, there's nothing so bad that it couldn't be worse.'

Again, we do not know if an anti-awfulizing statement is truly healthy unless it has two parts: an assertion that it is bad that an unpreferred event has occurred, for example, and a denial of the position that nothing could be worse. If only the first part is present in the person's statement (e.g. 'It is bad that you have not treated me with respect'), then this statement could really represent an unhealthy belief as when the following implicit addition (shown in brackets) is discovered: 'It is bad that you have not treated me with respect (and come to think of it, it is not only bad it is terrible that you have done so)'. Thus, we need the two parts of this belief to be explicitly present (i.e. an assertion of badness and a denial of awfulness) for it to qualify as a true anti-awfulizing belief as in the following: 'It is bad that you have not treated me with respect, but it is not the end of the world.'

Another way to represent the flexible nature of an anti-awfulizing belief is to say that the person holding such a belief places a negative critical activating event along a continuum of badness from 0 to 99.99%. In doing so, the person recognizes that a higher rating could be given and therefore it is not awful that the event has occurred (see p. 10 for a definition of awful).

People often accuse REBT's advocacy of anti-awfulizing as a healthy belief as ignoring the existence of tragedies and catastrophes. However, this is not the case. REBT theory does acknowledge the existence of tragedies and catastrophes, but maintains that they are unfortunately part of life and can be transcended. If they were truly awful (meaning nothing could be worse) it would not be possible for anybody to transcend them. We know, however, that this is not true and that human beings can transcend holocausts and other tragedies/catastrophes. As such, according to REBT, tragedies and catastrophes are not awful.

High Frustration Tolerance Beliefs

High frustration tolerance (HFT) beliefs are healthy when they point to the fact that an individual can tolerate a negative critical activating event that the person would prefer not to face, but which is worth tolerating. HFT beliefs are expressed in such statements as: 'It would be difficult for me to put up with not joining the club, but I could tolerate it'; 'It would be hard for me to stand it if I were not accepted by my reference group, but I could bear it if that were to occur'; 'The fact that you have not treated me with respect is difficult for me to tolerate it, but I can stand it'; and 'I find it difficult to bear the fact that I do not get up every morning at 8.00 a.m. to exercise for twenty minutes, but it is tolerable'.

In each of these statements, the person acknowledges that the negative critical event that he or she is facing is difficult to tolerate, but asserts that it is bearable. This is how we know that the belief expressed truly represents high frustration tolerance. If only the first part is present in the person's statement (e.g. 'The fact that you have not treated me with respect is difficult for me to tolerate', then this statement could really represent an unhealthy belief as when the following implicit addition (shown in brackets) is discovered: 'The fact that you have not treated me with respect is difficult to tolerate (and therefore it is intolerable)'. Thus, once again, we need the two parts of this belief to be explicitly present (i.e. an assertion of the difficulty of bearing the situation and a denial of unbearability) for it to qualify as a true HFT belief as in the following: 'The fact that you have not treated me with respect is difficult for me to tolerate, but I can stand it'.

Acceptance of Self, Others and the World/Life Conditions

Acceptance beliefs are healthy when they point to the fact that the person acknowledges that he or she is a fallible human being, other people are fallible human beings and the world is a complex place with positive, negative and neutral aspects. Since, this book is concerned with self-acceptance and will also touch on the issue of other acceptance I will here only deal with acceptance of the world/life conditions which are expressed in such statements as: 'If I do not join the club, that aspect of the world would be bad, but I can accept that the world is complex and made up of good, bad and neutral aspects'; 'If I were rejected by my reference group that would make that aspect of the world unfortunate, but the world would not be a bad place, but a place of mixed fortunes'; 'The fact that you have not treated me with respect is bad, but it does not reflect on life conditions as a whole which remain a mixture of the good, the bad and the neutral'; and 'I do not get up every morning at 8.00 a.m. to exercise for twenty minutes. That is bad, but it doesn't mean that the world is a rotten place for allowing such things to happen. Rather, I can accept that the world is a complex place where good, bad and neutral things happen.'

In each of these statements, the person acknowledges that an aspect of the world is bad, but asserts that this aspect does not completely define the world, which is acknowledged to be a complex place where good, bad and neutral events take place. This is how we know that the belief expressed truly represents acceptance of the world/life conditions. If only the first part is present in the person's statement (e.g. 'The fact that you have not treated me with respect is bad') then this statement could really represent an irrational belief as when the following implicit addition (shown in brackets) is discovered: 'The fact that you have not treated me with respect is bad (and therefore life conditions are rotten for allowing this to happen).' Thus, yet again, we need the two parts of this belief to be explicitly present (i.e. an assertion of the badness of the critical activating event and an assertion of the complexity of the world which is accepted as being made up of good, bad and neutral aspects) for it to qualify as a true world acceptance belief, as in the following: 'The fact that you have not treated me with respect is bad, but it does not reflect on life conditions as a whole which remain a mixture of the good, the bad and the neutral.'

Having considered each healthy belief in turn I will now discuss the four unhealthy beliefs one at a time.

Rigid Demands

Rigid demands point to what you believe you must have or must not have in life. They come in the form of statements such as: 'I must join the club'; 'I absolutely have to be accepted by my reference group'; 'You absolutely must treat me with respect'; and 'I absolutely should get up every morning at 8.00 a.m. to exercise for twenty minutes'.

The defining characteristic of these beliefs is absolutism. In other words, the individuals concerned are rigid in what they believe. Thus, the person who believes 'I absolutely have to be accepted by my reference group' does not allow, in his or her belief system, for the fact that he or she may be rejected by the reference group.

Although the person may transform a partial preference into a rigid demand (e.g. 'I want to be accepted by my reference group and therefore they have to accept me'), it is not possible for that person to hold a full preference and a rigid demand at precisely the same time with the same level of conviction. Thus, if a person believes 'I want to be accepted by my reference group, but they don't have to accept me', then that person cannot hold the following belief at the same time with the same level of conviction: 'I absolutely have to be accepted by my reference group.' However, the person can hold these two beliefs at the same time at different levels of intensity. Thus, it is common for clients in REBT to say something like: 'Yes, I can understand that while I may want to be accepted by my reference group, I don't have to receive this acceptance. But I don't believe this very strongly. I believe more strongly the idea that I have to be accepted by my reference group, even though I can understand that it is unhealthy.'

It is a major goal of REBT therapists to help clients to strengthen their conviction in their healthy beliefs and weaken their conviction in their unhealthy beliefs.

Awfulizing Beliefs

Awfulizing beliefs point to what you believe at the time is worse than the worst thing in the world. They come in the form of statements such as: 'It would be awful if I did not join the club'; 'It would be horrible if I were not accepted by my reference group'; 'It is the end of the world that you did not treat me with respect', and 'It is terrible that I do not get up every morning at 8.00 a.m. to exercise for twenty minutes'.

The defining characteristic of these beliefs is extreme exaggeration. In other words, the individuals concerned are extreme in evaluating the negative critical activating events that they encounter. Thus, the person who believes 'It would be horrible if I were not accepted by my reference group' does not allow, in his or her belief system at that time, that anything could be worse.

Although the person may transform a partial anti-awfulizing statement into an awfulizing belief (e.g. 'It would be bad not to be accepted by my reference group and therefore it would be awful if this happened'), it is not possible for that person to hold a full anti-awfulizing belief and an awfulizing belief at precisely the same time with the same level of conviction. Thus, if a person believes 'It would be bad not to be accepted by my reference group, but it wouldn't be horrible', he or she cannot hold the following belief at the same time with the same level of conviction: 'It would be horrible if I were not accepted by my reference group.' However, the person can hold these two beliefs at the same time, at different levels of intensity. Thus, it is common for clients in REBT to say something like: 'Yes, I can understand that while it would be bad, but not horrible not to be accepted by my reference group, I don't believe this very strongly. I believe more strongly the idea that it is horrible not to be accepted by my reference group even though I can understand that it is unhealthy.'

Don't forget that it is a major goal of REBT therapists to help clients to strengthen their conviction in their healthy beliefs and weaken their conviction in their unhealthy beliefs.

Low Frustration Tolerance Beliefs

Low frustration tolerance beliefs point to what you believe you cannot tolerate. This means that at the time you think you will either disintegrate or forfeit any chance of future happiness as long as the negative critical activating event that you think you cannot bear exists. LFT beliefs come in the form of statements such as: 'It would be unbearable if I did not join the club'; 'I could not stand it if I were not accepted by my reference group'; 'I cannot tolerate the fact that you did not treat me with respect'; and 'I can't put up with the fact that I do not get up every morning at 8.00 a.m. to exercise for twenty minutes'.

The defining characteristic of these beliefs is a perceived inability to tolerate what is in fact tolerable. In other words, the individuals concerned believe that they are unable to put up with the negative critical activating events that they in fact can tolerate. Thus, the person who believes 'I could not stand it if I were not accepted by my reference group' does not allow, in his or her belief system at that time, that he or she would be able to tolerate this event, that he or she will not disintegrate, nor will he or she forfeit the prospect of future happiness if this event were to occur.

Although the person may transform a partial HFT statement into an LFT belief (e.g. 'It would be difficult for me to tolerate it if I were not accepted by my reference group and therefore I could not stand it if this happened'), it is not possible for that person to hold a full HFT belief and an LFT belief at precisely the same time with the same level of conviction. Thus, if a person believes 'It would be difficult for me to tolerate it if I were not accepted by my reference group, but I could stand it if this happened', then he or she cannot hold the following belief at the same time with the same level of conviction: 'It would be intolerable if I were not accepted by my reference group.' However, he can hold these two beliefs simultaneously, at different levels of intensity. Thus, it is common for clients in REBT to say something like: 'Yes, I can understand that while it would be difficult to tolerate not being accepted by my reference group, I can tolerate it if it happened, but I don't believe this very strongly. I believe more strongly the idea that I couldn't stand it if I were not accepted by my reference group even though I can understand that it is unhealthy.'

It is once again a major goal of REBT therapists to help clients to strengthen their conviction in their healthy beliefs and weaken their conviction in their unhealthy beliefs.

Depreciation of Self, Others and the World/Life Conditions

Depreciation beliefs point to situations where a person assigns a global negative rating to oneself, other people and the world. Since, this book is concerned with self-depreciation and will also briefly deal with other depreciation, I will, in this chapter, only deal with depreciation of the world/

life conditions which are expressed in such statements as: 'If I do not join the club, the world is a rotten place for depriving me'; 'If I were rejected by my reference group, the world would be completely bad'; 'The fact that you have not treated me with respect means that life conditions are completely lousy'; and 'I do not get up every morning at 8.00 a.m. to exercise for twenty minutes. This proves that life conditions are thoroughly bad.'

The defining characteristic of these beliefs is a global depreciation of a complex system. It therefore involves an arrant overgeneralization where the world is given a global negative rating on the basis of a negative rating of a part of it, i.e. the critical activating event that the person has encountered. Thus, the person who believes 'If I were rejected by my reference group, the world would be completely bad' implicitly rates such rejection as being bad, and on the basis of this, concludes that the world would be completely bad.

Although the person may transform a partial acceptance statement into a depreciation belief (e.g. 'If my reference group rejects me, that would be bad and therefore the world would be completely bad)', it is yet again not possible for a person to hold a full acceptance belief and a depreciation belief at precisely the same time with the same level of conviction. Thus, if a person believes 'If I were rejected by my reference group that would make that aspect of the world unfortunate, but the world would not be a bad place, but a place of mixed fortunes', he or she cannot hold the following belief simultaneously with the same level of conviction: 'If I were rejected by my reference group, the world would be completely bad.' However, the person can hold these two beliefs simultaneously, at different levels of intensity. Once again, it is common for clients in REBT to say something like: 'Yes, I can understand that while it would be bad if I were rejected by my reference group, the world would not be a bad place for allowing this to happen, but a place of mixed fortunes, but I don't believe this very strongly. I believe more strongly the idea that the world would be a bad place I were rejected by my reference group even though I can understand that it is unhealthy.'

It is worth stressing yet again that a major goal of REBT therapists is to help clients to strengthen their conviction in their healthy beliefs and weaken their conviction in their unhealthy beliefs.

C

In the ABCDEs of REBT, C stands for the consequences of holding beliefs at B about the critical activating event at A. REBT theory states that there are three major consequences of such beliefs: emotional, behavioural and cognitive. I will deal with each in turn.

Emotional Consequences

In the previous section, I have taken great care to distinguish between healthy beliefs and unhealthy beliefs. It is important that you keep this distinction fully in mind while reading this section for I will consider a key REBT hypothesis. This hypothesis states that when people hold healthy beliefs about negative critical activating events, then they will experience healthy negative emotions at C in the face of these activating events. By contrast, when people hold unhealthy beliefs about those same negative critical activating events, then they will experience unhealthy negative emotions at C in the face of these events.

Table 1.1 outlines the terms that REBT theory attaches to healthy negative emotions and their unhealthy counterparts. In considering the two lists in this table, it is important that you bear in mind two points. First, clients will not automatically understand the differences between unhealthy negative emotions and healthy negative emotions and therefore you need to clarify this point for them. Second, clients may have their own idiosyncratic emotional lexicon, and it is therefore important that you discover what this is and perhaps use this in working with them to distinguish healthy negative emotions from their unhealthy counterparts rather than foist the REBT lexicon on them.

Table 1.1: Unhealthy and Healthy Negative Emotions

Unhealthy negative emotions	Healthy negative emotions
Anxiety	Concern
Depression	Sadness
Guilt	Remorse
Hurt	Sorrow
Shame	Disappointment
Unhealthy anger	Healthy anger
Jealousy	Concern for one's relationship
Unhealthy envy	Healthy envy

As I mentioned above, whether a person experiences a healthy negative emotion or an unhealthy negative emotion depends on whether he or she holds a healthy or an unhealthy belief. In addition, what determines whether someone experiences anxiety or concern as opposed to depression or sadness, for example, are the inferences that relate to the critical activating event that the person focuses on at A. Table 1.2. gives examples

Table 1.2: Illustrative Inferences Related to Emotional Pairings

Inference	Emotional pairing
Threat	Anxiety/Concern
Loss	Depression/Sadness
Moral code violation by self	Guilt/Remorse
Betrayal by significant other	Hurt/Sorrow
Falling very short of one's ideal	Shame/Disappointment
Other acts badly	Unhealthy anger/Healthy anger
Other poses a threat to one's relationship	Jealousy/Concern for one's relationship
Other has something that one prizes and desires	Unhealthy envy/Healthy envy

of inferences that are typically involved in the experience of healthy and unhealthy negative emotional pairing. Please note that this table is illustrative rather than exhaustive. For a more thorough listing of such inferences the reader is directed to Chapter 1 of *Brief Rational Emotive Behaviour Therapy* (Dryden, 1995) which appears in the same series as the current text.

Many people think that healthy negative emotions are weaker than their unhealthy counterparts. Thus, if you suggest to a client that concern is a viable alternative to anxiety, he may balk at the idea because he may wrongly think that you are asking him to adopt an emotion whose intensity does not do justice to the negativity of his critical activating event. Thus, it is important for you to appreciate for yourself and to tell your client that both healthy and unhealthy negative emotions vary in intensity from mild, moderate and intense. Thus, if your client is experiencing intense anxiety and you suggest concern as a viable emotional alternative, the client may reject your suggestion because he construes concern as a weaker emotion than intense anxiety, for the reasons discussed above. However, if you explain to your client that both anxiety and concern vary in intensity, and that intense concern is the healthy alternative to intense anxiety, he is more likely to accept your suggestion.

The intensity of a negative emotion depends on the strength of conviction in the relevant belief. The stronger a person's conviction in an unhealthy belief, for example, the more intense will be his or her unhealthy negative emotion about the critical activating event. And if that person's belief is healthy the stronger his conviction in that belief, the more intense will be his or her healthy negative emotion about the same event.

There are three main reasons why healthy negative emotions are more constructive than unhealthy negative emotions. First, as I have shown, unhealthy negative emotions stem from healthy beliefs whereas unhealthy negative emotions stem from unhealthy beliefs. Second, as I will show, unhealthy negative emotions lead to more functional actions and action tendencies than do unhealthy negative emotions. Finally, as I will also show, healthy negative emotions lead to more realistic cognitive consequences than do unhealthy negative emotions.

Behavioural Consequences

C also represents the behavioural consequences of holding a belief about a critical activating event. These behavioural consequences may be an action that a person actually performs or they may be a tendency to act which is not acted on. The latter is known as an action tendency. The distinction between an action and an action tendency is very important in REBT theory, and in clinical practice REBT therapists often encourage their clients to act against their action tendencies. A common instance of this occurs in the treatment of anxiety where clients are urged to confront situations (actual behaviour) that they would rather avoid (action tendency).

REBT acknowledges that behaviour can be triggered by a person's belief about a critical activating event without that person experiencing an emotional consequence. When this occurs it is because the behaviour has a defensive function, i.e. it serves to protect the person from experiencing an emotion that the person believes he or she cannot tolerate, for example. However, more often than not, emotional and behavioural consequences go together.

When a person holds a belief about a critical activating event and experiences a negative emotion, then that person is likely to act in certain ways. Different action tendencies (and, of course different actions) are associated with different negative emotions. REBT theory argues that the actions and action tendencies that are associated with healthy negative emotions are more functional than the actions and action tendencies associated with unhealthy negative emotions. Table 1.3 lists some of the actions and action tendencies associated with different healthy and unhealthy negative emotions. Both, you will recall, stem from rational and irrational beliefs respectively. Again, this table is illustrative rather than comprehensive and the reader is directed to Chapter 2 in Dryden (1995) for greater detail on this issue.

Cognitive Consequences

Finally, C stands for cognitive consequences of holding beliefs about critical activating events. This may be confusing so it needs careful

Table 1.3:   Negative Emotions and Actions/Action Tendencies

Negative emotion	Type	Action/Action tendency
Anxiety	Unhealthy	Avoidance of threat
Concern	Healthy	Confronting threat
Depression	Unhealthy	Prolonged withdrawal from enjoyable activities
Sadness	Healthy	Engagement with enjoyable activities after period of mourning
Guilt	Unhealthy	Begging for forgiveness
Remorse	Healthy	Asking for forgiveness
Hurt	Unhealthy	Sulking
Sorrow	Healthy	Assertion
Shame	Unhealthy	Averting one's eyes from the gaze of others
Disappointment	Healthy	Maintaining eye contact with others
Unhealthy anger	Unhealthy	Shouting
Healthy anger	Healthy	Assertion
Jealousy	Unhealthy	Prolonged suspicious questioning of the other
Concern for one's relationship	Healthy	Brief open-minded questioning of the other
Unhealthy envy	Unhealthy	Spoiling the other's enjoyment of the desired possession
Healthy envy	Healthy	Striving to gain a similar possession for oneself

explanation. In the ABCDE model cognitions can occur at each of the five components. Since I have so far considered the ABC part of the model, I will restrict my discussion to these three components. Cognitions can and frequently do occur at A in the form of inferences. Inferences are cognitive hunches about reality which give meaning to it. They go beyond observable reality and as such they need to be tested against the available evidence.

For example, let's suppose that a client relates an experience where a friend passed her in the street without acknowledging her. The client infers that her friend has ignored her. This is an inference (i.e. a cognitive hunch) about what had happened. In REBT, we do not challenge inferences at this point because we want to identify the client's unhealthy negative feelings about this incident and the beliefs that underpin such feelings. Let's suppose that the client reports feeling hurt because she believes (at B) that her friend must not ignore her. Now, clearly this belief is a cognition and the essence of beliefs is that they are evaluative cognitions in that they appraise the critical activating event at A. So far, then, the client experiences cognitions at A and at B.

The client then goes on to say that the friend who ignored her will then turn her other friends against her and she will lose a number of her other friends. What the client has gone on to reveal are also cognitions. These cognitions are, in fact, inferences that stem from the client's irrational belief at B.

In summary, cognitions that occur at A are inferences, the most critical of which triggers beliefs at B. These beliefs, which are evaluative cognitions, then produce a further set of inferences at C, and these are referred to as cognitive consequences.

Table 1.4 lists the kinds of cognitions associated with different healthy and unhealthy negative emotions that stem from rational and irrational beliefs respectively. This table is illustrative rather than comprehensive and the reader is once again directed to Chapter 2 in Dryden (1995) for greater detail on this issue.

PSYCHOLOGICAL INTERACTIONISM

So far, I have presented the first three components of the ABCDE model as if they were separate from one another. However, in reality this is not the case. Indeed, an important principle in REBT is that known as psychological interactionism. This principle states that As, Bs and Cs interact with one another often in complex ways (see Ellis, 1991, and Dryden, 1994, for a thorough discussion of this issue). It also states that in the area of psychological functioning pure cognition, pure behaviour and pure emotion in all probability do not exist. Let me illustrate this principle with some examples.

When you hold an unhealthy belief at B, as we have seen, you also tend to feel, act and think in certain ways at C. These tendencies are part of the experience of holding the unhealthy belief at C. However, holding such a belief also influences the type of inferences you make at A. Thus, if you believe that you must be approved by significant others and one such person disagrees with you, then this unhealthy belief will make it more likely that you will think that the person dislikes you than you would if you held a healthy belief about approval (see Bond & Dryden, 1996, for a review of research demonstrating the impact of beliefs on inferences).

Table 1.4: Beliefs, Emotions and Cognitive Consequences

Belief	Emotion	Cognitive consequence
Unhealthy	Anxiety	Overestimates negative features of the threat
Healthy	Concern	Views the threat realistically
Unhealthy	Depression	Only sees pain and blackness in the future
Healthy	Sadness	Able to look into the future with hope
Unhealthy	Guilt	Assumes more personal responsibility than the situation warrants
Healthy	Remorse	Assumes appropriate level of personal responsibility
Unhealthy	Hurt	Thinks that the other has to put things right of own accord first
Healthy	Sorrow	Doesn't think that the other has to make the first move
Unhealthy	Shame	Overestimates the 'shamefulness' of what has been revealed
Healthy	Disappointment	Sees what has been revealed in a compassionate self-accepting context
Unhealthy	Unhealthy anger	Sees malicious intent in the motives of others whether or not there is evidence for this inference
Healthy	Healthy anger	Does not see malicious intent in the motives of others unless there is evidence for this inference
Unhealthy	Jealousy	Tends to distrust partner even though there is no clear reason to do so
Healthy	Concern for one's relationship	Tends not to distrust partner unless there is clear reason to do so
Unhealthy	Unhealthy envy	Tends to denigrate the value of the desired possession
Healthy	Healthy envy	Honestly admits to oneself that one wants the desired possession

Holding beliefs can also influence the type of events that you encounter at A. For example, if you believe that you must have the approval of significant others, you may stay away from situations where you think you will not receive approval and only put yourself in situations where you think such approval is virtually guaranteed. In this away you determine the type of actual events that you face in life.

Emotional and behavioural consequences at C also overlap with As and Bs. Thus, if you avoid people whom you don't know at C, you strengthen your unhealthy belief at B. For as you choose to withdraw you are telling yourself something like: 'I cannot risk being with this group of people because there is a chance that they might disapprove of me and I need their approval.' Your avoidance will also limit the type of activating events that you encounter at A and will also have a direct impact on the kind of inferences that you make at A. Thus, avoiding a group of people at C tends to increase in your mind the probability that these people will disapprove of you at A and does not give you any chance to test such an inference. By contrast, facing these people will enable you to test your hunch and is likely to give you experiences which go against this inference, thereby decreasing in your mind the probability that they will disapprove of you.

Finally, the As that you encounter closely interact and overlap with Bs and Cs. Thus, if you stay away from people and spend a lot of time on your own at A, your beliefs at B will tend to be more unhealthy than they would be if you spent more time with people. Being on your own may well help to strengthen your unhealthy idea that you need approval and that you are no good if you don't have it. Also, being on your own may well serve to increase your sense of loneliness and isolation. While this effect will be exacerbated by unhealthy beliefs, it will still exist without such cognitive mediation.

Having outlined and illustrated the principle of psychological interactionism, we can now proceed to consider the D component of the model.

D

In REBT theory, D stands for disputing irrational beliefs. Disputing involves the therapist cognitively challenging the person's unhealthy beliefs and teaching the person to challenge his or her own unhealthy beliefs using a variety of cognitive, emotive and behavioural methods.

Cognitive Disputing

DiGiuseppe (1991) and his students analysed a large sample of audiotapes of Albert Ellis's therapy sessions and discovered that Ellis used a variety of disputing styles and arguments which were directed at different irrational beliefs. Furthermore, this work was done at differing levels of specificity. Here is a brief résumé of DiGiuseppe's findings.

Styles

In his research, DiGiuseppe and his students found that Ellis used four basic disputing styles:

1. *Socratic.* Here, Ellis would ask his clients a number of open-ended questions which were designed to help them to think for themselves why their unhealthy beliefs were unhealthy and why the healthy alternatives to such beliefs were healthy. During Socratic disputing sequences, Ellis would refrain from making any didactic explanations.
2. *Didactic.* Here, Ellis would explain to his clients why their unhealthy beliefs were unhealthy and, conversely, why their healthy beliefs were healthy. When you employ didactic disputing you are in effect teaching your clients to think healthily. However, while you may accurately teach these principles of REBT, it is what clients learn that is the crucial issue here. Consequently, it is important that you check your clients' understanding of your teaching points so you can gauge whether or not they are effectively learning what you want them to learn. This is perhaps best encapsulated in the phrase: 'There is no good course without a test.'
3. *Use of humour.* Here, Ellis would make a humorous intervention designed to encourage his clients to laugh at their unhealthy beliefs and see how self-defeating these ideas are. The important point to remember when using a humorous disputing style is that you are directing your interventions at your clients' ideas and not at the clients themselves (Ellis, 1994; Dryden, 1996).
4. *Metaphorical.* Here, Ellis would tell his clients metaphorical stories designed to challenge his clients' unhealthy beliefs. As you gain experience as an REBT therapist you will build up a fund of such stories. Once again, when using this disputing style, it is important to check whether or not your clients have understood the point of such metaphorical stories. In REBT, we believe in the importance of being explicit and are sceptical that clients will necessarily understand the point of such stories just because we have related them.

Arguments

Ellis was found to use three major arguments while disputing his clients' unhealthy beliefs. Since I will consider these in greater depth when discussing how to challenge clients' self-depreciation beliefs in Chapter 7, I will cover these arguments briefly here. The three major arguments employed by Ellis are as follows:

1. *Empirical.* Here, Ellis helped his clients to see that there were no laws of the universe which allowed for the existence of their unhealthy beliefs. They were, in short, inconsistent with reality or false. Also, Ellis helped his clients understand that the healthy alternatives to their unhealthy beliefs were consistent with reality and that evidence could be found for their veracity.
2. *Logical.* Here, Ellis helped his clients to understand that their healthy beliefs were intrinsically sensible, but that their unhealthy beliefs could not be logically derived from these healthy beliefs.
3. *Pragmatic.* Here, Ellis helped his clients to see clearly that their unhealthy beliefs led to dysfunctional emotional, behavioural and cognitive consequences and, by contrast, their healthy beliefs led to functional consequences in the same three areas.

The Targets of Disputing: Different Unhealthy Beliefs

DiGiuseppe and his students found that Ellis disputed all four unhealthy beliefs that I discussed earlier in this chapter (see pp. 9–12), i.e. rigid demands, awfulizing beliefs, LFT beliefs and depreciation beliefs.

Disputing Unhealthy Beliefs at Different Levels of Specificity

Unhealthy beliefs occur at different levels of specificity. Thus, a client may believe 'I must be approved by my boss'; 'I must be approved by people that I work with'; or 'I must be approved by everyone'. These three beliefs range from the specific to the general. In DiGiuseppe's (1991) research, Ellis was found to dispute unhealthy beliefs across the entire specific-general continuum. Normally in REBT we begin the disputing process by challenging our clients' specific unhealthy beliefs, and only after we have obtained more data about their belief system do we move on to identify and challenge their general (or core) unhealthy beliefs.

Emotive Disputing

Emotive disputing of unhealthy beliefs is distinguished from cognitive disputing by the greater emphasis placed on the strength, vigour or energy with which these beliefs are challenged. When using emotive disputing methods with themselves, for example, clients are encouraged do so initially with a forceful overt voice, speaking their disputes out loud with great firmness.

They are then encouraged to maintain this vigour while disputing their unhealthy beliefs *sotto voce* and, finally, they are advised to maintain the same level of force that they use to challenge their unhealthy beliefs silently. I will discuss emotive disputing methods in greater detail in Chapter 10.

Behavioural Disputing

Prior to 1993, Rational Emotive Behaviour Therapy was known as Rational-Emotive Therapy. The reason for the introduction of the word 'Behaviour' into the title of the therapy was to counteract views which stated that RET (as it was known then) neglected the use of behavioural methods. In fact, this has never been the case, and as far back as the early 1960s when the first edition of Ellis's (1962) seminal book *Reason and Emotion in Psychotherapy* was published, REBT made liberal use of behavioural techniques. The major purpose of these techniques then was the same as it is now: to promote cognitive change and, more specifically, to help clients practise acting in ways that are consistent with their healthy beliefs and inconsistent with their unhealthy beliefs.

In reality, REBT therapists encourage their clients to use behavioural techniques in concert with cognitive techniques, For example, if a client has a dire need for his friend's approval, a conjoint behavioural-cognitive technique might be to encourage the client to disagree with his friend while showing himself that while it may be good to have his friend's approval, he does not need it.

While REBT therapists favour the use of conjoint behavioural-cognitive techniques, they recognize that without behavioural change any cognitive change that the client might achieve will be theoretical. Thus, a therapy that emphasizes the use of cognitive change techniques without also emphasizing behavioural techniques will be advocating cognition without ignition (Dryden, 1985). Thus, it is the use of behavioural methods that often ignites the change process.

Vicissitudes of the Disputing Process

The purpose of disputing is to encourage clients to weaken their conviction in their unhealthy beliefs and strengthen their conviction in their healthy beliefs. As may be imagined, the disputing process usually does not go perfectly smoothly and clients do experience a number of difficulties along the way (see Ellis, 1985, and Neenan & Dryden, 1996, for a thorough discussion of such difficulties and how they may be handled in therapy). It is important to alert clients to the fact that the disputing process may not go smoothly and encourage them to join with you in adopting a problem-solving approach to episodes when this process goes awry. In doing so you can both work to identify and overcome obstacles to client change.

E

E stands for the effects of the disputing process at stage D in the ABCDE model. If the disputing process has gone well and clients have practised a range of cognitive, emotive and behavioural disputing methods sufficiently often, and have successfully negotiated obstacles to change, then the effects of this disputing process will be as follows. First, clients will have changed their unhealthy beliefs to their healthy equivalents. This process is rarely if ever a once-and-for-all process and thus clients will need to be vigilant in case they transform their new healthy beliefs back into unhealthy beliefs.

However, assuming that clients have largely modified their unhealthy beliefs and now have greater conviction in their healthy equivalents, the effects of this change will be dependent on two factors: (i) the level of specificity of the unhealthy beliefs that have been changed; (ii) the number of unhealthy beliefs that have been changed. Basically, the more general the unhealthy belief that has been modified, the more wide-ranging will be the effects of this change. Thus, if a client has changed the general unhealthy belief 'I must be approved by others' and now believes 'I would prefer to be approved by others, but I don't have to have their approval', he will experience more pervasive constructive effects than if he had changed a specific unhealthy belief such as 'I must be approved by my boss' to 'I would like to be approved by my boss, but I don't have to have her approval'.

The constructive effects of successfully disputing unhealthy beliefs are the same as the emotional, behavioural and cognitive consequences of holding healthy beliefs (see Tables 1.1, 1.3 and 1.4). This is the case since the goal of disputing is for clients to strengthen their conviction in their healthy beliefs. In addition, if clients hold a set of healthy beliefs strongly they are more likely to make accurate inferences about the activating events that they encounter than if they continue to hold a set of unhealthy beliefs.

In this chapter, I have outlined the major theoretical and practical cornerstone of REBT – its ABCDE model. As you have seen, this model spells out how REBT therapists conceptualize psychological problems and outlines the major steps that need to be taken for clients to overcome these problems. In the next chapter, I will outline the concept of ego disturbance and discuss the REBT view of unconditional self-acceptance.

2

EGO DISTURBANCE AND THE REBT VIEW OF UNCONDITIONAL SELF-ACCEPTANCE

In this chapter, I will consider the concept of ego disturbance and REBT's view of unconditional self-acceptance. This material provides therapists with the theoretical underpinnings for running self-acceptance groups.

In the first chapter, I outlined the REBT's ABCDE model. I showed there that REBT hypothesizes that there are four major unhealthy beliefs that underpin much psychological disturbance: demands, awfulizing beliefs, LFT beliefs and depreciation beliefs. REBT theory goes further and distinguishes between two different types of psychological disturbance. These are known as discomfort disturbance and ego disturbance.

Discomfort disturbance arises when a person's sense of comfort (broadly defined) is threatened and is underpinned by demands, awfulizing, LFT and other/world depreciation beliefs. When self-depreciation beliefs are present they are very much secondary to the aforementioned beliefs. Ego disturbance, on the other hand, arises when a person's self-esteem is threatened and is underpinned by demands and, of course, self-depreciation beliefs. When awfulizing, LFT and other/world depreciation beliefs are present they are secondary to self-depreciation beliefs.

REBT theory holds that ego and discomfort disturbance interact, often in complex ways. However, in this book I will focus primarily on ego disturbance and its remediation and will only deal with discomfort disturbance as it prevents group members from working on themselves to build self-acceptance.

In the first part of this chapter, I will elaborate on REBT's concept of ego disturbance before considering how REBT views self-acceptance.

EGO DISTURBANCE

According to REBT theory, ego disturbance occurs when a person makes a demand on himself or herself, others or the world which is not met and then self-depreciates in some way. The following are examples of themes that are commonly involved in ego disturbance. You will note from Chapter 1 that these themes are inferential in nature and that clients react to them as if they are true, whether they are or not.

1. Failing to achieve an important target or goal.
2. Acting incompetently (in public or private).
3. Falling short of one's ideal.
4. Failing to live up to one's standards.
5. Breaking one's ethical code.
6. Being criticised.
7. Being ridiculed.
8. Not being accepted, approved, appreciated or loved by significant others.

You will recall from Chapter 1 that, according to REBT theory, people do not disturb themselves about events because of the inferences they make about these events; rather they disturb themselves because they hold unhealthy beliefs about these inferential events.

Ego Disturbance Beliefs in the Emotional Disorders

As will now be shown, when ego disturbance predominates in people's problems their unhealthy beliefs largely take the form of rigid demands and self-depreciation beliefs. Ellis (1994) has argued that self-depreciation beliefs are derived from rigid demands although empirical evidence on this point is equivocal (Bond & Dryden, 1996). However, since I am putting forward the classical REBT position in this book, I will adopt Ellis's view here.

This view is shown in the following list of emotional disorders, which outlines the associated unhealthy ego beliefs. I am not saying that such beliefs completely account for the existence of such emotions whenever they occur because such emotions are also underpinned by unhealthy discomfort beliefs. However, in the following list I will assume that each emotion is largely ego-related and will thus be underpinned by unhealthy ego beliefs. It is these beliefs that are listed below.

- *Anxiety.* 'If I fail at my upcoming test which I must not do, I would be a failure.' 'If he rejects me as I think he will do soon, but which he must not do, I would be no good.'
- *Depression.* 'Because I have failed the test, as I absolutely should not have done, I am a failure.' 'Since my partner has rejected me, as she absolutely should not have done, this proves that I am no good.'
- *Guilt.* 'I have hurt the feelings of my parents, which I absolutely should not have done. I am therefore a bad person.' 'I failed to help a good friend in trouble. The fact that I did not do what I absolutely should have done proves that I am a rotten person.'
- *Hurt.* 'My ex-girlfriend is going out with my best friend, which absolutely should not happen. Since it is happening, this proves that I am unlovable.'
- *Shame.* 'I have acted foolishly in front of my peers which I absolutely should not have done, and this proves that I am an inadequate person.' 'I have let down my reference group. I absolutely should not have done this and I am less of a person for so doing.'
- *Unhealthy anger.* 'You absolutely should not have criticized me. Your criticism reminds me that I am a failure.'
- *Jealousy.* 'If my husband looks at another woman, which he must not do, it means that he finds her more attractive than me. This must not happen, but if it does it proves that I am worthless.'
- *Unhealthy envy.* 'My friend is making better progress than I am in our respective careers. I must have what he has and because I don't this makes me less worthy than I would be if I had what he has.'

SELF-DEPRECIATION

You will have seen from the above statements that ego disturbance occurs when people make demands on themselves, others or the world and depreciate themselves in some way when their demands are not met. In this section, I will consider the concept of self-depreciation.

Self-depreciation is based on the following unhealthy principles.

1. *Human beings can be given a single global rating.*

In the previous section, I gave several examples of the ways in which people depreciate themselves: 'I am a failure', 'I am no good', 'I am a bad person', 'I am a rotten person', 'I am an inadequate person', 'I am less of a person', 'I am unlovable', 'I am worthless', 'I am less worthy'.

Each of these examples involves the person giving himself (in these cases) a single global rating. Indeed, the concept of self-esteem is based on this principle. While high self-esteem involves the person assigning to himself a single, positive, global rating, low self-esteem involves the person in assigning a single, negative global rating. This means that self-esteem is variable and can go up and down, leaving the person vulnerable to emotional disturbance.

2. *Human beings are perfectible.*

When a person depreciates himself by, for example, not achieving as well as he believes he must, then he is operating on the principle that, as a human being, he is perfectible. When he makes a demand, he holds the view that he must, literally, achieve the standard that he sets for himself. If he was perfectible then he would be able to achieve as well as he demands he must. Obviously this is not the case, but his demanding and self-depreciating beliefs do not reflect the essential nature of human beings, i.e. we are not perfectible and often are not able to achieve to our preferred standards.

3. *A person's global self-rating varies according to changing conditions.*

As I have already pointed out, the concept of self-esteem is based not only on the principle that a person can be assigned a global rating, but also on the idea that this rating is variable. This variation is usually contingent on changing conditions. Thus, when a person believes that he is a failure when he fails an important test, it is unlikely that he would make this rating of himself if he did very well on the test. And when that person believes that he is unlovable when he discovers that his ex-girlfriend is dating his best friend, it is unlikely that he would believe this of himself if his ex-girlfriend was not going out with anyone.

Again, as pointed out above, when a person gives himself a global rating, he is clearly emotionally disturbed when this rating is negative, but is vulnerable to such disturbance when this rating is positive. This latter point is the case because the person rates himself positively when a favourable set of conditions exists. However, should this set of conditions change to a negative set of conditions, then the person will probably rate himself negatively. Thus, if a person rates himself positively when he does well on an important test, he is vulnerable to giving himself a negative global rating should he do poorly in a future test.

4. *Human beings differ in worth.*

The principle that human beings differ in worth is linked to the aforementioned principle that a person's rating of himself varies according to changing conditions and is found most frequently when a person compares himself with others. Thus, when a person demands that he must do as well as others and he does not do so, then he tends to rate himself as less worthy than these other people. This principle is present when a person experiences shame and unhealthy envy. In both these emotions the person rates himself more negatively than he rates others. Thus, when a person experiences shame, he considers himself to be insignificant or defective and views others as more significant or perfect. When a person experiences unhealthy envy, he thinks that he has less worth than others who have what he demands he must have.

There are times when a person may well rate himself as being more worthy than others. This can be a true reflection of how a person views himself or it can sometimes be a compensatory strategy. When it is a compensatory strategy, if the person did not view himself as being better than others, he would depreciate himself.

The principle of people having differing worth is sometimes institutionalized as in some caste systems whereby an individual sees himself as either more worth while or less worth while than others, depending upon his membership of a particular caste.

5. *Rating oneself globally involves committing errors of overgeneralization.*

When a person rates himself globally he makes an error of overgeneralization or what is called the part–whole error. When a person commits this error he first infers that he has failed at an important task, for example, and evaluates this failure negatively. This represents an evaluation of part of that person. The person then concludes that because he failed at the task this proves that he is a failure. In other words, he evaluates himself negatively as a person. This represents an evaluation of the whole of that person. The part–whole error occurs, therefore, when a person gives himself a global rating of his whole self on the basis of making an evaluation of part of himself.

6. *Global negative self-rating is based on a rigid demanding philosophy.*

As I have pointed out already in this chapter, Albert Ellis's (1994) position is that self-depreciation beliefs and the global self-rating which underpins these beliefs are derived from rigid demands. This position is represented in the examples outlined on p. 26 and is summed up in Ellis's memorable phrase: 'Shouldhood leads to shithood. You're never a shit without a should.'

7. *Global negative self-rating promotes self-defeating action.*

When a person rates himself in a global, negative manner, he tends to act in self-defeating ways. This is consistent with the REBT position which states that unhealthy beliefs at B in the ABCDE model tend to lead to unconstructive behavioural consequences at C. For example, if a person considers himself to be a failure for failing at an important test, then it is likely that he will tend to give up and not take the test again. Or if he decides to retake the test his self-depreciation belief may lead him to study too hard and exhaust himself so that he increases the chances of failing again.

UNCONDITIONAL SELF-ACCEPTANCE

According to REBT theory, unconditional self-acceptance is the healthy alternative to self-depreciation. Unconditional self-acceptance is found when people hold preferences about the way they want themselves, others and the world to be, but do not then transform these preferences into rigid demands. The following are examples of negative themes that people face when they accept themselves. They are the same themes that are involved in ego disturbance. Again you will note that these themes are inferential in nature and that clients react to them as if they are true, whether they are or not.

1. Failing to achieve an important target or goal.
2. Acting incompetently (in public or private).
3. Falling short of one's ideal.
4. Failing to live up to one's standards.
5. Breaking one's ethical code.
6. Being criticized.
7. Being ridiculed.
8. Not being accepted, approved, appreciated or loved by significant others.

You will recall from Chapter 1 that, according to REBT theory, when people experience healthy negative emotions about actual or inferred negative activating events they do so because they hold healthy beliefs about these events.

Self-acceptance Beliefs in Healthy Negative Emotions

As will now be shown, when people experience healthy negative emotions their beliefs largely take the form of flexible preferences and self-acceptance beliefs. Here I will again follow Ellis's (1994) view that self-acceptance beliefs are derived from flexible preferences. The list of healthy negative emotions and the healthy beliefs that underpin them are the healthy alternatives to the list of emotional disorders listed on p. 26.

- *Concern.* 'I would rather not fail at my upcoming test, but there is no law of the universe to prevent me from doing so. If I do fail, I would not be a failure. Rather, I would be a fallible human being who has failed.' 'If he rejects me, as I think he will do soon, I can still accept myself as a unique unrateable human who would rather not be rejected, but recognizes that there is no evidence in favour of the idea that this must not happen. His rejection would not make me a no good person.'
- *Sadness.* 'I would have preferred to have passed the test, but there is no reason why I had to do so. Failing the test proves that I am a fallible human being and not a failure.' 'I would have preferred it had my partner not rejected me, but there is no reason why she must not have done so. Even though she rejected me, I am still a fallible human being. There is no evidence that I am no good.'
- *Remorse.* 'I have hurt the feelings of my parents. I would rather not have done so, but there is no reason why I absolutely should not have done so. I am a fallible human being for doing the wrong thing rather than a bad person.' 'I failed to help a good friend in trouble. The fact that I did not do what I would much rather have done makes me fallible and not a rotten person. There is no reason why I absolutely should have gone to my friend's aid.'
- *Sorrow.* 'My ex-girlfriend is going out with my best friend. I would much rather that she did not do this, but I don't have to get this desire met. The fact that she is going out with him has no bearing on the way I view myself. I am fallible rather than unlovable.'
- *Disappointment.* 'I have acted foolishly in front of my peers. There is no reason why I absolutely should not have done so even though I would have preferred it if I hadn't. I am not an inadequate person for acting in the way that I did. Rather I am a complex unrateable human being.' 'I really did not want to let down my reference group, but I am human and am not immune from doing so. As such, I am not less of a person for so doing.'
- *Healthy anger.* 'I would rather you hadn't criticized me, but there's no reason why you absolutely should not have done so. Your criticism reminds me that I am fallible and not a failure'.
- *Concern for one's relationship.* 'I would much prefer it if my husband did not look at another woman or did not find her more attractive than me. However, there is no law to forbid him from doing either. If he does, I can still accept myself as a fallible human being. It does not prove that I am worthless.'

- *Healthy envy.* 'My friend is making better progress than I am in our respective careers. I would prefer it if I was doing as well as him, but there is no law which states that this has to be the case. I am not less worthy than I would be if I had what he has. Rather I am the same fallible human whether I have what he has or not.'

The Principles on which Self-acceptance is Based

As you can see in each of the aforementioned examples, the person held a self-accepting belief. Let me now consider the principles upon which self-acceptance is based. Before I do so, I want to stress that I use the terms 'self-acceptance' and 'unconditional self-acceptance' interchangeably in this book.

1. *Human beings are too complex to legitimately be given a single global rating.*

REBT theory argues that it is not possible legitimately to give a person a single global rating, be it positive or negative. The problem with the concept of self-esteem is that it implies that you can rate a person globally. Let me show what I mean by defining clearly the terms 'self' and 'esteem'.

First, let me take the term 'self'. Hauck (1991: 33) has provided a very simple, but profound, definition of the self. He says that the self is 'every conceivable thing about you that can be rated'. This means that all your thoughts, images, feelings, actions and bodily parts are part of your 'self' and all these different aspects that belong to you from the beginning of your life to the moment of your death have to be included in your 'self'.

Now let me consider the term 'esteem'. This word is derived from the verb 'to estimate' which means to give something a rating, judgement or estimation.

The question then arises: 'Can we give the self a single legitimate rating, estimation or judgement which completely accounts for its complexity?' The answer is clearly 'no'. As Hauck (1991) notes, it is possible to rate different aspects of one's 'self', but a person is far too complex to warrant a single, legitimate, rating.

Even if it were valid to give a person a single global rating – a task which would involve a team of objective judges and a computer so powerful that it could analyse the millions upon millions of data produced by that person – as soon as that global judgement was made, it would become immediately redundant, since that person would continue to produce more data. In other words, a person is an ongoing ever-changing process and thus defies the ascription of a single, static, global judgement.

By contrast, the concept of unconditional self-acceptance does not involve any such rating or evaluation. Rather, accepting yourself involves acknowledging that you are a complex, ongoing, ever-changing process that defies being legitimately rated by yourself or by others. However, and this is the crucial point, unconditional self-acceptance does allow you to rate different aspects of yourself. Indeed, it encourages this type of evaluation, since doing this allows you to focus on your negative aspects and, if possible, do something to improve them without self-blame. Conversely, if you focus on your negative aspects from the standpoint of self-rating or self-esteem, then you are less likely to change them, because you are sidetracked by giving your 'self' a global negative rating for having these aspects. It is difficult to change anything while you are berating yourself for having these aspects in the first place.

2. Human beings are essentially fallible.

REBT theory holds that if human beings have an essence it is probably that we are essentially fallible. As Maultsby (1984) put it, humans have an incurable error-making tendency. I would add that we frequently make more serious mistakes than we are prepared to accept and that we often keep repeating the same errors. Why do we do this? Hauck (1991) argues that we keep repeating errors out of stupidity, ignorance or because we are psychologically disturbed. Ellis (1994) noted that humans find it very easy to disturb ourselves and difficult to undisturb ourselves. Self-acceptance, then, means acknowledging that our essence is fallibility and that we are not perfectible.

3. A person's global self-rating does not vary according to changing conditions.

Thus far, I have argued against the idea that human beings can be rated. It therefore follows that this position is against the notion that human beings have worth since worth is an evaluative concept, and when it applies to humans it supports the idea that humans can be legitimately rated.

As I will demonstrate in Chapter 5, some clients are loathe to surrender the idea that humans have worth. With these clients you can employ the healthy use of the concept of human worth.

The main problem with the concept of human worth is that people normally make their 'worth' contingent on variables that change (for example, 'I am worth while if I do well in my exams', which implies that if I do not do well in them then I am not worth while). Even if a person fulfils the conditions of worth at any given moment, he or she is still vulnerable to emotional disturbance if those conditions are not continually met.

The only way that a person can apply the concept of worth or use any other kind of global self-rating in a healthy manner is to make her (in this case) worth or self-rating contingent of one of three constants. First, she can believe that she is worth while (or other relevant self-rating) because she is human. Second, she can believe that she is worth while (or other relevant self-rating) as long as she is alive. This second form of self-rating can even be employed by people who believe in an afterlife (e.g. 'I am worth while as long as I am alive in this life or any future life that I may have'). Third, the person can believe that she is worth while because she is unique. Since one's humanness, aliveness and uniqueness is constant during one's lifetime, then this use of unconditional self-rating will not leave that person vulnerable to emotional disturbance as long as she makes such self-ratings.

However, the difficulty with such unconditional self-rating beliefs is that they are somewhat arbitrary. A person cannot prove that she is worth while because she is human, alive or unique. She can just as easily say that she is worthless because she is human, alive or unique. This is equally unprovable. While clients who prefer to use some form of self-rating can be encouraged to rate themselves positively and unconditionally, this tactic will not work for those who believe that they are worthless for being alive, human or unique. This group of clients need to be taught the principles of unconditional self-acceptance as outlined above.

4. *All humans are equal in humanity, but unequal in their different aspects.*

If the essence of being human is fallibility, then all humans are equal in their humanity, and since human beings cannot be rated it follows that no human is worthier than any other. This principle reveals Rational Emotive Behaviour Therapy as one of the most humanistic, if not the most humanistic of all psychotherapies. However, this principle of parity, as it is sometimes called, does not deny that there is a great deal of variation among human beings with respect to their different aspects. Thus, Adolf Hitler may be equal in humanity to Mother Theresa, but in terms of their compassion, the latter far outscores the former.

5. *Unconditional self-acceptance avoids errors of overgeneralization.*

When a person accepts himself (in this case) unconditionally, he avoids making overgeneralizations or what have been called 'part–whole' errors. Earlier in this chapter, I pointed out that when a person rates an aspect of himself negatively (e.g. 'It is bad that I have failed') and then gives himself a global negative rating as a result (e.g. 'therefore I am a failure'), he makes an error of overgeneralization, or what is called the part–whole error.

Applying the concept of unconditional self-acceptance to this example, the person would still infer that he has failed in some respect and would still evaluate this failure negatively. However, his conclusion that his failure proves that he is a fallible human being and not *a failure* would be perfectly logical and would not involve an overgeneralisation.

6. *Unconditional self-acceptance is based on a flexible, preferential philosophy.*

Earlier in this chapter, I pointed out that, according to Ellis (1994), self-depreciation beliefs are based largely on rigid demands. It follows, then, that unconditional self-acceptance beliefs are based largely on flexible, preferential beliefs.

For example, if you believe that you are inadequate because you acted in a socially inappropriate manner, then this self-depreciation belief is based on your rigid demand: 'I must not act in a socially inappropriate manner.' A self-accepting alternative belief would involve you accepting yourself as a fallible human being who may have acted inappropriately, but who is not an inadequate person. This self-accepting belief, in turn, would be based on the following, flexible, preferential belief: 'I would prefer not to act in a socially inappropriate manner, but there is no reason why I absolutely must not do so.'

7. *Self-acceptance leads to healthy emotional and behavioural results.*

Accepting yourself in the face of negative activating events will result in your experiencing healthy emotion results such as concern, sadness, remorse, disappointment, sorrow, healthy anger, concern for your relationship and healthy envy. As I have shown in Chapter 1, these emotions will lead you to act in constructive ways. However, if you adhere to the principle of self-esteem, you may consider yourself to be worth while when you face positive activating events, but when you face negative activating events you will depreciate yourself, which will lead you to experience unhealthy negative emotions such as anxiety, depression, guilt, hurt, shame, unhealthy anger, jealousy and unhealthy envy. As I have shown in Chapter 1, these emotions will lead you to act in unconstructive ways.

8. *Self-acceptance promotes constructive action, not resignation.*

If we can accept ourselves as fallible human beings, with all that this means, paradoxically we have a much better chance of minimizing our errors and psychological problems than if we depreciate ourselves for having them in the first place. Self-acceptance enables us to do this because it helps us to focus on what we do as humans rather than on how worth while we are for what we do (as is the case if we buy into the concept of self-esteem and depreciate ourselves for our errors). As self-acceptance is based on a philosophy of desire, it also motivates us to take constructive action as we focus on what we don't do well. Self-acceptance does not, therefore, encourage resignation, as many think it does.

Resignation is based on the idea that there is nothing we can do to improve aspects of ourselves, so there is no point in trying. Indeed, self-depreciation is far more likely to lead to resignation than self-acceptance. Thus, if you believe that you are a failure for failing, you are much more likely to conclude that there is little you can do to succeed than if you accept yourself for failing. Believing yourself to be a failure implies that you will not be able to succeed (and therefore why try?), while believing that you are fallible implies that you can both succeed and fail (and therefore it is worth trying to succeed).

In Chapters 5–14 I will show how Rational Emotive Behaviour Therapists apply the theoretical ideas that I have covered in this chapter in the context of a ten-week educational group designed to help clients begin the journey towards self-acceptance. But first, in the next chapter, I will discuss the role adopted by REBT therapists in the therapeutic process. In doing so, I will pay particular attention to their role in running brief, educational self-acceptance groups.

3

RUNNING SELF-ACCEPTANCE GROUPS: THE ROLE OF THE RATIONAL EMOTIVE BEHAVIOUR THERAPIST

In this chapter, I will outline the therapeutic role of the Rational Emotive Behaviour Therapist with special reference to the main theme of this book: running self-acceptance groups. In particular, I will consider the following issues:

1. First, I will outline the REBT position on the 'core conditions'.
2. Second, I will explain why REBT therapists generally adopt an active-directive therapeutic style and why this is especially the case in running self-acceptance groups.
3. Third, I will consider the role of the REBT therapist as a psychological educator.
4. Finally, I will consider the gate-keeping role of the REBT therapist in running self-acceptance groups and will stress the particular importance of structuring group sessions and effectively managing communication within the group.

REBT's POSITION ON THE 'CORE CONDITIONS'

In 1957, Carl Rogers, published an article which has become one of the most seminal papers in the field of counselling and psychotherapy. In this article, among other issues, Rogers outlined a number of core therapeutic conditions which needed to be present if therapeutic change was to occur. His original list has subsequently been refined, and the present consensus in the field is that there are three such conditions. These are empathy, respect and genuineness, and are collectively known as the core conditions.

In this section I will outline REBT's position on each of the core conditions, for this is somewhat different from Rogers' original views. First, I will consider REBT's view on the status of these core conditions in the therapeutic process. In his original paper, Rogers (1957) opined that these conditions were both necessary and sufficient for therapeutic change. This means two things: (i) they have to be present and (ii) no further conditions are necessary if therapeutic change is to occur. Since Rogers' original formulation, some theorists, such as Carkhuff (1983) and Egan (1994), have argued that these three core conditions are necessary but not sufficient for the occurrence of therapeutic change. This position states that empathy, respect and genuineness are necessary but not sufficient for such change. This means three things: (i) these conditions have to be present otherwise therapeutic change will not occur; (ii) the existence of these conditions is not enough for the occurrence of such change and (iii) other additional conditions have to be present if therapeutic change is to ensue.

REBT's position on this issue is quite different from the two that have been outlined. It is a position that has remained basically the same since Ellis (1959) responded to Rogers' (1957) original paper. It is that while the presence of the core conditions may well be desirable, they are neither necessary nor sufficient for therapeutic change to occur. This means three things: (i) the core conditions may well aid therapeutic conditions; (ii) their absence does not preclude the occurrence of therapeutic change and (iii) other additional conditions have to be present if such change is to occur. Having outlined the REBT position on the core conditions, let me consider REBT's stance on each in turn.

Empathy

REBT distinguishes between two types of empathy: affective empathy and philosophic empathy. When REBT therapists communicate affective empathy they show their clients that they understand how the latter feel. However, when they communicate philosophic empathy, they show their clients that they also understand the beliefs (or philosophies) that underpin the latter's feelings. As such, philosophic empathy is a theory-driven type of empathy by which I mean that this type of therapist understanding is influenced by REBT theory which states that emotions are largely determined by the beliefs that people hold about the activating events that they encounter.

While both types of empathy are important in the practice of REBT, philosophic empathy is especially important. While affective empathy is important in that it helps clients to 'feel' that their REBT therapists understand their emotional experience, on its own it does not take clients much further. The addition of philosophic empathy helps clients to understand the factors that explain why they feel as they do. It thus has an educational value that is not offered by the communication of affective empathy.

Since philosophic empathy is a theory-driven concept in that it communicates the REBT view of why clients feel as they do, it is important to make this clear to clients. Effective REBT therapists do not think that they have the monopoly on truth. They are secure enough in their practice to make clear that theirs is but one approach to the understanding and amelioration of psychological disturbance and there are other different perspectives in the field of counselling and psychotherapy. This is particularly important for clients who do not resonate with the REBT model. When this is the case, my practice is to refer the client to a practitioner whose approach to therapy will be more acceptable to that client.

Also, since philosophic empathy is a theory-driven concept, it is important that when offering this type of understanding, you put it forward as a hypothesis rather than as a fact. For example, it is better to say something like 'I may well be wrong and if I am please do correct me, but my hunch is that the reason why you feel anxious about meeting your new employer is that you believe that you must make a good impression on him. Am I right or wrong about that?' than to declare 'The reason you feel anxious about meeting your new employer is because you believe that you must make a good impression on him'. The first statement is tentatively put and the client is given the freedom to confirm or deny the accuracy of the therapist's attempt to empathize with the reason for the client's anxiety. As such it involves the client in the therapeutic process and strengthens the therapeutic alliance between the two. The second statement, on the other hand, is put forward as a fact and the client is given no opportunity to confirm or deny its accuracy. As such it does not foster the therapeutic alliance and discourages client involvement in the therapeutic process. Effective REBT therapists, therefore, are more likely to couch their theory-driven empathic communications in the manner of the first statement than the second.

Unconditional Acceptance

This condition was originally called unconditional positive regard and has subsequently been called respect or prizing. It represents the therapist's basic attitude towards the client as a human being. In REBT, we call this condition unconditional acceptance.

Unconditional acceptance is different from unconditional positive regard and the other terms in that it does not imply a global positive rating of the client, which the other terms do. Rather, it advocates that the therapist accepts that the client is unrateable as a person and is a fallible human being with good, bad and neutral aspects. As such, the client is no better or no worse than anyone else. This attitude is held unconditionally in that there are seen to be no exceptions to this principle. When the therapist departs from this basic attitude towards clients, this is viewed as evidence that the therapist holds an unhealthy belief about the client and not that the client warrants such a departure in attitude. The concept of acceptance was considered in greater depth in the previous chapter where I fully discussed the REBT view of self-acceptance.

Genuineness

As the term makes clear, genuineness points to the extent to which therapists are being truly themselves in the therapeutic encounter or the extent to which they are adopting a therapeutic façade. In REBT we think that it is important for therapists to be themselves within the professional and ethical context of the practice of psychotherapy. This latter phrase is very important because it reminds us that there is a context to be taken into account when we consider genuineness. Having stressed this point, REBT therapists do not hide behind any façade. We will generally answer clients' questions honestly when asked – if they are therapeutically relevant – and we will engage in self-disclosure if doing so has a therapeutic point. In being ourselves, however, we are acutely aware that we are therapists and are guided by the following principle: 'First, do no harm.' Thus we will not honestly give an opinion or answer a question if we think that clients may disturb themselves about what we have to say.

For example, sometimes a client makes the accusation that I do not care about him or her. If I think that the client can take my answer, I may say something like:

> 'If by caring you mean do I love you or do I think about you a lot when you are not here, the answer is that I don't care for you in this way. I don't care for you or any of my clients as I care for my family or close friends. But this doesn't mean that I do not care about your well-being. Far from it. When you are here I care enough to give you 100% of my attention and my expertise. In other words, I care passionately about helping you over your problems.'

Now most clients can take such an honest response and see that my job is to provide professional caring and nothing else. However, a small minority of clients may well disturb themselves about what I have just said and with these clients I would tone down what I say. So, in summary, the REBT position on genuineness is this: By all means be honest, but don't forget that you are a therapist and that your job is to help clients overcome their emotional problems. Therefore, do no harm and make sure that your disclosures are therapeutically relevant.

REBT FAVOURS AN ACTIVE–DIRECTIVE THERAPEUTIC STYLE

All approaches to counselling and psychotherapy can be located on two continua with respect to the therapeutic style favoured by practitioners of these approaches: the activity level of the therapist and the amount of direction provided by the therapist. For example, those who offer a listening service will tend to be placed towards both the very low end of the level of activity continuum and the very low end of the directiveness continuum. This means that listeners are neither active nor directive in their stance towards their clients. Carl Rogers, the pioneer of person-centred therapy, would have been placed towards the high end of the level of activity continuum and towards the low end of the directiveness continuum. This means that Rogers was active in therapeutic style but did not provide much direction to his clients.

Rational Emotive Behaviour Therapists would tend to be placed towards the high end of both the level of activity and the directiveness continua. In other words, they tend to be highly active and highly directive in therapeutic style, particularly at the beginning of the therapeutic process. In brief they are known for their active–directive style of conducting therapy.

What is the rationale for this active–directive approach? Let me address this issue by considering each aspect of this therapeutic style separately. Rational Emotive Behaviour Therapists have a definite view of how clients disturb themselves and what they need to do to overcome their psychological problems. This view is encapsulated in the ABCDE model discussed in Chapter 1. We believe, furthermore, that, left to their own devices, clients will not generally discover this model for themselves and even if they do so they are very unlikely to know how to apply the model to help themselves. Consequently, they need to be directed towards and educated in the model and how to use it. Let me state that effective REBT therapists direct their clients to this model in a sensitive way, mindful of the pace at which their clients learn and how much information they can assimilate at any point in time.

In directing their clients to the ABCDE model, REBT therapists are active in the therapeutic process. They actively involve their clients in a Socratic dialogue, helping them to identify, challenge and change their unhealthy beliefs by asking many questions designed to encourage their clients to think carefully and independently about the empirical, logical and pragmatic status of both their unhealthy beliefs and their healthy alternatives. They also actively use didactic explanations about different aspects of the ABCDE model, taking care to check frequently that they are making themselves clear. If they were passive in this process, then this would mean that the process of REBT would be much longer than it otherwise needs to be. Thus, the active–directive style of practising REBT is deemed to be not only more effective but also more efficient than any other style of practising this approach to psychotherapy.

If REBT therapists favour an active–directive style in individual therapy, this is especially the case when running self-acceptance groups. As you will see, you have a number of tasks to accomplish in the ten weeks over which these groups are typically run and you also have to manage the therapeutic communication between yourself and the group members on the one hand and among the group members on the other. This cannot be achieved if you were to be either passive or non-directive in therapeutic style. I will have more to say on this issue later in this chapter.

Having said this, REBT is a flexible approach to therapy and there is scope for varying your therapeutic style with different clients. While this variability is more likely to occur in individual therapy since you are communicating with one person at a time, you can still vary your therapeutic style while running self-acceptance groups when communicating individually to group members. However, when you are addressing the group as a whole your therapeutic style will be active–directive in nature.

REBT THERAPISTS AS PSYCHOLOGICAL EDUCATORS

One way of conceptualizing the role of Rational Emotive Behaviour Therapists is to see us as psychological educators. Psychological education may be seen as 'the systematic approach to helping clients use the model and method advocated by the counsellor'. Thus, REBT therapists are psychological educators to the extent that they help their clients to use the ABCDE model of problem conceptualization and change. Certainly, in this book, I will present a structured approach to teaching clients the REBT perspective on self-depreciation and its healthy alternative, self-acceptance and a number of key techniques that they can use to become more self-accepting.

As I am teaching clients a specific perspective, I will expect that they will be prepared to use the methods that stem from this perspective. However, in order for them to do this they will have to understand this perspective and consider that it has potential to help them overcome their self-depreciation problems. Whether they come to these conclusions will depend on two factors: (i) my ability to communicate the REBT model in a persuasive manner; and (ii) their own views on the determinants of their self-depreciation problems and how these can be best addressed.

Two of the hallmarks of psychological education are explicitness and relativity. My goal as a psychological educator is to teach explicitly the REBT model of self-depreciation and its remediation. However, I will also want to make clear to the clients in the group that this perspective is not the only one used in the field of counselling and psychotherapy. There are other perspectives, and if any of the group members do not find the REBT model helpful, I will be quite happy to refer them to a therapeutic approach with which they are likely to resonate.

These qualities of explicitness and relativity means that clients are in the position to make an informed choice concerning the potential usefulness of REBT to their self-depreciation problems. If they do not find it useful they are given other treatment possibilities.

If they do find REBT potentially useful in overcoming their self-depreciation problems, they are then provided with a full understanding of REBT's position on these problems (see Chapter 2) and are given explicit training in REBT methods which they can use as they strive to overcome these problems and work towards greater self-acceptance. It is both the explicit teaching of the REBT conceptualization of self-depreciation problems and the explicit instruction in relevant REBT change techniques that characterize the psychological–educational features of REBT.

REBT THERAPISTS AS GATE-KEEPERS OF THERAPEUTIC COMMUNICATION IN SELF-ACCEPTANCE GROUPS

In Chapters 5–14 of this book, I will outline a session-by-session guide to running self-acceptance groups. One of the defining features of these groups is that they are structured. From an educational perspective, these groups follow a set curriculum of topics that are important to cover if clients are to be given the tools which they can use after the groups finish. However, clients are not passive recipients of the therapist's wisdom in the group process. They are encouraged to be active in the therapeutic process in providing relevant self-referent information which can be worked on during the group sessions. They are also encouraged to voice their doubts, reservations and objections to the REBT view of self-depreciation and self-acceptance and to the change techniques that are taught during the life of the group. Finally, they are encouraged to communicate with one another to share similar experiences and to encourage each other as they all embark on the journey towards self-acceptance.

Despite the fact that clients are encouraged to be active during self-acceptance groups, REBT group therapists need to keep on track with respect to the therapeutic curriculum. In other words, they have a number of tasks to perform during the life of the group. Consequently, therapists need to adopt and maintain a gate-keeping role in managing the therapeutic communication that occurs between themselves and the group members as well as that which transpires among the group members themselves. Thus, therapists need to dissuade clients from engaging in lengthy asides, communication that is not relevant to the topic of building self-acceptance. They also need to discourage group members from offering one another solutions to the problem of self-depreciation which do not involve changing the unhealthy beliefs that are at the core of this problem in the first place. This means that therapists intervene whenever group members offer one another palliative, pollyana-ish, incorrect or dangerous solutions to self-depreciation problems and explain why these solutions will not work in the long term.

It is important that REBT group therapists explain to group members why they are adopting this gate-keeping role and remind them of this healthy belief as they make gate-keeping interventions. When they make interventions designed to keep the group on track, they need to do so firmly but non-pejoratively, explaining to the group the nature of the deviation from task-relevant discussion and then continuing with the group's on-task focus. In doing so it is helpful to build any bridges between the task-irrelevant behaviour that the group is currently engaged in and the task-relevant behaviour that the therapist will now bring them back to. For example:

FRANK: That reminds me of the time I sold my bike to get more money for my holiday in Europe.

JENNY: I've been to Europe. Where did you go?

THERAPIST: Those sound like interesting journeys, but let's get back to our respective journeys towards self-acceptance. Now as I was saying.

At times, REBT group therapists may have to interrupt clients in mid-sentence if they are to interrupt the task-irrelevant interchanges among group members. In doing so, the therapist concerned should avoid

making perjorative or rude comments to group members as these will
threaten the therapeutic alliance between the therapist and the group
members and will reveal the offending therapist as a poor role model for
healthy communication.

When therapists intervene to stop group members giving one another
poor advice, once again they need to explain why the advice will not help
the member concerned to develop self-acceptance in the long run.
However, the group member giving the advice should be reinforced for
making the effort to help a fellow group member. For example:

JOHN: My boss criticized me and I felt badly about myself and I'm not
    sure what I need to do to develop self-acceptance in the face of his
    criticism.

THERAPIST (*to the group*):   Any ideas, group?

JOAN: You could always tell yourself something like: 'He's just envious
    of you. That's why he's criticizing you.'

THERAPIST: Thanks for suggesting that, Joan. However, there's a problem
    with that intervention. That's what we call changing the A, Joan. You're
    encouraging John to change the way he views his boss, rather than
    changing his unhealthy beliefs about being criticized. Can you see that if
    John follows your advice he won't develop self-acceptance when he
    most needs it? i.e. when the going gets tough and his boss criticizes him.

As the group members become increasingly familiar with the REBT
model and its change techniques, then the therapist can ask them to
comment on one another's poor suggestions. Thus, the therapist can ask
for a volunteer to comment on the group member's suggestion or can ask
a named individual. Here's an example of the latter:

JOHN: My boss criticized me and I felt badly about myself and I'm not
    sure what I need to do to develop self-acceptance in the face of his
    criticism.

THERAPIST (*to the group*):   Any ideas, group?

JOAN: You could always tell yourself something like: 'He's just envious
    of you. That's why he's criticizing you.'

THERAPIST: Thanks for that suggestion, Joan, but there's a problem with
    it. Keith, can you see what that problem is?

If Keith correctly identifies the problem with Joan's suggestion, the therapist should acknowledge that. However, if he is incorrect, the therapist

should first thank him for his suggestion and then provide the right answer. By the 'right answer' here I mean from the perspective of REBT theory.

Some therapists would ensure that a group member should provide the right answer and would hold back in providing it themselves, believing that it is empowering and that it facilitates group learning if group members are all involved in considering an issue such as what is wrong with Joan's suggestion to John. Here, the therapist would ask each member in turn for his or her input and would only provide the answer when it became clear that none of the members is able to do so. While there is much to say for this approach to running groups, the main problem with it is that it is too time consuming. If one had twenty or thirty sessions to run such a group, this approach would have much to commend it. However, with ten 90-minute group sessions, there is insufficient time to adopt this approach and to cover everything on the therapeutic curriculum. Consequently, a compromise has to be struck.

Taking the example of evaluating Joan's suggestion to John, a suitable compromise would involve the therapist encouraging one or two group members to comment on Joan's suggestion and then providing the correct answer if the group members fail to.

In this chapter, I have explained why, in their quest to help clients build self-acceptance, REBT therapists are best seen as active–directive, psychological educators within the context of offering these clients an empathic, accepting, genuine, but firmly managed therapeutic relationship. However, the success of brief, educationally based self-acceptance groups also depends on the careful selection of clients who can benefit most from such groups. Consequently, in the next chapter, I will turn my attention to the formation of these groups.

4

SETTING UP A SELF-ACCEPTANCE GROUP

In this chapter, I will discuss the issues that an REBT group leader needs to consider in setting up a self-acceptance group. In doing so, I will first outline the basic assumptions that underpin the practice of such groups before discussing a number of nitty-gritty issues. Here, I will deal with the issue of advertising for and selecting group members and look at the context in which the group is run and the impact that this may have on group process. I will also focus on the immediate setting in which the group is run and the materials that are needed by the group leader and group members if important tasks are to be successfully completed during the life of the group.

Before I begin my discussion, I want to stress an important point which you should keep in mind as you read this chapter. There is often a difference between running self-acceptance groups under ideal conditions and running them under the actual conditions one will invariably face in therapeutic practice. If you are an idealist and are only prepared to run self-acceptance groups if ideal conditions are met, then you will not run self-acceptance groups. It is as simple as that. I am not advocating that you should run such groups no matter what conditions exist; however, you do need to adopt a pragmatic approach both when you plan your group and when you run it.

I have run self-acceptance groups in a university setting, a NHS hospital, a private psychiatric clinic and a prison, and in all these contexts I have been called upon to make compromises with my ideal practice. I will highlight and discuss these compromises throughout this chapter.

Having made this important caveat, let me consider the basic assumption which underlies the practice of time-limited, educationally focused self-acceptance groups. It is this assumption which guides the way these groups are structured and run and which influences the thinking of REBT therapists as they set them up.

BASIC ASSUMPTION

The self-acceptance groups that I run, and which are the focus of this book, are based on the basic assumption that the philosophy of unconditional self-acceptance can be taught. The REBT view, as discussed in Chapter 3, is that while it is highly desirable that these ideas are taught by an accepting therapist, this is neither a necessary nor sufficient ingredient of the group experience for group members. While REBT therapists recognize that group members will not be able to accept themselves fully in a short period of time, they do ascribe to the view that these members can be taught both the basic principles of self-acceptance and a variety of tools which can aid their practice of these principles during the ten weeks when the group meets. This assumption means that the goal of self-acceptance groups is to equip group members for the journey towards self-acceptance and to encourage them to begin this journey. It does not claim to help them achieve self-acceptance in ten weeks.

THE FORMAT OF SELF-ACCEPTANCE GROUPS

There are very many different types of therapy groups. If we just take two salient variables – time and group membership, for example – we have brief open groups, brief closed groups, long-term open groups and long-term closed groups. The self-acceptance groups that are the focus of the present text are run as brief closed groups. Why? I will answer this question by considering each variable in turn.

Let me begin by considering the question of time. Self-acceptance groups are brief for two reasons. First, they are brief because their aim is to help group members begin the journey towards self-acceptance and to give them the necessary knowledge and skills to make this journey. In my experience this can be achieved in ten weekly 90-minute group sessions. Second, they are brief for pragmatic reasons. Thus, when self-acceptance groups are run in a private psychiatric hospital, the group leader has to be mindful of the fact that group members are likely to be limited with respect to insurance cover. While a minority of private clients may be prepared to finance their attendance themselves, the majority are reliant on their fees being met by their insurance companies. Since it is likely that such clients are concurrently attending other therapy groups and have regular contact with their psychiatrists, their insurance companies will not usually fund their attendance at a long-term group. This is particularly the case as these companies are currently introducing managed care principles into their funding of mental health services.

The issue of how much therapy is offered to patients is also salient in the National Health Service with its increasing emphasis on market principles. Increasingly, patients are being offered brief therapy, and if this can take place in the context of groupwork, so much the better. It is far more likely that patients will be offered the opportunity to attend self-acceptance groups in the NHS if these groups are brief than if they are long-term.

Second, let me consider the issue of group membership. The choice of whether to make membership of self-acceptance open or closed follows logically from the decision to make such groups brief and time-limited. As I have just stated, self-acceptance groups are held over ten weekly 90-minute sessions. As I will show you in Part 2 of this book, these group sessions are tightly structured and, in effect, follow a therapeutic curriculum. As such, it is crucial that the membership of such groups is closed. If it was open, the group leader would have to spend valuable group time introducing and explaining the principles of self-acceptance (as discussed in Chapter 2) every week, thus taking time away from teaching the skills that group members need to learn and practise in the group if they are to apply these principles outside the group.

Also, making self-acceptance groups closed has other therapeutic advantages. First, it means that group members can learn to trust one another and disclose their problems at a deeper level than would be possible in an open group. Second, in doing so, group members can learn that their problems are not unique and that they are not weird people for having universally shared problems. Third, closed groups allow for the development of a sense of group cohesiveness, so important to a good therapeutic outcome (Yalom, 1995).

It is for these reasons that self-acceptance groups are run briefly and with a closed membership. In the next section, I will discuss the issue of advertising for potential members of such groups.

ADVERTISING SELF-ACCEPTANCE GROUPS

Therapeutic groups are not magically established. A lot of planning usually has to go into their formation. The first obvious step to setting up a self-acceptance group is that you have to let people know of its existence. There are usually two groups of people whom you have to inform that you are planning to run a self-acceptance group: (i) relevant professionals who might refer suitable clients to your group and/or whose responsibility it is to decide whether or not your group should be incorporated into the therapeutic services offered by the organization in which you work and (ii) the client population from whom you hope to draw the membership of your group.

Liaising with Professionals whose Permission you Need to Run your Self-acceptance Group

If you are not directly responsible for organizing therapy services in the place where you work, it is very advisable that you liaise with the professionals who are thus responsible, since in all probability you will require their permission to run your group. In my experience this is best done at a face-to-face meeting where you should be prepared to talk about:

- the nature and aims of the group
- how long the group will run for
- its cost-effectiveness
- who is most likely to benefit from the group
- the importance of interviewing potential group members prior to the first group meeting
- the importance of having a room large enough to accommodate comfortably eleven people and small subgroups of clients who may talk without being overheard by other subgroups
- the materials and equipment you and the group members will need, and
- which referring agents should be contacted if permission to run the group is granted.

It is important that you prepare yourself thoroughly for this meeting so that you can talk succinctly and confidently about these points. You will also need to anticipate the kinds of questions that the person you will be meeting is likely to ask and prepare answers to these questions. Finally, you need to be responsive to the requirements of the other person. For example, if the organization cannot provide certain materials, you will need to find a way around this problem.

Identifying and Informing Relevant Referring Agents about the Group

If you are given permission to run the group, I suggested above that you need to ask the person who has granted this permission to identify referring agents whom you need to inform about the group's existence. Most therapeutic organizations have an implicit, if not an explicit, protocol about how referring agents should be contacted and it is best that you learn and abide by this protocol. Failure to do so is likely to lead to permission to run your self-acceptance group being withdrawn, as well as to other problems.

Most organizations have a standard list of referral agents, but will differ concerning how these people can be contacted. Some organizations will allow you to contact referral agents directly, while others will want to do this themselves. If the former is the case you will probably need to draft a letter informing referral agents about the group. It is wise to send a draft of this letter to the appropriate person in your organization for comment before you send it out. If the latter is the case, the person concerned will either want you to draft a letter or will want to write it personally, based on the information you have supplied. If this is the case, it is wise to ask to see this letter before it is sent so that you can correct any misconceptions in it. For example, you may discover in a draft that the course is being advertised as a self-esteem course and not one designed to foster self-acceptance. This is something that you need to correct and you need to do so tactfully to the person concerned.

What information do you need to include in such a letter to referral agents? I suggest the following:

- the type of group you are running
- the type of client problems the group is designed to address
- the aims of the group, and
- who might benefit from attending the group.

Here you can let referring agents know your inclusion criteria (see below, pp. 53–55). It is important to stress that you will conduct an intake interview to ensure that only clients likely to benefit from the group will be included. Other information includes:

- the dates on which group sessions will be run
- who will be running the group
- where the group sessions will be held
- the cost of attendance (if relevant)
- how and to whom referrals can be made, and
- the feedback that you will provide to the referrer about any clients referred after the group has finished.

While a letter including the above information is likely to be the most frequent mode of communication to referring agents, you may work in an organization where you could make a personal presentation to referring agents. Thus, in a private psychiatric hospital where I used to run self-acceptance groups, the consultant psychiatrists use to meet weekly for what was called the 'consultants' lunch'. Before I ran a self-acceptance group at that hospital for the first time, I obtained an invitation to attend such a lunch, where I spoke about my plans to run such a group. This proved to be a very successful way of obtaining referrals. I followed up my presentation with a letter of thanks to each consultant, outlining in that letter the information contained in the ten points presented above.

Advertising the Self-acceptance Group to Potential Clients

If you are in a position to inform potential clients directly of your plans to run a self-acceptance group – and once again you will probably need to gain permission to do so – you will probably need to prepare written advertising material. This may be in the form of advertising posters or letters sent directly to a targeted client population. In both instances you will need to provide the following information (which you will note is similar to the information provided to referring agents):

- the type of group you are running
- the type of client problems the group is designed to address
- the aims of the group
- who might benefit from attending the group
- the dates on which group sessions will be run
- who will be running the group
- where the group sessions will be held, and
- the cost of attendance (if relevant).

Figure 4.1 shows an example of advertising material that I prepared for clients attending a day care unit in a private psychiatric hospital that incorporated much of this information (the remainder was given by the therapy services manager at the hospital).

SELECTING GROUP MEMBERS

Let me assume that you have advertised the existence of your self-acceptance group and have now received the names of potential group members. The next step is to interview them to determine whether or not they are suitable for the specific group you are planning to run. Yalom

---

Do You Suffer From Low Self-Esteem?

Do you often think of yourself in the following terms?:

'I'm a failure'
'I'm unlovable'
'I'm defective'
'I'm insignificant'
'I'm a bad person'

Do you think that other people will reject you if they got to know you or that they will find you boring?

If so, you probably have low self-esteem. Low self-esteem is often at the core of emotional problems such as *depression, guilt, shame, anxiety, anger, jealousy, hurt* and *envy.*

However, you can learn to develop a much healthier attitude towards yourself. Windy Dryden, Britain's first Professor of Counselling, has developed a ten-week group programme in which you will learn:

- Why self-acceptance is the healthy alternative to low self-esteem.
- Techniques that you can use to help you to develop self-acceptance during the weeks in which the group meets, and afterwards too.

If you are interested in joining this group and can commit yourself to attending all ten weekly group sessions, contact Sue in the office for further details.

Figure 4.1:   An Example of Advertising Material for a Self-acceptance Group

(1995) has noted that there is little research evidence to help us to determine who will benefit from which kind of therapy group. He also notes that it is easier to specify who is not likely to benefit in a particular group rather than who is. In other words, the exclusion criteria are more likely to be obvious than the inclusion criteria.

Another point to consider is the number of people who have expressed an interest in joining your group. If you have ten spaces (which I consider the maximum number for a brief self-acceptance group), you are much more likely to set stricter inclusion criteria the greater the number of interested applicants you have beyond ten. If you have ten or less then exclusion criteria rather than inclusion criteria are likely to play a much greater control in the selection process.

Having said all this let me outline inclusion and exclusion criteria for brief, educationally focused self-acceptance groups.

Inclusion Criteria

Inclusion criteria for self-acceptance groups are factors that make clients particularly suitable for these groups. The following is a list of such criteria:

1. *The person agrees to focus on ego disturbance problems in the group.*

If you recall from Chapter 1, REBT posits two major types of psychological disturbance: ego disturbance and discomfort disturbance. As the name indicates, self-acceptance groups are designed for clients whose major problems are in the area of ego disturbance (see Chapter 2 for a discussion of ego disturbance). It is likely that many clients also have problems in the realm of discomfort disturbance. However, if their main problems concern lack of self-acceptance or they wish to focus on ego disturbance issues in the group, even if their main problems are to do with discomfort disturbance, they are suitable for inclusion in a self-acceptance group.

2. *The educational focus of the group makes sense to the person and joining the group is considered to be a helpful experience.*

As I will discuss below, when you interview potential group members, you will use that opportunity to inform them in broad terms about the nature of self-acceptance groups. In particular, you will want to tell them about the educational focus of the group. Thus, you will explain that you will provide a particular framework within which they will be shown that unhelpful beliefs about the 'self' lie at the root of self-depreciation problems and you will teach them techniques to help them begin the journey towards self-acceptance. Explaining this enables the potential members to make an informed decision concerning whether or not the group makes sense to them and whether or not they think that it has the potential to be helpful to them. If the potential members indicate that the group makes sense to them and they think it may be helpful to them, then these are positive inclusion criteria.

3. *The person is prepared to practise outside sessions what is learned in sessions.*

As I pointed out in Chapter 1, the self-acceptance groups that are described in this book are based on the principles and practice of Rational Emotive Behaviour Therapy (REBT). As is well known, REBT is an approach which falls within the wider cognitive-behavioural tradition of psychotherapy. One of the hallmarks of this tradition is the emphasis that is placed on clients helping themselves between sessions. Put another way, clients are expected to carry out relevant regular 'homework' tasks so that they can practise outside therapy sessions what they learn during these sessions.

This emphasis on homework tasks is a prominent feature of self-acceptance groups and, as such, clients who are prepared to do this work are suitable for these groups. If they are not willing to do so, they may well be suitable for the group on other inclusion criteria, but they will derive little benefit from the group unless they practise outside the group what they learn within it. It is my practice, therefore, not to include clients who state at intake interview that they are not prepared to do between-session homework tasks.

4. *The person understands and assents to the modest aims of the group.*

In the same way as Maslow (1968) explained that one cannot achieve self-actualization, rather one can only work towards it, a person cannot achieve full self-acceptance. So while one can acquire a self-acceptance belief and strengthen it, one cannot strengthen it to such an extent that one never loses it. I have already pointed out that the aims of self-acceptance groups are modest. They are to equip group members with the knowledge and skills to enable them to embark on the journey to-wards self-acceptance rather than to help them achieve self-acceptance, once and for all. It is important to explain this aim to potential clients at the intake interview. Those who understand and assent to it are par-ticularly suitable for inclusion in self-acceptance groups.

5. *The person is able to attend group sessions regularly.*

As you will see in Part 2 of this book, self-acceptance groups have a tightly structured curriculum. There is a lot to cover in ten group sessions and I have already pointed out that this necessitates such groups having a closed membership (see pp. 47–48). It also explains why regular attend-ance at such groups is very important. Clients who are willing and able to make a commitment to attend all group sessions are also particularly suitable to join these groups.

6. *The person is willing to discuss problems in a group setting.*

Not all clients are willing to join a group because they find the idea of discussing their problems in a group context quite frightening. Such people are not likely to volunteer for any kind of therapy group, or if they do come forward, do so with a great deal of ambivalence. On the other hand, other clients are quite willing to join a group and discuss their problems in a group setting. They see the benefits rather than the costs of doing so. Such clients make good group members on this criterion.

7. *The person is willing to help other group members.*

Good members of self-acceptance groups are those who not only wish to be helped in a group setting, but who also wish to help other group members. If some members are only there for themselves, then this will not be productive for the other members of a self-acceptance group. Since membership of the group involves cooperation in group exercises, a person who is involved when the focus is on him or her, but non-participipative when the focus is on others, will ultimately interfere with the level of cooperation in the group. While this issue might be productively taken up, explored and worked through in a longer-term group, there is insufficient time to do this in a brief, educationally focused, self-acceptance group. The converse problem lies with the member who gains self-esteem through helping others. This issue, however, is easier to take up within the context of a self-acceptance group since it fits more readily with the theme of the group than does the member who is self-preoccupied.

In summary, people who have the joint motivation of helping themselves and helping others are good candidates for self-acceptance groups on this criterion. Those whose major motivation is to help others can be included if they meet other inclusion criteria, while those whose sole motivation is to help themselves should not be included unless you need those people in the group to make it viable in terms of numbers.

Exclusion Criteria

Exclusion criteria for self-acceptance groups are factors that make clients unsuitable for these groups. The following is a list of such criteria:

1. *The person will not interact productively in the group.*

As I mentioned earlier, the success of a self-acceptance group depends, in part, on there being a level of cooperation between group members. There are three major threats to this cooperative spirit which, if detected at intake interview, constitute exclusion criteria. These threats are (i) the member who monopolizes the group; (ii) the member who wishes to relate only to the therapist and (iii) the withdrawn member. In other words, people posing such threats should not be selected for self-acceptance groups, even if their exclusion means that the group has to be postponed until other more suitable group members are found, and even if the group has to be cancelled, I would rather not run a self-acceptance group than run one knowing that it will not be a productive experience for the majority of group members. Let me deal with these three situations in turn.

(i) *The member who monopolizes the group.* Clients who monopolize self-acceptance groups are disruptive for two main reasons. First, they slow up the momentum of the group and make it very difficult for the group leader to take charge of the group process – something which is necessary if the curriculum is to be covered. Dealing with clients who monopolize the group is difficult for the group leader because interventions have little lasting impact on their behaviour. They may briefly stop speaking in response to the leader's request or intervention, but will very soon return to their monopolizing ways. As such, other group members become increasingly irritated with those members and energy is taken away from the central task of the group: learning and practising the techniques of unconditional self-acceptance. Also, such clients often wander off the point and introduce too many irrelevancies into their communications. This also serves to move the group away from its central task.

Second, clients who monopolize the group do not give other group members sufficient opportunities to participate in the group process. They prevent others from elaborating on their own points and this means that others are given less time to relate the concepts and techniques that are being taught in the group to their own experience. Consequently, clients who monopolize the group interfere with the learning of other group members who derive less benefit from the group than would be the case if those people were not present. For these reasons, people who are likely to monopolize self-acceptance groups should be excluded from them.

(ii) *The member who wishes to relate only to the therapist.* Some clients find it difficult to participate productively in self-acceptance groups because they wish to relate only to the therapist. As such they do not actively join in small group or peer exercises and remain on the edge of interactions that do not involve the therapist. The reasons that such people take this stance are often complex, but include not being able to share the therapist with other group members and viewing the therapist as the expert and the only person in the group who has anything of value to the group. This is disruptive in that, over time, these members become marginalized and this may serve to reinforce their own self-depreciation attitudes. While this process can be worked with productively in a longer term group, doing so would take up too much time in a brief, structured self-acceptance group. Thus, it is best if such individuals are excluded from joining these groups.

(iii) *The withdrawn member*. Clients who are likely to be withdrawn and non-participative in self-acceptance groups should not be included in these groups for two reasons. First, it is unlikely that they will derive much personal benefit from these groups. Being a member of a self-acceptance group calls upon group members to communicate openly about their self-depreciation problems and to engage actively in small group and peer exercises. If such members are withdrawn, they will not be willing to talk about their problems when others are present. Consequently, the therapist will not be able to help them to apply self-acceptance concepts and associated techniques to their problems. Thus, what they learn from the group will be strictly theoretical. Second, when members are withdrawn they will not be in a position to help others in small group and peer exercises and thus their presence will inevitably interfere with other group members' learning.

2. *The person has significant learning difficulties.*

Another category of clients who should be excluded from brief, educationally focused self-acceptance groups are those with significant learning difficulties. The issue here is time. As you will see from Part 2 of this book, there is a lot of material to cover in ten weeks and the therapist does not have a great deal of time to spend with people who may require more time than is available in understanding and digesting the concepts and techniques that need to be covered. Consequently, if you work as a therapist with clients who have significant learning difficulties and you wish to run self-acceptance groups for such clients, you will need to spend much more than ten 90-minute lessons covering the material that I will be describing in the second part of this book. Also, you will need to simplify much of the material. As this topic falls outside my brief, interested readers might wish to consult Knaus and Haberstroh (1993) and Gandy (1995) for a discussion of how REBT concepts generally may be applied with clients who have significant learning difficulties.

3. *The person is not in the right frame of mind psychologically to benefit from a self-acceptance group.*

The third exclusion criterion is somewhat similar to the second in that they both focus on a person's capacity to understand and put into practice the material that will be covered during the life of a self-acceptance group. However, while the second exclusion criterion focused on the intellectual ability of the person wishing to join the group, here I am more concerned with the person's psychological state.

As will be seen from Part 2 of this book, group members do need to be in a fairly good state of mind to benefit from a self-acceptance group. For example, the concept of unconditional self-acceptance is fairly difficult to understand and the techniques that you will teach group members to use both within and between group sessions require that clients are able to concentrate quite hard on these methods. Consequently, clients who are not sufficiently in a good state of mind to focus on the concepts and techniques that they will be taught are not good candidates for a self-acceptance group. This group would include clients who are (i) undergoing ECT; (ii) severely depressed or (iii) acutely anxious. However, clients who are moderately depressed or anxious can, on this criterion, be accepted as group members.

4. *The person is, at the same time, a client in a markedly conflicting approach to therapy.*

The fourth exclusion criterion that I wish to discuss concerns a situation where a person who wishes to join a self-acceptance group is, during that period, a client in a different and markedly conflicting approach to therapy. I use the word 'markedly' advisedly here because the very fact that a person is in a different, conflicting approach to therapy is not itself reason enough to exclude the client.

However, when there is a marked conflict between an REBT-based self-acceptance group and another therapeutic approach, then it is best for the person concerned and the rest of the group that he or she is not invited to join the group. The marked conflict to which I refer may concern very different stances adopted by the two approaches to self-esteem and self-acceptance. Some approaches to therapy make self-esteem and the self-rating that underpins it a major goal for clients to achieve. This markedly conflicts with the REBT view on unconditional self-acceptance being a major goal of therapy. This would not necessarily be a problem if the other therapeutic approach did not make self-rating such a central lynchpin, but if it does then it is best to exclude the client who may otherwise become very confused in attempting to make sense of two very different concepts. One possible consequence of this is that such a person may take up too much of the group's valuable time in trying to resolve his or her confusion, and the leader cannot devote that amount of time to any one individual.

Two other potential areas of marked conflict between a self-acceptance group and a client's other therapy concern more broader issues. First, the other approach may downplay, disregard or ridicule the role that cognition and behaviour play in people's emotional problems. This position is, of course, at marked variance with the REBT view and again the client may become too confused about these differing ideas to benefit from the self-acceptance group. Second, the active–directive, educational role of the group leader (see Chapter 3 for a full discussion of this subject) may be markedly at variance with the style adopted by the client's other therapist. If a client is used to seeing a therapist who is reflective and relatively non-directive in style, then the client may take too long to get used to the REBT group leader's very different style. Once again, this may lead to confusion in the mind of the client who may not derive much benefit from the self-acceptance group as a result.

In summary, if you judge that a client is likely to become very confused due to the marked differences between an REBT-oriented self-acceptance group and some other therapy, it is best to exclude that client from the group.

5. *The person does not have the support of the psychiatrist or key worker.*

It may well be the case that clients who are interested in joining a self-acceptance group have a psychiatrist or key worker who has overall responsibility for their case. If that person has suggested to the clients that they join the group and has made a referral to that effect, then this constitutes an inclusion criterion. However, if the clients have, of their own accord, applied to join the group, but their psychiatrist or key worker does not support their application, then including them as group members may be problematic for the clients in the long run and may cause professional difficulties for yourself. When I first started to run self-acceptance groups in a private psychiatric hospital, I did include in my self-acceptance groups two clients who did not have the support of their psychiatrists. I did so in the belief that as they were paying directly for the group they were entitled to join it. However, once the psychiatrists found out about their membership, they put pressure on the clients to withdraw from the group and told me in no uncertain terms that they would decide whether or not their patients would join such a group, not the patients nor myself. Whatever one may think of such behaviour, one does have to work within an organization and respect its norms if one wants to continue to work there. Consequently, if a client's application to join a self-acceptance group does not have the support of the person who has overall responsibility for the client's treatment, then it is best not to include that client in the group.

Conducting Intake Interviews

Whenever possible it is important to interview prospective members for self-acceptance groups. These interviews are known as intake interviews and allow you, as group leader, to accomplish the following important tasks.

1. You can explain to clients more about the nature of self-acceptance groups and your role as group leader in greater detail.
2. You can specify that you expect group members
   - to attend regularly
   - to discuss their self-depreciation problems with other members of the group
   - to participate in small group and peer exercises
   - to practise in between group sessions what they learn in these sessions
   - to ask questions and disclose doubts about any concept or exercise introduced in the group.
3. You can outline the practical requirements of participating in the group, such as
   - where and when the group is going to meet
   - any fees required and how these can be paid
   - to let you know in advance if attendance at any group meeting is not possible.
4. You can answer any queries the person has about the group and his or her participation within it.
5. You can discover whether the client is suitable to join the group or whether he or she should be excluded. Here your interviewing will be informed by the inclusion and exclusion criteria discussed above. Let me present these criteria again and illustrate the type of questions you might ask.

Inclusion Criteria

1. The person agrees to focus on ego disturbance problems in the group.
   - How would you describe your main problems? (In response to the person's answer, you will want to differentiate between problems based on ego disturbance and those based on discomfort disturbance.)
   - In what situations do you think badly about yourself as a person?
   - Are you willing to focus on your self-depreciation problems in the group?
2. The educational focus of the group makes sense to the person and joining the group is considered to be a helpful experience.
   - Now that I have explained the educational focus of self-acceptance groups, do you think that joining such a group will be a helpful experience for you? If so, in what way?

3. The person is prepared to practise outside sessions what is learned in sessions.
   - A major feature of self-acceptance groups is that you will be expected to put into practice outside sessions what you learn in sessions. What is your reaction to this?
4. The person understands and assents to the modest aims of the group.
   - As I have explained, the purpose of self-acceptance groups is to equip you to begin the journey towards self-acceptance and not to help you achieve self-acceptance once and for all. What is your reaction to this aim?
5. The person is able to attend group sessions regularly.
   - Will you be able to attend sessions regularly?
   - Can you think of any reason why you will not be able to attend group sessions regularly?
6. The person is willing to discuss problems in a group setting.
   - How do you feel about discussing your problems with other group members?
7. The person is willing to help other group members.
   - Are you willing to help group members as well as allowing them to help you?

Exclusion Criteria

1. The person will not interact productively in the group.
   - Have you previously been a member of a therapy group? If so, what was that experience like for you?
   - What difficulties do you think you may have in interacting with other group members?
   - What difficulties do you think you may have interacting with me as a group leader?
2. The person has significant learning difficulties.
   - Do you have any difficulties learning about new concepts when they are explained to you?
3. The person is not in the right frame of mind psychologically to benefit from a self-acceptance group.
   - Are you currently undergoing or have you recently undergone a course of ECT?
   - How depressed are you at this point in your life?
   - How anxious are you at this point of your life?
4. The person is, at the same time, a client in a markedly conflicting approach to therapy.
   - Are you at present a client in any other therapy? Please tell me about the therapy you are having.

5. The person does not have the support of the psychiatrist or key worker.
   – Have you told your psychiatrist/key worker that you want to join a self-acceptance group? If so, what was their response?

You will be able to form an opinion concerning whether or not a person is suitable for a self-acceptance group on most of these criteria by gauging the responses to your initial questions and any follow-up questions you choose to ask on the basis of these responses. However, you will also wish to keep in mind how the person interacts with you in the intake interview as another way of helping you to decide whether or not he or she is suitable to join a self-acceptance group. In particular, you will want to note the following:

1. If the person monopolizes the intake interview and consistently interrupts you, then that person may also monopolize a self-acceptance group and may not be suitable as a member of the group as a result.
2. If the person is very withdrawn in the intake interview and will only give monosyllabic answers to your open-ended questions, then that person may also be very withdrawn in a self-acceptance group and may not be suitable as a group member as a result.
3. If the person finds it very difficult to understand your explanations about the nature of self-acceptance groups, then that person may not be able to understand the concept of self-acceptance and the techniques that you will be teaching during the life of the group. Consequently, the person may not be suitable for the group.
4. If the person appears very depressed or anxious in the intake interview, then that person may also be very depressed or anxious in the group and may not be suitable as a member of the group as a result.

While I strongly advocate that you conduct intake interviews, this may not always be possible; in which case, someone will have to either conduct the interviews for you or select group members without interview. In either situation, you will need to provide that person with as much information as possible about the group and the inclusion and exclusion criteria discussed above. Thus, I once ran a self-acceptance group in a prison with people who had committed murder. Given the constraints of the prison system it proved impossible for me to conduct intake interviews with the men and it also proved too difficult for any of the prison psychologists to do these interviews. So I met one of the psychologists who knew the men at whom the group was targeted, explained to her the nature and aim of the group, gave her a list of the inclusion and exclusion criteria and she chose eight men who she thought were suitable. When I ran the group it transpired that only five were suitable and two of the other men dropped out of the group quite early. The group was still viable, but it would have been better if I had been able to select group members myself.

Gaining Information about Clients from Other Sources

If you are still uncertain about whether or not a particular client is suitable to join a self-acceptance group having conducted an intake interview, then you may turn to two other informational sources to help you make your decision. These involve (i) seeking information from other professionals and (ii) using questionnaires.

Seeking Information from Other Professionals

There may be times when you wish to consult other relevant professionals about a client to test out a suspicion you may have about that person. This is likely to be the case if you think that the person (i) may not interact productively in the group, (ii) may have a significant learning difficulty or (iii) may be too psychologically impaired at that time to benefit from the group.

In the first case listed above, if you work in an organization where that person is currently participating or has participated in other groups, it is useful to consult the leaders of those groups to seek information about that person's interactional style as it was manifest in a group setting. I tend to be guided by the views of colleagues since they have first-hand experience of how the person related to other group members and to the group leader. Such information is especially helpful if the group in which the person was a member was brief and educational in nature. In the other two cases listed above, it is very helpful to test your suspicion with the person's psychiatrist and/or other key worker who will often be in an ideal position to confirm or deny your impressions.

Using Questionnaires

The use of questionnaires in this context particularly relates to the psychological impairment criterion. For example, if you think that a person may be too depressed to benefit from a self-acceptance group, you can ask him or her to complete the Beck Depression Inventory (BDI). If the person scores between 26 and 30 or above on the BDI, indicating severe depression, then you will probably wish to exclude the client from a self-acceptance group at that time. Also, if you think that the person is too anxious to benefit from the group, you can ask him or her to fill in the Beck Anxiety Inventory (BAI). If the person scores 30 or above on the BAI, indicating severe anxiety, then again you will probably wish to exclude that person. If the person is otherwise suitable to join a self-acceptance group, you can suggest that he or she may join the group once the level of depression or anxiety has dropped to a point where he or she is able to concentrate fully on the content of the group.

CREATING A 'GOOD ENOUGH' SETTING

A number of years ago, I was at a conference presentation on group therapy at which a member of the audience, during question time, bemoaned the context in which he ran groups. 'How can I be expected to work under these conditions,' he complained about the NHS setting in which he 'conducted' a slow, closed group. 'Every week when I run my group the chairs are different.' 'You think you've got problems,' I responded. 'Every week when I run my group, the chairs are the same, but the people are different.' I was referring to the open groups that I run in a private psychiatric hospital. This amusing interchange points to the importance of the setting in which groups are run. In this part of the chapter, I will outline the minimum conditions that are necessary for the successful running of self-acceptance groups.

Room Requirements

When you set up a self-acceptance group, you will need a room that is large enough to accommodate a maximum of eleven people (you and ten group members), in which three subgroups and five peer groups can talk without interrupting or being interrupted by others carrying out the same exercises. If you can get one large room and several smaller rooms then this is ideal, but one large room will suffice. If you can only get one medium sized room, you will need to determine whether or not this room is large enough by getting ten people (and yourself) to sit in it as a whole group in three sub-groups and five peer groups to see if they can talk without interrupting or being interrupted by others. If this is not possible, my advice is not to run the group because you have less than the minimum conditions necessary to run a SUCCESSFUL self-acceptance group. I have stressed the word 'successful' here. You can, of course, pack eleven people into a broom cupboard, but the resulting group will not be successful!

Time Requirements

I have run many self-acceptance groups in a variety of different organizational contexts and have finally determined that ten 90-minute sessions are sufficient to cover what may be viewed as a self-acceptance curriculum. Consequently, once you have found a suitably sized room (or suite of rooms) you will require this accommodation for ten consecutive weeks, at the same time, for 90 minutes. This may be easier said than done, because large therapy rooms are usually at a premium no matter where one works.

Obviously having the same accommodation every week is ideal, but I would have no objection to having different rooms each week as long as they are large enough to accommodate the group and as long as sufficient notice (at least a week in advance) is given. Unlike psychodynamic groups, REBT-influenced self-acceptance groups do not need the constancy of a single group room to achieve their objectives.

Equipment and Other Practical Requirements

As I have stressed several times already in this book, self-acceptance groups are educational in nature. As such, you will need certain equipment to get your points across. Thus, you will definitely need one and preferably two white boards or flipcharts with suitable marker pens. You will need this equipment every week, and therefore they should either be left in the room or locked away in a safe place to which you have access. In particular, you need to make regular checks that the marker pens still have ink since they tend to run out quickly, especially if their tops are not replaced.

You should also ensure that pens and paper are available for the group members to make notes. While most clients will bring writing material regularly, some will not and I'd rather provide such material than make a therapeutic issue out of it since failure to bring in writing materials is more likely to be due to discomfort disturbance than ego disturbance and therefore not the main focus of the group. There may also be practical reasons for providing writing materials to group members. For example, I once ran a self-acceptance group in a prison, where inmates were not allowed to bring their own pencils or paper to the group and these had to be made available on a regular basis.

I have pointed out several times already in this book that REBT clients in general, and self-acceptance group members in particular, are required to carry out homework tasks. As such, it is important that you keep a record of both group tasks (i.e. assignments that all members of the group are expected to do) and homework tasks that are specific to individuals. You will probably have incorporated group assignments into your curriculum as I routinely do (as you will see in Part 2), but you will need a way of keeping track of members' individual assignments. My recommendation is to use a 'no carbon required' (NCR) notebook. This enables you to write out a written reminder of the task for the group member to retain and to make and keep an automatic copy of what you have given your client.

Finally, I recommend that you use as a course text a self-help book written by Paul Hauck (1991) on the subject of self-acceptance and how to work towards achieving it. It covers a lot of the ground that you will teach in group sessions and gives clients an opportunity to reflect on the concepts at their leisure between group sessions. As you will see, I use about half of Hauck's book, but I recommend that clients do not read Chapter 2. This makes the case that self-depreciation is a major feature of a variety of personality disorders, but does so in such a way that clients may imagine they are suffering from a number of personality disorders when this is not the case.

It is helpful to have a plentiful stock of Hauck's book so that group members can purchase it from you or from the organization running the group, otherwise clients will order it from their local bookstore, and by the time it arrives the group will be almost at an end.

Limiting Disruptions

It is an axiom of good therapeutic practice that therapy sessions should be carried out free from external disruption. This is true whether we are referring to individual therapy, couple therapy or group therapy. Therefore, the group should be held in a room that is not used for any other purpose, otherwise you may be interrupted on several occasions, even if you put a 'Do Not Disturb' sign on the door!

It is likely, however, that the room in which the group meets will be used for other groups before and after your own group. Given this, I suggest that you aim to end on time so that you do not delay the beginning of the next group. Hopefully, the leader of the group preceding your own will show you the same courtesy. If not, and the start of own group is delayed then you should meet the person concerned and courteously ask him or her to end that group on time. If the person does not respond to this request you should discuss the issue with your line manager, whose job it is to resolve such matters.

This just leaves disruption caused by group members leaving the group early and joining the group late. In my experience of running self-acceptance groups in a private psychiatric hospital, this problem is caused either by patients scheduling appointments with other mental health professionals, or psychiatrists insisting that they see their patients during the group when it is convenient for them to do so, but inconvenient for the patients. The first problem is more easily dealt with than the second.

When a client is late in attending the group or leaves the group early to keep an arranged appointment to see another mental health professional, then as a group leader you need to remind that person that, during the intake interview, he or she had agreed to attend all sessions. You should reiterate that regular attendance is crucial if the client is not to miss important parts of the curriculum. You can then ask the client to reaffirm his or her commitment to attend regularly. You should then tell the client that, if the same situation arises again, he or she will be asked to leave the group. If the situation does indeed happen again where the client has arranged another appointment in group time, then you should indeed ask him or her to leave the group. This should be done without hostility and with an invitation for the person to join a different self-acceptance group once he or she is able to carry through with the commitment to attend regularly. I should add that I have never had to ask someone to leave a self-acceptance group, but on two occasions I have confronted members who have had to leave the group early to keep an appointment that they have themselves initiated.

If a member has to leave a group early or join a group late in order to keep a psychiatrist-initiated appointment, then the situation is quite different. My practice is to check whether or not the person has informed the psychiatrist that the appointment clashes with the group. If the psychiatrist has not been informed or if the psychiatrist has insisted on booking the appointment anyway, I ask the client if he or she could have been more assertive with the psychiatrist. If the answer is no (as it often is), I mention that his or her lack of assertion may be due to 'low self-esteem' and ask the client to introduce this issue in the group at some relevant time. In the meantime I will have a word with the psychiatrist and request that he or she does not book appointments with the client during group time. If the psychiatrist then refuses, I will raise the issue with the relevant hospital administrator. If the matter is still unresolved I will allow the client to continue to attend the group and tape-record the relevant parts of the sessions that are missed to ensure that he or she does not fall behind the rest of the group. However, I will not accept any other patients of that particular psychiatrist in future self-acceptance groups. I should add that this has only happened to me on one occasion.

We are now ready to move on to the second part of this book, in which I will provide a session-by-session practical guide to conducting self-acceptance groups.

Part 2

The Therapeutic Curriculum in Self-acceptance Groups

5

SESSION ONE: WHY SELF-ACCEPTANCE AND NOT SELF-ESTEEM?

As I stated in the first part of this book, brief educationally oriented self-acceptance groups are run over the course of ten consecutive weeks, each group session lasting for ninety minutes. In this part of the book, I will cover the self-acceptance curriculum and detail what you need to cover in each of the ten group sessions. In this chapter, I focus on the first session.

In the first session of a ten-week self-acceptance group, you should:

- ask group members to introduce themselves to the group
- explain any guidelines you want group members to follow
- consider the concept of self-esteem and its disadvantages
- consider the concept of self-acceptance and its advantages
- stress the value of homework tasks
- assign the first task.

MAKING INTRODUCTIONS

Your first task in the group is to introduce yourself as the group leader and to ask group members to introduce themselves to the rest of the group. You can also ask each group member to say a little about the kind of self-depreciation problems they have at this point, but I prefer to wait until the second session to do this (see Chapter 6).

During the course of this book I will illustrate the concepts and techniques that I introduce by referring to eight people who were members of a particular self-acceptance group that I ran in the context of a private psychiatric hospital. The people to whom I will refer are not real individuals, but are each a composite of clients that have been members of one of my self-acceptance groups. I have taken this approach to preserve the confidentiality of past members of my groups. However, I have tried to make the people as lifelike and as representative of actual group members as possible. Here are the eight people and their main presenting problems.

RONALD, a 45-year-old businessman who has been depressed over being made redundant.

BETTY, a 37-year-old singer who is afraid to perform in public.

SARAH, a 22-year-old university student who is considering dropping out of her course because she thinks that she will fail her exams.

LIONEL, a 56-year-old golf professional who is ashamed about playing because he has lost his form.

CAROL, a 60-year-old retired widow who feels guilty about remarrying.

BRIAN, a 34-year-old salesman who can't say no to people.

FIONA, a 28-year-old accountant who describes herself as a people pleaser and suffers from anxiety.

LIAM, a 23-year-old systems analyst who is severely jealous of his girlfriend.

OUTLINING GROUP GUIDELINES

Your next task is to outline any guidelines that you think are important for members of the group to adhere to. My practice is to outline three such guidelines. These refer to attendance, confidentiality and members meeting with one another outside sessions.

First, with respect to attendance, I stress that it is important that members of the group should ideally attend group sessions regularly and remind them that they agreed to this in their intake interview with me (assuming that I conducted such an interview with them).

Second, with respect to confidentiality, I explain that everything that members say should be treated in strict confidence. This means that group members should not discuss with anyone outside the group what was disclosed in the group. I stress that there are two exceptions to this rule. I explain that I will break confidentiality if a member threatens his or her own life or that of another person and refuses to tell his or her psychiatrist about these intentions.

Third, I tell the group that their psychiatrists and/or key workers may ask me about their progress in the group. I explain that in the context of conducting therapy groups in the hospital, it is usual practice for the group leader to provide such information when asked. I state that I will do so unless the member tells me otherwise.

Finally, with respect to group members meeting one another outside the hospital (members may well see each other in other therapy groups in the hospital), I explain that I have no objection to this in principle. However, I ask that group members guard against colluding with one another. For example, if one member knows that another has not carried out a home-work task then he (in this case) should bring this up if that group member pretends that she has completed it.

CONSIDERING THE CONCEPT OF SELF-ESTEEM

As I discussed in Chapter 2, REBT theory considers that the concept of self-esteem is problematic and advocates the concept of self-acceptance instead. However, group members will generally think that self-esteem is a healthy concept and will wish to raise their self-esteem. It is important to address this issue as early as possible and my practice is to do this at this point in the first group session.

The style in which I introduce these ideas involves a mixture of didactic and Socratic methods. Thus, sometimes I will teach an idea didactically and at other times I will try to tease out the idea from group members by asking them questions and, in response to their answers, guide them with further questions until the idea has been flushed out. I am some-times asked what determines my use of didactic techniques as opposed to Socratic methods and vice versa. It seems to me that I am more likely to use Socratic techniques with group members who show that they can involve themselves in a productive Socratic dialogue and I can only determine this by trial and error. In addition, I am more likely to use didactic techniques when time is running short in a session and when it is clear that the Socratic method is not proving effective in teasing out a particular idea. When using didactic methods it is important to ensure that group members understand the point being conveyed. While time does not allow you to check each group member's level of comprehen-sion on every point, it is useful to ask one or two group members, at various points, to put into their own words their understanding of what you have said. While I demonstrate this once or twice in this part of the book, space prevents me from showing the frequency with which I check group members' understanding. I ask readers to bear in mind that I do this much more frequently than is conveyed here. I also recommend that you frequently check your group members' level of comprehension of didactically presented points when running your own self-acceptance groups.

Another feature of my style is that I seek to involve all group members in the therapeutic dialogue. Thus, if some group members are not forthcoming, I will involve them in the group discussion by asking them direct questions or by inviting them, by name, to give an opinion on the point under discussion.

In what follows, I will present a typical dialogue that occurs when I teach a group why self-esteem is a problematic mental health concept and why unconditional self-acceptance is its healthy alternative. Please note that I have already suggested to group members that they may take notes if they wish and have handed out writing materials to those who don't have any with them. I have further suggested that, as this group is primarily educational, it would be useful if they would bring with them a notepad and pen every week.

Who Wants High Self-Esteem?

I begin by asking group members who amongst them would like to have high self-esteem or feel better about themselves. In response to this question, virtually everyone in the group raises his or her hand. I then ask each member to indicate what would boost his or her self-esteem and I write their responses on a flipchart. Here is what each group member said:

RONALD: Getting another job.

BETTY: Being able to sing in public.

SARAH: Passing my exams.

LIONEL: Regaining my form at golf.

CAROL: Having the blessing of my son and daughter about getting married again.

BRIAN: Being able to assert myself with people.

FIONA: Knowing that I'm liked.

LIAM: Knowing that my girlfriend loves me.

Defining the Terms 'Self' and 'Esteem'

I next suggest that group members take a closer look at the concept of self-esteem and do this by asking them to define the terms 'self' and 'esteem'. I have two purposes here. First, I want to teach group members the REBT concept of self-esteem and why it is problematic and, second, I want to make sure that all group members take part in the learning process. Thus, I will at times ask them questions to involve them in the discussion. You will see how I achieve these two purposes from the following dialogue.

WINDY: OK. Let's have a look at what self-esteem means. Now if we break this concept into its two component parts we have the term 'self' and the term 'esteem'. Let's start with the term 'self'. What is the self?

[A period of silence follows.]

Well, Lionel, are your thoughts part of your 'self'?

LIONEL: Yes.

WINDY: So, I'll put that on the flipchart.

[I turn to the flipchart, write 'SELF' in capital letters, underline it and write the word 'Thoughts' underneath.]

What else is part of your 'self'?

LIAM: Your behaviour?

WINDY: Right.

[I write the word 'Behaviour' on the flipchart under the word 'thoughts'.]

What else should we put up on the flipchart?

FIONA: Your dreams?

WINDY: Right, your dreams.

[I add 'Dreams' to the list.]

What else?

BRIAN: Your feelings.

WINDY: Right, your feelings or emotions.

[I add 'Feelings' to the list.]

Anything else?

BETTY: Your body?

WINDY: Definitely. All your bodily parts are part of your 'self'.

[I add 'Bodily parts' to the list.]

What else?

[A period of silence follows.]

Well, what about the sensations you experience. Are they part of your 'self'?

CAROL: Yes.

WINDY: OK.

[I add 'Sensations' to the list.]

Anything else?

[Another period of silence follows.]

What about images? Are they part of your 'self'?

SARAH: Aren't they the same as dreams?

BRIAN: I think they're different.

RONALD: So do I.

WINDY: So should I add images to the list?

[The group generally indicates its assent, so I add 'Images' to the list.]

What about personality characteristics? Are they part of your 'self'?

SARAH: Most definitely.

WINDY: So let me add these to the list. So let's see what what we have. The following are parts of your 'self':

SELF

Thoughts
Behaviour
Dreams
Feelings
Bodily parts
Sensations
Images
Personality characteristics

Now, how old are you, Lionel?

LIONEL: Fifty-six.

WINDY: How many thoughts have you had from the day you were born until now?

LIONEL: Millions.

WINDY: At the very least. Sarah, how many behaviours have you carried out from the day you were born until now?

SARAH: Again, millions.

WINDY: That's right and does the same apply to dreams, feelings and the rest of the headings?

BETTY: Yes.

WINDY: So, is the 'self' a simple thing or is it very complex?

BETTY: It's extremely complex.

WINDY: Right, it's extraordinarily complex. Now does the 'self' stay the same or does it change over time?

SARAH: It changes over time.

WINDY: Right, so the 'self' constantly changes and it is extremely complex.

[I write 'Extremely complex' and 'Constantly changing' on the board.]

<u>SELF</u>

Thoughts
Behaviour
Dreams
Feelings
Bodily parts
Sensations
Images
Personality characteristics

Extremely complex
Constantly changing

This fits with the definition of the 'self' given by my American colleague, Paul Hauck. He says that the 'self' is 'every conceivable thing about you that can be rated'. Let me write this up on the chart. I'll put it just under the heading 'SELF'

<u>SELF</u>

The self is 'every conceivable thing about you that can be rated':

Thoughts
Behaviour
Dreams
Feelings
Bodily parts
Sensations
Images
Personality characteristics

Extremely complex
Constantly changing

Now that we have defined the 'self', let's have a close look at the concept of 'esteem'. What verb does 'esteem' come from?

CAROL: Estimate?

WINDY: That's right. To estimate, to judge or to rate. Now let's put these two terms together. What does 'self-esteem' mean, Ronald?

RONALD: Rating the 'self'?

WINDY: Right, and what is the 'self', Fiona?

FIONA (*reading from the chart*):   Every conceivable thing about you that can be rated.

WINDY: Now, let me ask you all a very important question. Can we give the 'self' a single rating, estimation or judgement which completely accounts for its complexity and its changingness?

BRIAN: No, you can't.

WINDY: Why not? . . . (*silence*), Betty?

BETTY: Because as you've said one's 'self' is too complex and it keeps changing.

WINDY: Right, now do you all see that? You can't legitimately give the 'self' a single rating because it is too complex and is constantly in flux. Shall I write that up on the flip chart?

LIONEL: Yes (*and other group members nod in agreement*).

[I do so.]

SELF

The self is 'every conceivable thing about you that can be rated'

> Thoughts
> Behaviour
> Dreams
> Feelings
> Bodily parts
> Sensations
> Images
> Personality characteristics
>
> Extremely complex
> Constantly changing

You can't legitimately give the 'self' a single rating because it is too complex and is constantly in flux.

WINDY: Now that is why the concept of self-esteem is problematic. It assumes that you can legitimately give your 'self' a rating, but as we've just seen you can't do that because your 'self' is too complex to merit a single rating, and even if you could give it a single rating that rating would very soon become redundant because you keep generating more data. In other words, your 'self' is constantly changing.

Let me give you an example. Fiona, you said that the one thing that would raise your self-esteem was having people like you. If people were to like you, how would you rate yourself in your own head?

FIONA: I would think of myself as a worthwhile person.

WINDY: Right, group. Let's consider Fiona's statement. She said that she would be a worthwhile person if other people liked her. Now Fiona's 'self' is represented by the word 'I'. What is the rating she is making about herself?

LIAM: That she is worth while.

WINDY: But Fiona isn't worth while because she is too complex to merit this single rating.

FIONA: So if I'm not worth while, are you saying that I am worthless?

WINDY: Certainly not. Why am I not saying that, Fiona?

FIONA: Because the term 'worthless' is also a single rating. Yes, I see now.

BRIAN: But if Fiona isn't worth while and she isn't worthless, what is she?

CONSIDERING THE CONCEPT OF UNCONDITIONAL SELF-ACCEPTANCE

With Brian's question the group is ready to consider and discuss the concept of unconditional self-acceptance. Let's rejoin the group and continue the dialogue.

WINDY: That's a very important question, Brian. It hits at the very heart of why we are here. Do you remember what this group is called?

RONALD: A self-acceptance group.

WINDY: That's right. It's called a self-acceptance group and not a self-esteem group because, as we have seen, the concept of self-esteem has problems which the concept of self-acceptance does not have. So, let's see what the concept of self-acceptance involves and then we can answer Brian's question about what rating, if any, we can apply to Fiona. Is that OK, Fiona?

FIONA: Fine.

WINDY: So now I'll go over the eleven principles of self-acceptance. The first principle is one that will now be familiar to you. I'll just write it up on the flipchart here.

[Under the heading 'THE ELEVEN PRINCIPLES OF SELF-ACCEPTANCE', I write the following principle.]

1. *As a human being you cannot legitimately be given a single rating, but parts of you can be rated, as can what happens to you.*

WINDY: So far we have seen that the 'self' is too complex to be given a single rating and that, even if it could be so rated, that rating would soon be obsolete because the 'self' is a process, which means that it is constantly changing. As soon as you rate it, it would have changed. However, although you can't rate your 'self' as a whole, you can rate parts of your 'self'. Thus, you can focus on an instance of your behaviour and you can rate it. Thus, if Betty sings poorly in public, it would be sensible for Betty to say something like: 'It is bad that I sang poorly in public on this occasion.' Betty, do you know why it would be sensible for you to rate your behaviour in this respect?

BETTY: I'm not sure.

WINDY: Anyone else?

RONALD: Because it alerts her that there is a problem to be solved.

WINDY: That's an excellent answer, Ronald. If Betty didn't rate her singing negatively, she would not realize that she had a problem and she would therefore not be motivated to do anything about it. So, the main point here is that you can rate aspects of your 'self', like your behaviour, your emotions and your thoughts, and it is also helpful to do so, because you can then set about making appropriate improvements in those aspects. Any questions about that?

LIAM: So you are saying that it is OK to rate parts of our 'selves', but not the total whole.

WINDY: Exactly.

LIAM: That makes sense.

WINDY: I'm pleased it does. Now it also makes sense to rate what happens to us. For example, it would make perfect sense for Ronald to rate being made redundant as bad and to rate getting another job as good.

RONALD: I'm glad you said that.

WINDY: But it wouldn't make sense for Ronald to rate himself on the basis of having a job or not having a job. Do you see why, Ronald?

RONALD: Because I'm too complex to be given a single rating.

WINDY: That's exactly right. You are too complex to merit a rating, but having a job or not is a discrete enough situation to be rated. So let me recap on this point: 'Human beings cannot legitimately be given a single rating, but parts of them can be rated, as can what happens to them.' Any questions?

[There are no questions, so I move on to the second principle.]

Now let's move on to the second principle of self-acceptance. If human beings have an essence what do you think that essence is?

LIONEL: That we all have a soul?

WINDY: That's an interesting point. How many of the group think that we have a soul?

[Three people put their hands up.]

Well most people in the group think that having a soul isn't the essence of being human. Any other thoughts?

LIAM: Making mistakes?

WINDY: What does the group think of that?

[There is general verbal and non-verbal assent.]

That seems to be unanimous and I certainly agree with that. Does anyone know anybody who doesn't make mistakes?

BETTY: I know people who think they don't make mistakes.

RONALD: Don't we all.

[General laughter.]

WINDY: But do these people make errors? [General assent.] And their idea that they don't make mistakes is, in fact, proof that they are fallible because, as you've just agreed, that is a faulty idea. As one of my colleagues, Maxie C. Maultsby Jr, has said: 'humans have an incurable error-making tendency'. In other words, humans are fallible and that is their essential nature. Would anyone disagree?

[Members of the group indicate that they don't disagree with this proposition.]

Another essential feature of humans is their uniqueness. As the song goes: 'There will never be another you.' Any comment?

SARAH: That's quite right. Even identical twins have their own unique personalities.

WINDY: Good point, Sarah. So let me write the second principle on the flipchart:

2. *As a human being your essence is that you are fallible and unique.*

WINDY: Now let's move on to the third principle. This states that while humans are equal in humanity, when we compare people on different rateable aspects, it becomes clear that there is considerable variation. This is where humans differ. Thus, people differ markedly in their intelligence and in their kindness towards animals, to take two examples. What are your reactions to this principle?

BRIAN: So does this mean that it is sensible to compare yourself with others or not?

WINDY: That is a really good question, Brian. It means that it is sensible to compare aspects of yourself with those of other people, but it generally isn't constructive or indeed valid to compare your 'self' with the 'self' of others because the 'self' is far too complex to merit that kind of comparison. Thus, it might well be useful to compare your behaviour with that of others, for if you do you might learn something constructive, but it is really a nonsense to compare 'selves'.

BRIAN: I've never looked at it that way. That's really useful.

WINDY: Any other comments? . . . No? . . . So let me write the third principle on the flipchart.

3. *You are equal to other humans in terms of shared humanity, but unequal in many different specific respects.*

Now, let's go on to the fourth principle. Let's take what Sarah said would raise her self-esteem. Sarah, you said that if you passed your exams that would boost your self-esteem. How would you think about yourself if you failed your exams?

SARAH: That I would be a failure.

WINDY: Right, group, let's examine Sarah's statement that if she failed her exams she would be a failure. Now, does her conclusion 'I would be a failure' follow logically from her experience of failing her exams?

BRIAN: No.

WINDY: Why not?

BRIAN: Because it doesn't sound logical.

WINDY: OK, it doesn't sound logical and it isn't logical, but why do you think it isn't logical?

SARAH: Because failing exams is only a part of me and I'm judging the whole of me on the basis of that part.

WINDY: That's exactly it, Sarah. When you conclude that you are a failure for failing your exams, you are making a gross overgeneralization. This is sometimes also called the part–whole error; that is, you rate the whole of your 'self' on the basis of a part of your self. Now what would be a more logical conclusion?

FIONA: That if Sarah fails her exams this proves that she is an ordinary human being.

WINDY: That's right. We know that Sarah is human and we know humans are fallible. Therefore it makes perfect sense to say that if Sarah fails her exams, it follows that she is a fallible human being and is not and cannot be *a* failure. Any problems with this concept?

[Members of the group indicate that they agree with the concept.]

So let me write the fourth concept on the board.

4. *When you accept yourself unconditionally, you think logically and avoid making overgeneralization errors.*

WINDY: Now let's move on to principle number five. This principle states that self-acceptance and its unhealthy counterpart 'self-depreciation' or 'self-downing' are each linked to another philosophy. Not surprisingly this view says that the philosophy linked with self-acceptance is a healthy one and the philosophy linked with self-downing is unhealthy. Therefore, when you are putting your 'self' down for something, it is important to look for and challenge this other unhealthy philosophy.

Let's take Lionel's statement that his self-esteem will go up if he recaptures his form at golf. What's the self-acceptance alternative to this?

BETTY: That Lionel is a fallible human being whether his golf form improves or not.

WINDY: Correct, Betty. That's a very succinct way of putting it. Now let me outline the two philosophies and see if you can work out which belief goes with which. First, we have what is called a flexible preference. Here, Lionel would hold the following belief: 'I would really prefer to recapture my form at golf, but unfortunately there is no law of the universe to decree that I must do so.' Second, we have what is called a dogmatic demand. Here, Lionel would hold the following belief: 'I absolutely must recapture my form at golf.' Now which belief would be linked to Lionel's self-esteem fluctuating according to whether or not he recaptures his form at golf? Hands up those who think it is the flexible preference?

[No hands are raised.]

And the dogmatic demand?

[All hands are raised.]

Terrific. As you have seen, self-downing is based on a dogmatic demand or, as my American colleague, Albert Ellis, has put it: 'Should-hood leads to shithood. You're never a shit without a should.' Whereas the fifth principle, which I will now write on the flipchart, states:

5. *Unconditional self-acceptance is closely linked with a flexible, preferential philosophy.*

WINDY: Let's recap on the principles that we have covered so far (*walking over to the flipchart*). So far, we have seen that (i) self-acceptance reflects the complexity and changing nature of the self; (ii) the essential features of humans are that they are fallible and unique; (iii) humans are equal in their inhumanity, but unequal in their different aspects; (iv) when you accept yourself you avoid making illogical overgeneralizations; and (v) self-acceptance is based on a flexible preferential philosophy. Now, let's get pragmatic and consider the consequences of accepting yourself as opposed to rating yourself.

Let's take your case Liam, if we may. You said that your self-esteem would go up if you knew that your girlfriend loved you. Let's suppose that you knew that she did; how would you rate yourself?

LIAM: As a lovable person.

WINDY: And later if she said to you that she did not love you, how would you rate yourself then?

LIAM: As an unlovable person.

WINDY: And what emotions would go along with that belief?

LIAM: Depression.

WINDY: Now, let's go back to the situation where you know that your girlfriend loves you and you rate yourself as lovable. Now why doesn't thinking like that last?

LIAM: Because I start having doubts.

WINDY: And when you have those doubts, how do you feel?

LIAM: Jealous.

WINDY: About what?

LIAM: About her fancying someone else.

WINDY: Because if she did, how would you think of yourself?

LIAM: I'd be unlovable again.

WINDY: Right, so when Liam adheres to the concept of self-esteem, he is depressed when he doesn't have the love of his girlfriend, and when he does he is vulnerable to jealousy because he can't believe that her love will last. So does adhering to the concept of self-esteem have healthy results for Liam?

BRIAN: Certainly not.

LIAM: I agree with that wholeheartedly.

WINDY: Now let's see what difference adhering to the concept of self-acceptance would make to you, Liam. If you accepted yourself as a unique complex person, etc., how would you feel if you knew that your girlfriend loved you?

LIAM: I would still feel good.

WINDY: Right, because it is good to be loved by your girlfriend. Now let's assume that your girlfriend told you that she had fallen out of love with you and you still accepted yourself and did not put yourself down about that. How would you feel about that lack of love?

LIAM: Well, I still wouldn't like it, but I wouldn't be depressed.

WINDY: I would venture that you would feel sad for losing something important to you. Is that right?

LIAM: That's right.

WINDY: And feeling sad when you lose something or someone important to you is healthy because it allows you to adjust and move on with your life. Now, Liam, I want you to imagine that you are still accepting yourself. Now let's suppose that you still have the love of your girlfriend, but you start to think that you might lose her love. How would you feel about that if you accepted yourself?

LIAM: Well, I wouldn't feel jealous, but I would be on my guard.

WINDY: We normally call that vigilance 'concern about your relationship'.

LIAM: Right, I would be concerned.

WINDY: And again that would be healthy because it will motivate you to think about your relationship with your girlfriend and how to improve it if that is relevant.

Now, does the philosophy of self-acceptance lead to a healthier set of feelings and behaviours than the philosophy of self-esteem, or vice versa?

SARAH: From your discussion with Liam, you've shown that the philosophy of self-acceptance has the healthier results.

WINDY: Can everyone see that?

[Group members show their assent both verbally and non-verbally.]

OK. Let me write the sixth principle on the flipchart.

6. *When you accept yourself unconditionally, your emotions are healthy and your behaviour is constructive.*

WINDY: OK, now let's move on to the seventh principle. So far, I have argued against rating yourself; because, Carol?

CAROL (*consulting her notes*): Because the 'self' is too complex.

WINDY: That's one reason. Ronald, what's the second?

RONALD: Because the 'self' is a process and is constantly changing.

WINDY: Correct. And, third, because, as we've just seen, rating yourself will get you into trouble when you fail to achieve those conditions which you think have to exist in order for you to have high self-esteem. We'll return presently to the list of items that you gave me earlier of things that you thought would raise your self-esteem.

However, some people are very reluctant to give up the idea of self-rating altogether, so in case you are one such person, I will show you the healthy and unhealthy way of rating yourself. If you want to consider yourself worth while there are only three ways of doing it that won't get you into trouble. These relate to the three things about you that won't change. Now, what three things about you will not change?

RONALD: Your character?

WINDY: No, that will change over the course of your life. So, if you say I am worth while as long as I am extrovert, you will tend to put yourself down if and when you are more introverted, so that won't work. Any other suggestions?

BRIAN: You will always be human.

WINDY: Right, believing yourself to be worth while because you are human will work. What else?

CAROL: Your aliveness.

WINDY: Right, saying 'I am worth while because I am alive' will work and you can even renew that if you believe in an afterlife. What's the third condition?

[No response from the group.]

Well, your uniqueness won't change until we find a way of making a perfect clone of you. So If you say: 'I am worth while because I am alive, human and unique, that kind of self-rating won't get you into trouble emotionally. But if you say things like 'I am worth while as long as I am loved, successful or have a job, that won't work because these conditions may well change and if they do you will depreciate yourself.

So the seventh principle is:

7. *If you still want to rate yourself, judge yourself against conditions that do not change in your lifetime. Thus, think of yourself as worth while because you are human, alive and unique.*

WINDY: Before we consider the final four principles of self-acceptance. let's return to the question that Brian asked about Fiona. He asked: 'If Fiona isn't worth while and she isn't worthless, what is she?' Now what is the answer to that question, Fiona?

FIONA: I am a fallible human being who is too complex and changeable to be given a single rating.

WINDY: Right, but if you want to consider yourself to be worth while do so because you are human, alive and unique.

OK, now let's go on to the eighth principle. Some people are reluctant to adopt the principle of self-acceptance because they think that self-acceptance promotes resignation. They consider that if you accept yourself, then you won't be motivated to change aspects of yourself.

LIONEL: It's interesting that you've just said that, but I've had a similar thought.

CAROL: So have I.

WINDY: That's quite a common thought, but it's based on a misconception. Let me explain. When you accept yourself, as we've seen, you are in effect acknowledging that you are a unique, fallible human being who is constantly in flux and is too complex to merit a single rating or evaluation. However, adopting this attitude does not mean that you have no aspects that you would wish to change. Far from it. Since you are fallible, you have numerous faults that you can change. Now, remember that I have also shown you that self-acceptance is linked with a flexible preferential philosophy. This means that once you have identified, say, an aspect of your behaviour that is negative, it is likely that you will want to change this behaviour. This desire will motivate you to do something to change it. So, in fact, self-acceptance promotes change. If you were resigned to behaving negatively you would either be indifferent towards it or you wouldn't think that you could change it. Both of these situations are not related to self-acceptance. Any questions?

LIONEL: So accepting yourself means that you don't have to accept parts of yourself?

WINDY: Your question raises the issue of what we mean by acceptance. When acceptance is applied to the 'self', as we have seen it means acknowledging that you are fallible, human, unique, complex and in flux. When applied to negative behaviour it means that:

- you acknowledge that you have behaved negatively
- you regret acting in the way that you did
- all the conditions were in place for you to act that way
- you can learn from this experience and
- you can change your future behaviour if you so desire.

So you see, acceptance even of behaviour involves a desire to change that behaviour when you deem it to be negative. Any other questions? . . . No? . . . OK, let me write the eighth principle of self-acceptance on the flipchart.

8.   *Unconditional   self-acceptance   promotes   constructive   action,   not resignation.*

WINDY: Let's move on to the ninth principle. The ninth principle states that unconditional self-acceptance is a way of thinking that you can learn, but you cannot apply it perfectly. In other words, there will be times when you will depreciate yourself.

BETTY: So, do you mean that it's not like learning a fact like London is the capital of England which, once you have learned it, you won't ever forget?

WINDY: Partly, Betty. You can learn what self-acceptance means, and that is what we are doing now. But, when you apply this learning, there will be times, being human, when you will return to putting yourself down. The best you can do is to minimize your self-depreciating tendency, but it is unlikely that you will ever eradicate it entirely. Conversely, the best you can hope for is to keep striving for complete self-acceptance, while realizing that it is inhuman to expect that you will achieve this perfectly and that you will never return to depreciating yourself.

FIONA: Isn't that a pessimistic position?

WINDY: I don't think so. I think it is realistic. If I told you that you will reach a stage where you will accept yourself once and for all and that thereafter you will never deviate from such complete self-acceptance, I would be implying that you can achieve something superhuman. You may like what I have to say in the moment, but in the long term you may become discouraged when you realize that you have not reached perfect self-acceptance.

CAROL: So perfect self-acceptance is a myth.

WINDY: Right, and a myth is as good as a mile.

[General laughter.]

Any questions? . . . OK, let me put the ninth principle on the flipchart.

9.   *You can learn to accept yourself (but never perfectly, nor for all time).*

WINDY: Let's move on to the tenth principle. This principle follows on directly from the last. From what I have said, do you think that internalizing the philosophy of unconditional self-acceptance is easy and you can do it without working hard, or do you think that it is difficult and requires hard work?

BRIAN: It certainly isn't easy.

FIONA: Right, it sounds difficult.

WINDY: Does anyone think it is easy?

CAROL: The ideas that you have presented don't sound that difficult, but putting them into practice does sound difficult.

WINDY: That's well put, Carol. Understanding the concepts isn't that difficult. But putting them into practice so that they make a difference to the way you feel and behave is much more difficult and does require hard work on your part. How do you feel about that grim reality, group?

RONALD (*ironically*):   We're thrilled.

[General laughter.]

WINDY: Yeah, I can tell.

SARAH: But it is very realistic. If you had said that internalizing self-acceptance was a piece of cake, I would have lost faith in you and what you are trying to teach us.

WINDY: Good, that's why I'm going to encourage you to work hard so that you can get off to a good start going down the road towards self-acceptance. Any questions about this principle?

FIONA: What work do we have to do?

WINDY: That's what I will cover in later sessions. For the time being let me write up the tenth principle on the flipchart.

10. *Internalizing unconditional self-acceptance is difficult and involves hard work.*

WINDY: Finally, let's consider the eleventh principle. There are two major ways of internalizing the philosophy of self-acceptance. You can do it in a weak wimpish, manner or you can do it with force and energy in thought and deed. Which do you think will be more effective?

LIAM: Doing it with force and energy.

WINDY: Why?

LIAM: Because otherwise, you won't believe it.

WINDY: That's right. Even after you see that the philosophy of self-acceptance is true, more logical and yields better results than the philosophy of self-esteem, this latter philosophy will still be strong because you have held it for many years. Thus, showing yourself forcefully and with energy that self-acceptance beliefs are true, more logical and are better for your mental health than self-esteem beliefs is an example of fighting strength with strength. Any questions?

SARAH: How do we practise self-acceptance beliefs with force and energy?

WINDY: That's an important question, Sarah, which I will answer in a later session. What I'm concerned with at the moment are the principles of self-acceptance and not with the practical nuts and bolts of developing self-acceptance. But this will come, I promise. Any other questions? . . . No? . . . Right, so I'll write the eleventh and last principle of self-acceptance on the flipchart.

11. *Internalizing unconditional self-acceptance requires force and energy.*

Now that we've gone over the eleven principles of self-acceptance, let me give you all a handout with a list of these principles [see Table 5.1]. I suggest that you keep this list with you and review it several times a day.

Before I end this section, I want to stress that there are other ways of presenting the material on self-acceptance (see Palmer, 1997, for a review of these different methods). In Appendix 1, I discuss three techniques for teaching self-acceptance principles that I most commonly use.

Who Still Wants High Self-Esteem?

After I have finished explaining the eleven principles of self-esteem, I ask the group members to reconsider their answers to my question: 'What would raise your self-esteem?' I help them to see that whatever they

Table 5.1: The Eleven Principles of Self-acceptance
1. As a human being you cannot legitimately be given a single rating, but parts of you can be rated, as can what happens to you.
2. As a human being your essence is that you are fallible and unique.
3. You are equal to other humans in terms of shared humanity, but unequal in many different specific respects.
4. When you accept yourself unconditionally, you think logically and avoid making overgeneralization errors.
5. Unconditional self-acceptance is closely linked with a flexible, preferential philosophy.
6. When you accept yourself unconditionally, your emotions are healthy and your behaviour is constructive.
7. If you still want to rate yourself, judge yourself against conditions that do not change in your lifetime. Thus, think of yourself as worth while because you are human, alive and unique.
8. Unconditional self-acceptance promotes constructive action, not resignation.
9. You can learn to accept yourself (but never perfectly, nor for all time).
10. Internalizing unconditional self-acceptance is difficult and involves hard work.
11. Internalizing unconditional self-acceptance requires force and energy.

nominated does not raise their self-esteem, but are desirable things to have or achieve in their own right. I show them that self-esteem is contingent upon the existence of whatever they nominated and if that condition did not exist, then their self-esteem would plummet. Helping group members to understand that their adherence to the concept of self-esteem is a primary determinant of their problems and not their solution is liberating for most. Let me illustrate this point with an excerpt from my dialogue with one of the group members, which I will then widen to include the rest of the group.

WINDY: So, Fiona, if we return to what you said earlier about what would raise your self-esteem, you said that being liked would raise your self-esteem. Is that right?

FIONA: That's what I said.

WINDY: Now, going along with your previous statement that being liked would have raised your self-esteem, how would you have thought about yourself if you knew you were liked?

FIONA: As a worthwhile person.

WINDY: And how would you have thought about yourself if you knew that you were not liked?

FIONA: Worthless.

WINDY: Now can you all see how vulnerable Fiona is if she adheres to the principle of self-esteem. She places her worth in the hands of others. But let's apply to Fiona's situation what we've gone over today about self-esteem and its alternative, self-acceptance. Fiona, how does being liked make you worth while and not being liked make you worthless?

FIONA: Based on what we've gone over today, it clearly doesn't.

WINDY: And do you agree with what we've gone over today?

FIONA: Yes, it makes good sense.

WINDY: Now, using the principle of self-acceptance, what does being liked prove about your whole 'self'?

FIONA: Well, it doesn't prove anything about my whole 'self' other than that I am a fallible human being who cannot be rated.

WINDY: Right. And what does not being liked say about your whole 'self'?

FIONA: Again nothing other than I am a fallible human being who cannot be rated.

WINDY: Right again. Now, group, note that when Fiona adopts the principle of self-acceptance, her view of herself remains the same whether or not she is liked. Now obviously, Fiona is going to like being liked and she will dislike being disliked and that is healthy, but she can accept herself under both sets of conditions.

LIONEL: So what you are saying is that it makes sense for us to like the things we put on our raising self-esteem list, but these things don't in fact boost our self-esteem.

WINDY: That's brilliantly put, Lionel, although your observation doesn't make you a better person!

[General laughter.]

If we return to that list and use Lionel's observation, what can each of you conclude, Ronald?

RONALD: I'll like it very much if I get another job and I will actively dislike it if I don't, but I'm still the same fallible human, complex, changeable being whether or not I get another job.

WINDY: Good. Betty?

BETTY: It will be better for me if I can sing in public and worse for me if I can't, but I am the same person whether or not I sing publicly again.

WINDY: Right. Sarah?

SARAH: There are decided advantages for me if I pass my exams and definite disadvantages if I don't, but my 'self' doesn't change.

WINDY: Correct. Lionel, apply your own observation to yourself.

LIONEL: It would be very nice if I recapture my form at golf and not so nice if I don't, but again I remain the same fallible human being whether or not I get my handicap down.

WINDY: You'll still be an FHB, which is shorthand for fallible human being. Carol?

CAROL: Having the blessing of my son and daughter about getting married again would be great and not having their blessing would be bad news, but having their blessing doesn't make me a good person and not having it doesn't make me a bad person.

WINDY: So what are you in these different set of circumstances?

CAROL: I don't change. I'm fallible whatever happens.

WINDY: That's right. Brian, how about you?

BRIAN: Well I'm one of those people who still wants worth, so . . . Applying Lionel's point. I'm worth while if I am able to assert myself with people and I'm worth while if I can't. My worth depends on being alive and human.

WINDY: And being unique.

BRIAN: And being unique.

WINDY: OK, we've covered Fiona. Liam?

LIAM: I'm like Brian, I want to see myself as having worth. So knowing that my girlfriend loves me is great and knowing she doesn't love me sucks, but I'm a person of worth as long as I'm alive and kicking.

WINDY: And unique.

LIAM: And unique.

WINDY: Excellent. So, group, does anyone still want to raise their self-esteem?

[All members show verbally or non-verbally that they don't.]

HOMEWORK TASKS

At this point of the session, which will be at or near the end, I will stress the importance of homework tasks in the group process. Here is how I usually do so.

WINDY: Right, there's one more point to cover before we finish today. Do you remember when we met to see if this was the right group to join that I mentioned that you would be expected to do some work on yourself between sessions?

LIONEL: I do.

BETTY: So do I.

[The rest of the group nod in agreement.]

WINDY: Good. The purpose of these tasks is to reinforce what you learn in the group sessions and to give you an opportunity to practise what you've learned. If you just relied on what you learned during group sessions without doing anything between sessions, the group would be like an academic exercise. You'd learn the concepts but you wouldn't internalize them. Does that make sense?

LIAM: Absolutely.

[Other group members voice their agreement.]

WINDY: So the first homework task I'm giving you to do before next week is this. I want you to read Chapters 1 and 3 of my colleagues, Paul Hauck's, book on self-acceptance entitled *Hold Your Head Up High*. This will serve as a reminder of the ideas that we've gone over today. We've covered a lot of ground today and you may forget what you've learned. Hence these two chapters. Now, Chapter 1 outlines the problems that occur when people do not accept themselves and Chapter 3 presents the ideas of self-acceptance. If there are any points that you disagree with or are unsure of, make a note of them and we'll discuss them next week. OK?

[The group state 'OK'.]

While in structured educational self-acceptance groups homework tasks are assigned by the leader, group members have an opportunity to determine the content of the particular assignments. This is particularly the case in later sessions where the emphasis is on applying self-acceptance concepts and ideas to their own individual situations. However, when bibliotherapy is assigned this is unilaterally assigned by the group leader.

Before I close this session, I want to stress that it is important to help group members identify and overcome any obstacles to the completion of their homework tasks. It is important to do this before the end of each group session. While I will not deal with this issue in depth in this book, I refer readers to Appendix 2 which lists possible reasons why clients do not complete homework tasks. I also refer the interested reader to Ellis (1985) and Neenan and Dryden (1996) for a comprehensive discussion of this issue.

This marks the end of the opening group session.

6

SESSION TWO: GOALS AND PROBLEM ASSESSMENT

In the second session of a ten-week self-acceptance group, you should:

- review the previous week's homework task
- set goals with group members
- analyse a specific example of self-depreciation for each group member using the ABC framework
- set the next homework task.

REVIEWING THE PREVIOUS WEEK'S HOMEWORK TASK

One of the axioms of Rational Emotive Behaviour Therapy (REBT) is that if you assign or negotiate a homework assignment it is very important that you review this task with your client at the beginning of the following session. If you do not review homework tasks with members of a brief structured self-acceptance group, then you communicate to them that you do not consider these tasks to be an important part of the group experience. However, if you treat these tasks seriously then you show group members that these tasks are an important part of the group and should be treated as such by its members. It has been shown in many areas that if you expect a high level of performance from people then they are more likely to perform well than if your expectations are low (Rosenthal & Jacobson, 1968). Thus, if you let group members know that you expect them to carry out their homework tasks, then they are more likely to do them than if you take a *laissez-faire* attitude about homework task completion. Beginning each group session by reviewing group members' homework tasks is one important way that you convey to them that you expect them to have carried out these tasks.

You will recall from the previous chapter that I asked group members to read chapters 1 and 3 from Paul Hauck's (1991) book on self-acceptance entitled *Hold Your Head up High*. Here is an excerpt from a typical dialogue that I have with group members on their reactions to this material.

WINDY: So last week I suggested that you read Chapters 1 and 3 of *Hold Your Head Up High* and in particular to note any points with which you disagreed or wanted to discuss. Let me go round and get your reactions to this material. Who wants to start?

LIONEL: I'll start. I found it very useful. It served as a revision of points that you presented last week.

SARAH: I found the first chapter particularly helpful because it outlined the different guises that low self-esteem takes.

LIAM: I thought that too.

WINDY: OK, Brian, what comments do you have about those two chapters?

BRIAN: Again, like the others I thought they were useful. I did have one disagreement though. He says on page 15 that rejection isn't painful. Does he think that people shouldn't have feelings if they are rejected by someone they care about?

WINDY: That's an important point, Brian, and one that people in other self-acceptance groups have made. Let's have a close look at what Paul Hauck says. Turn to page 15 . . . Now you will note that he says that people who accept themselves:

> . . . understand very clearly that rejection is not emotionally painful unless they make it so. Only they can make it a painful experience. They do that by believing that being rejected proves they are awful and worthless persons and that the only way they can be respectable human beings is to be loved by certain people who are very important to them.

Well, Paul is showing here that if you make your worth contingent on being loved you will experience rejection as emotionally painful. However, the problem is with the word 'painful', which is quite a vague word.

Now the therapy that this group is based on distinguishes between healthy desires and unhealthy demands. We saw last week that demands are closely linked to self-esteem and preferences are closely linked to self-acceptance. Now when you make demands, for example, about being loved, then you will make yourself emotionally disturbed when you are rejected. However, when you prefer to be loved but don't insist that those close to you have to love you, you will still be very sad and disappointed about being rejected. Now what I do, which on this occasion Paul has not done, is to distinguish between healthy painful feelings like sadness, concern and disappointment and unhealthy painful feelings such as depression, anxiety and shame. So I would say that it is constructive for you to experience healthy painful feelings about being rejected because these feelings indicate that you are preferring but not demanding that you must be loved and your preference is not being met. However, it is not constructive to experience unhealthy painful feelings about being rejected because these feelings indicate that you are demanding that you must be loved.

So I would say that rejection is healthily painful when you want to be loved but do not demand that you must be. What's your reaction to that, Brian?

BRIAN: That makes a lot of sense to me because I wasn't sure, from what Dr Hauck had written, exactly what was a healthy response to rejection, and you've made that clear.

WINDY: Does anyone else want to comment on this issue?

CAROL: Let me clarify. You seem to be saying that if someone you care for rejects you, you do not have to feel badly about yourself, but it is healthy to feel badly about the rejection.

WINDY: That's very well put, Carol. Sometimes I use formulae to explain things and you've just reminded me of that. We can say (*writing this on the flipchart*):

Rejection + Self-Acceptance = Healthy Negative Feelings

Rejection + Self-Downing = Unhealthy Negative Feelings

OK, let's move on. Betty, what was your reaction to the chapters I asked you to read?

BETTY: Like other people, I found the material helpful. I didn't pick up on the point that rejection shouldn't be emotionally painful, but I do object to Paul Hauck's point that you shouldn't love anyone.

WINDY: That was on page . . .?

BETTY: On page 45.

WINDY (*turning to page 45 in the book*): This is the passage where Paul writes: 'From this day forward, never hate yourself, never love yourself, instead accept yourself. This also applies to others. Never hate others, and never love others. Accept others as they are, or try to change them if you can.'

Then Paul goes on to say: 'Then, if they can still satisfy your deepest desires and needs, you will love all the wonderful things they do for you. You will not think they are better persons than others simply because they make you very happy.'

What I think Paul is getting at here is that if you say that you love someone you tend to give them a global positive rating. Since he has already cautioned against the rating of human beings he is cautioning against loving a person. Rather he advocates that we love all the wonderful things they do for us. I agree with Paul that we cannot logically give someone a global positive rating, but I think that it is unrealistic to expect people to stop thinking in terms of loving others. So if you say that you love someone, and really mean by this that you think that the other person is wonderful, then show yourself that you are in love with a fallible human being who may have wonderful traits, but is emphatically not a wonderful person.

But if you say that you love someone and mean by this you know that this person is fallible and you recognize that he or she meets your deepest desires, then saying that you love that person is not a problem as far as I can see. Does that make sense, Betty?

BETTY: I think so.

WINDY: What's your understanding of the point that I've just made?

BETTY: That the healthy meaning of loving someone is recognizing that they are human and not wonderful and that they currently meet your deepest desires. And the unhealthy meaning of loving someone is thinking that they are great rather than fallible.

WINDY: That's on the ball, Betty. The problem is in the meaning of 'I love you' and not in the words themselves. Good, Fiona, what were your reactions to the reading material?

FIONA: I go along with what's already been said.

WINDY: No other problems with the material?

FIONA: No, it all made good sense.

WINDY: Ronald?

RONALD: Like Fiona, it all made perfect sense to me. I agreed with Brian about the issue of rejection not being emotionally painful, but your explanation helped to clear up that confusion.

WINDY: Has anyone got any other points to make before we move on?

[Group members indicate that they want to move on.]

Before I finish this section, I do wish to stress that, on occasion, group members will not have completed their homework tasks. This will be true of any group and with any homework assignment. If this occurs, it is important to help the group member concerned identify how he (in this case) stopped himself from doing the set task. Once you have helped him to identify this obstacle you can then help him to address and overcome the obstacle before suggesting that he does the task before the next group session. It is important that you conduct this discussion without blaming the group member. Accept him as a person who has not completed a homework task and encourage him to adopt the same attitude towards himself. A full discussion of how to deal with clients who have not completed their homework tasks warrants a separate book and two such books have been published. I refer you then to Ellis (1985) and Neenan and Dryden (1996). As I mentioned in the previous chapter, Appendix 2 lists possible reasons why clients do not carry out homework tasks. You can use this form as a framework for exploring the nature of the obstacle or you can ask the group member to complete the form himself.

SETTING GOALS WITH GROUP MEMBERS

I have already stressed several times that the purpose of self-acceptance groups is not to help members to achieve full self-acceptance. That would not be possible, and certainly not after ten 90-minute sessions. Rather, the basic aim of these groups is to help members to begin the journey towards greater self-acceptance and to equip them with the knowledge and skills they will need as they embark on this journey. In line with this basic aim, the next task that I describe involves helping members to set realistic goals for the end of the group. Here is how I generally do this.

WINDY: What I want to focus on now is to help each of you to set a goal that you can aim to achieve by the end of the group. I'm going to ask you to split up into two groups to do this. But first, I'll demonstrate this process with one of you. Who'd like to volunteer?

BETTY: I'll volunteer.

WINDY: OK, Betty. Now, if you recall, the purpose of this group is to equip you with the knowledge and skills to begin the journey towards greater self-acceptance. What then, Betty, would you have achieved by the end of the group that would show you that you have begun to make that journey? Try to make your answer as specific as possible.

BETTY: I would like to have sung in public.

[This is a reasonably specific goal, but to make it even more specific, I ask the following.]

WINDY: On how many occasions?

BETTY: Let's say twice.

WINDY: Fine, Betty, that's what we call your behavioural goal. We also need you to set a self-acceptance goal along with your behavioural goal. An example might be as follows: 'I want to sing in public on two occasions and accept myself as a fallible human being if people aren't appreciative.' Do you see what I mean?

BETTY: Right, then my goal would be: 'Singing in public on two occasions and accepting myself as a fallible human being if I sing poorly.'

WINDY: Now if you did sing poorly and you accepted yourself for it, how would you feel about singing poorly?

BETTY: I'd feel very disappointed.

WINDY: Right, you'd feel disappointed and that would be healthy because singing poorly is a negative activating event. But if you depreciated yourself for singing poorly, how would you feel?

BETTY: I'd feel ashamed.

WINDY: And shame is an unhealthy negative emotion because it is based on a self-depreciating belief and it also leads to avoidance. If you feel ashamed about singing poorly in public you are much more likely to avoid singing in front of others than if you felt disappointed, but not ashamed about singing poorly. That's great, Betty. Why don't you make a note of your goal?

OK, group, let me give you precise instructions for this task which I'll write up on the flipchart.

1. *Set a behavioural goal.*

This will be something that you would like to do, but at the moment you are scared to do. Be as specific as you can and bear in mind that we are looking at what you can realistically achieve in ten weeks' time.

2. *Develop a self-acceptance statement which you can practise along with the desired behaviour listed above.*

This self-acceptance statement should be designed to help you deal with negative events you might encounter along the way. Thus, Betty's self-acceptance statement would help her if she sang poorly. For Betty, singing poorly is a negative activating event.

CAROL: Can I ask a question at this point?

WINDY: Go ahead.

[If Carol asked an irrelevant question, I would not have answered it at this point, but would tell Carol that I would deal with it after the goal-setting exercise that I am asking the group to do. In the event, Carol asked a very pertinent question, which I was very happy to answer.]

CAROL: Doesn't thinking about negative events make it more likely that they will occur?

WINDY: Do you mean that if Betty develops a self-acceptance statement about the possibility of singing badly, then she increases the chances of singing badly?

CAROL: Exactly.

WINDY: Actually, the reverse is probably true. Let me explain. the important thing here is not whether or not Betty entertains the possibility that she might sing poorly, but her attitude about that event. Thus, if she depreciates herself for singing poorly, she will tend to avoid singing in public. Under these conditions she won't think about the possibility about singing in public because she won't take the risk of doing so. If she does decide to do so, her self-depreciating attitude will lead her not only to think about singing poorly, but she will convince herself that this will happen.

Now if Betty accepts herself for singing poorly in public, she will be far less anxious about singing in front of others and thus much more likely to take the risk and do so. This attitude will enable her to realistically assess the likelihood of singing poorly versus singing well. Does that make sense, Carol?

CAROL: Yes, the important point is Betty's attitude about singing poorly rather than whether or not she thinks that she might.

WINDY: Exactly, Carol. Now the third instruction is as follows:

3. *Specify a healthy negative emotion that you would experience if the negative event happened and you accepted yourself.*

Remember: Betty said that she would feel disappointed if she sung poorly and accepted herself for it. It is constructive to experience healthy negative emotions such as concern, sadness, disappointment, for example, if negative events occur because it means that you are not getting what you want, but you accept yourself in the face of such negativity.

I suggest that you write down these three guidelines, which are again (*pointing to the flipchart and reading*):

1. Set a behavioural goal.

2. Develop a self-acceptance statement which you can practise along with the desired behaviour listed above.
3. Specify a healthy negative emotion that you would experience if the negative event happened and you accepted yourself.

Right, now split up into two groups of four and one at a time help one another to set goals. I'll give you about twenty minutes to do this task and I'll be around to answer any questions if you get stuck.

[The whole group then divides into two smaller groups and I wander from group to group listening to some of the discussion, making suggestions where appropriate and answering questions that group members have. After which I reconvene the whole group.]

WINDY: OK, let's go round and see which goal each person came up with. Liam?

[Going round in a clockwise direction, the group members identified the following goals. My interventions are shown whenever I help a member clarify some aspect of his or her goal.]

LIAM: My goal is to watch my girlfriend talk to another man at a party, to be concerned about it, and in the event that she finds him attractive, regard myself as a worthwhile person because I'm unique, alive and fallible.

LIONEL: Playing a round of golf a week, and showing myself that I am a fallible human being if I play poorly in front of others. In this way I will feel disappointed, but not ashamed about this eventuality.

CAROL: Telling my son and daughter that I plan to get married again and if they disapprove of me, to feel sorry about that, but not guilty. To accept myself as a fallible human in the face of hurting my children's feelings.

BRIAN: To assert myself with four people and to consider that I still have worth even if they reject me. To feel sad if they reject me, but not depressed.

SARAH: To speak up at every seminar that I attend and to accept myself if I say something stupid. To feel less anxious about saying something stupid.

WINDY: OK, let me come in here. The problem with aiming for being 'less anxious' is twofold. First, 'less anxious' as a goal has its problems because it is not very specific. Second, since your anxiety is based on a self-depreciating philosophy, opting to feel 'less anxious' means that you are still adhering to that philosophy. If you were to strive to feel concerned rather than less anxious about saying something stupid in your seminar groups, these two problems would disappear since (i) concern as a goal is specific and (ii) it is based on a self-accepting, not a self-depreciating philosophy. What do you think?

SARAH: That sounds reasonable.

WINDY: So what is your goal now?

SARAH: To speak up at every seminar that I attend and to accept myself if I say something stupid. To feel concerned about saying something stupid.

WINDY: Good. Let's move on. Ronald, what is your goal?

RONALD: To telephone a number of my business contacts, tell them that I have been made redundant and ask them to help me get another job. To feel disappointed about revealing my plight, but to accept myself for being in the situation that I'm in.

WINDY: That's fine, Ronald. Can I just ask you to specify a minimum number of business contacts that you will contact since 'a number' is a little vague.

RONALD: OK, I'll contact at least ten.

WINDY: Fine, so your goal is now . . . ?

RONALD: To telephone at least ten of my business contacts, tell them that I have been made redundant and ask them to help me get another job. To feel disappointed about revealing my plight, but to accept myself for being in the situation that I'm in.

WINDY: Good, Fiona?

FIONA: To talk to people who I think don't like me and to feel disappointed about the possibility that they don't like me. To think that I am an unrateable, fallible human whether they like me or not.

WINDY: Talk to how many people?

FIONA: To ten such people.

WINDY: So your goal is?

FIONA: To talk to ten people who I think don't like me and to feel disappointed about the possibility that they don't like me. To think that I am an unrateable, fallible human whether they like me or not.

WINDY: And, finally, let's remind ourselves of Betty's goal.

BETTY: To sing in public on two occasions, to accept myself as a fallible human being if I sing poorly and, if this happens, to feel disappointed about it.

WINDY: Thank you, group. What I will do now, if you think it would be helpful, is to write up what's on the flipchart and give you all a copy of everyone's goals. What do you think?

[Group members indicate that it would be helpful to have such a list, which is reproduced in Table 6.1.]

ANALYSING A SPECIFIC EXAMPLE OF SELF-DEPRECIATION USING THE ABC FRAMEWORK

The next task is to ask group members to select a specific example of a situation in which they depreciated themselves in some way. My usual

Table 6.1: List of Group Members' Goals to be Achieved by the End of the Group

LIAM:	To watch my girlfriend talk to another man at a party and to be concerned but not jealous about it. In the event that she finds him attractive, to regard myself as a worthwhile person because I'm unique, alive and fallible.
LIONEL:	Playing a round of golf a week, and showing myself that I am a fallible human being if I play poorly in front of others. In this way I will feel disappointed, but not ashamed, about this eventuality.
CAROL:	To tell my son and daughter that I plan to get married again and if they disapprove of me, to feel sorry about that but not guilty. To accept myself as a fallible human in the face of hurting my children's feelings.
BRIAN:	To assert myself with four people and to consider that I still have worth even if they reject me. To feel sad if they reject me, but not depressed.
SARAH:	To speak up at every seminar that I attend and to accept myself if I say something stupid. To feel concerned, but not anxious, about saying something stupid.
FIONA:	To talk to ten people who I think don't like me and to feel disappointed, but not hurt, about the possibility that they don't like me. To think that I am an unrateable, fallible human whether they like me or not.
BETTY:	To sing in public on two occasions and accept myself as a fallible human being if I sing poorly. To be concerned about singing poorly, but not anxious.
RONALD:	To telephone at least two of my business contacts, tell them that I have been made redundant and ask them to help me get another job. To feel disappointed about revealing my plight, but to accept myself for being in the situation that I'm in, and thereby not feel ashamed.

practice at this stage is to recommend to group members that they choose a problem that is related to the goal that they have selected. However, if they want to choose a different problem I do not object as long as it is an example of self-depreciation. I ask each group member in turn to talk about the experience briefly to the rest of the group and I use the ABC framework of REBT to help him or her to assess it. You will recall from Chapters 1 and 2 that A stands for the activating event, B for the beliefs that the person holds about the event and C for the emotional and behavioural consequences of holding this belief. Let me provide two examples of how I did this with Ronald and Fiona.

WINDY: The first step towards self-acceptance is to analyse situations in which you put yourself down. So, I'll go over one such example with each of you and in doing so I'll use a framework called the ABC framework to help you to see why you feel badly about yourself. It might be better if you were to choose a situation that is relevant to your goal, but I'll leave that to you. Who'd like to start?

RONALD: I will. I get anxious whenever I think of calling one of my business contacts.

WINDY: Can you give us a specific example?

[In REBT we prefer at the outset to work with specific examples of a problem. This level of specificity aids the assessment process.]

RONALD: It never gets that far. As soon as I think of it, I dismiss it from my mind.

[Because Ronald is unable to identify a specific example, I work with him at a more general level.]

WINDY: What are you most anxious about?

RONALD: That they'll find out that I've been made redundant.

WINDY: What's scary about them finding out that you've been made redundant?

RONALD: They'll think I'm a has-been.

WINDY: Let's just suppose for the moment that they'll think you're a has-been. What's anxiety-provoking about that?

RONALD: It would mean that I would feel badly about myself.

WINDY: What would the precise self put-down be?

RONALD: I'm not worth much.

WINDY: So when you think about calling your business colleagues what are you demanding?

RONALD: That they mustn't think that I'm a has-been.

WINDY: Let me put what you've said into the ABC framework, Ronald. I'll put it on the flipchart.

A = My business colleagues will think I'm a has-been if I tell them that I have been made redundant.
B = (i) They mustn't think that I'm a has-been.
     (ii) If that happens, I'm not worth much.
C = Anxiety.

Is that accurate, Ronald?

RONALD: Yes it is.

WINDY: Right, so what I've done, group, is to take Ronald's major emotion, anxiety, which is his C, discovered what he was most anxious about at A and then identified his beliefs at B, namely his demand and self-depreciation statement. Let's move on to Fiona. What situation do you want to discuss, Fiona?

FIONA: Well, whenever I am talking to someone I think doesn't like me, I get all flustered and I try very hard to get them to like me.

WINDY: Can you give us an actual example?

[Because Fiona is referring to events that have occurred, it is likely that she will be able to identify a specific example. Remember, specificity aids the assessment process.]

FIONA: Yes, over the weekend, I was invited to a dinner party and I was talking to a woman who I thought didn't like me. I got all flustered and tried desperately to think of something to say so that she would like me. This just made things worse because my mind just went blank.

WINDY: I'm not sure what you mean by flustered. What emotion do you experience when you say you were flustered?

[In REBT, we encourage our clients to be as precise as they can be about their emotions. This helps us to check whether their negative emotions are healthy or unhealthy (see Chapter 1 for more information on this point).]

FIONA: I felt anxious.

WINDY: And what were you most anxious about?

FIONA: About this woman not liking me.

WINDY: What's anxiety-provoking for you if it was true that she didn't like you?

FIONA: I'd feel worthless.

WINDY: One last thing. When you were anxious what were you demanding?

FIONA: That she must like me.

WINDY: Let me put what you've said into the ABC framework and you can correct me if I'm not on target. Again I'll put it on the flipchart.

A = The woman at the party may not like me.
B = (i) She must like me.
  (ii) I'd be worthless if she didn't like me.
C = Anxiety. Desperately trying to find some way of making her like me.

Is that accurate?

FIONA: That's exactly it.

WINDY: So again what I've done, group, is to take Fiona's major emotion at C, which is again anxiety, discovered what she was most anxious about at A and then identified her beliefs at B, namely her demand and self-depreciation statement.

At this point I continue to go round the group, asking group members for relevant situations in which self-depreciation was an issue for them and assessing these situations using the ABC framework. Here are the remaining ABC assessments that I carried out.

Brian

A = My unassertiveness is a weakness.
B = (i) I must not have this weakness.
  (ii) I am a weak, defective person for being unassertive.
C = Ashamed.

[This ABC shows an important feature of REBT practice. It appears from his initial goal statement (see p. 102) that Brian fears asserting himself in case he is rejected. In REBT, this is his primary problem. However, as the above ABC shows, he also feels ashamed about his lack of assertion. Brian's shame constitutes what I have called (Dryden, 1995) his meta-emotional problem – literally an emotional problem about an emotional problem. Meta-emotional problems are often expressed by self-acceptance group members for they tend to depreciate themselves for experiencing such emotions as unhealthy anger, depression, anxiety and other unhealthy negative emotions as well as self-defeating behaviours such as avoidance, overeating and procrastination.]

Liam

A = Thinking that when my girlfriend spoke to another man yesterday, it meant that she was interested in having a relationship with him.
B = (i) She must only be interested in me.
(ii) If she is interested in another man it means that I am not good enough as a person.
C = Jealousy.

Carol

A = Hurting my children's feelings by telling them that I am going to get married.
B = (i) I absolutely must not hurt my children's feelings
(ii) If I do so I am a rotten person.
C = Guilt.

Betty

A = Imagining singing poorly in public.
B = (i) I must not sing badly in public.
(ii) If I do it will prove that I am a complete fool.
C = Shame.

Sarah

A = Thinking that I may say something stupid and people will laugh at me.
B = (i) I must not say something stupid and others must not laugh at me.
(ii) If I do say something stupid in public and others laugh at me, these two things prove that I am a thorough jerk.
C = Anxiety.

Lionel

A = Thinking that I have played poorly in front of my golf colleagues and they look down on me.
B = (i) My colleagues must not look down on me if I play poorly.
(ii) If they do, it means that I am an insignificant person.
C = Ashamed.

After I have helped all the members of the group to develop an ABC assessment of a specific example when they depreciated themselves, I then outline a step-by-step guide to how they can conduct such an assessment for themselves (see Table 6.2).

Table 6.2:   A Step-by-step Guide to Assessing a Self-depreciation Episode using the ABC Framework

STEP 1: Identify a specific situation where you depreciated yourself in some way.

STEP 2: Use the ABC framework to analyse the episode. Write on a piece of paper the following:
A =
B = (i)
      (ii)
C =

STEP 3: Identify your major unhealthy negative emotion. Choose one from the following emotions: anxiety, depression, guilt, hurt, shame, unhealthy anger, jealousy or unhealthy envy. Write this emotion next to C =.
A =
B = (i)
      (ii)
C = Major unhealthy negative emotion.

STEP 4: Ask yourself the following question: What was I most _____ about? (where the line indicates the unhealthy negative emotion you listed under C). Write this next to A =
A = The aspect of the situation I was most _____ about.
B = (i)
      (ii)
C = Major unhealthy negative emotion.

STEP 5 Identify the demand you were making about A (expressed in the form of a must, absolute should, have to or got to) and write this under B = (i).
A = The aspect of the situation I was most _____ about.
B = (i) Demand.
      (ii)
C = Major unhealthy negative emotion.

STEP 6: Identify the self-depreciating statement you made and write this under B = (ii).
A = The aspect of the situation I was most _____ about.
B = (i) Demand.
      (ii) Self-depreciating statement.
C = Major unhealthy negative emotion.

SETTING THE NEXT HOMEWORK TASK

The next homework task follows logically from the work that you have done in the session. Ask group members to identify and analyse another situation in which they depreciated themselves using the ABC framework and the six steps that you have just outlined. It is helpful to give each group member these six steps in the form of a handout.

This brings the second group session to a close.

7

SESSION THREE: QUESTIONING DEMANDS, SELF-DEPRECIATION BELIEFS AND THEIR HEALTHY ALTERNATIVES

In the third session of a ten-week self-acceptance group, you should:

- review the previous week's homework task
- teach group members how to question their demands and related self-depreciation beliefs as well as the healthy alternatives to these beliefs
- assign homework designed to help group members practise their new questioning skills.

REVIEWING THE PREVIOUS WEEK'S HOMEWORK TASK

You will recall from the last chapter that I asked group members to use a six-step guide to assessing self-depreciation episodes and write out an ABC analysis of one such episode. At the beginning of this session I ask each member of the group to read out his or her ABC analysis which I then write up on the flipchart for all to see. My role in this process is to check the accuracy of group members' ABC assessments, to correct obvious errors and to encourage the whole group to participate in this checking exercise. I also reinforce what each group member has done, taking care not to imply that I am rating the person as a whole. To help group members distinguish between reinforcement of their achievements and person rating I generally introduce some humour into the proceedings and say something like 'That was a good ABC, but that doesn't make you a more worthwhile person!' or, more sardonically, 'You did well, Lionel. Go to the top of the worth league!'

Before I give an excerpt from the self-acceptance group that I am presenting for illustrative purposes, let me consider various difficulties that group members have with the ABC assignment and how these can be addressed.

Common Difficulties with the ABC Assessment Exercise

In this section, I will detail the common difficulties that group members have with following the step-by-step guide to assessing self-depreciation problems outlined in the previous chapter (see p. 109). These difficulties become manifest as group members read out their particular ABCs. I will discuss these difficulties as they occur at each of the six steps.

STEP 1: *Identify a specific situation where you depreciated yourself in some way.*

The most common difficulty that group members show at this initial step is in choosing a specific example of their self-depreciation. What they do instead is to select a general theme or an example which is in fact an amalgam of several incidents. The reason why it is important that group members select a specific example of self-depreciation is that specificity enhances the assessment process. It makes it more likely that the person concerned will identify the actual unhealthy negative emotion that she (in this case) experienced at the time and what she was most disturbed about. This has the knock-on effect of facilitating an accurate assessment of the person's self-depreciating belief and associated demand. By contrast, a more general example of self-depreciation yields more general (and thus less valid) information about the person's emotion, relevant activating event and unhealthy beliefs.

When a group member selects an example which is not specific enough to analyse, it is important that you respond by explaining why the example lacks the necessary concreteness and review with the member one of his or her more recent examples of self-depreciation which is specific enough to analyse. Then show the member why that example meets the specificity criterion and contrast this with some of his or her other examples which do not.

STEP 2 *Use the ABC framework to analyse the episode. Write on a piece of paper the following:*

A =
B = (i)
    (ii)
C =

In general, group members do not experience difficulty with this step since they are only being asked to copy the ABC format as laid out.

STEP 3: *Identify your major unhealthy negative emotion. Choose one from the following emotions: anxiety, depression, guilt, hurt, shame, unhealthy anger, jealousy or unhealthy envy. Write this emotion next to C =.*

If group members do not find step 2 difficult, this cannot be said of step 3. In my experience, they make two errors at this step, both of which involve ignoring the instructions that they were given. The first main error that group members make in identifying their major negative emotion is that they provide a vague emotion. Instead of choosing one of the specific emotions listed in the instruction (see above), they say, for example that they felt upset, distressed or bad. This is too imprecise for an accurate REBT assessment and consequently clients should be helped to be more precise in identifying their target emotion. Occasionally, however, group members may not be able to be more precise and as a group leader you should accept this and try to infer the precise emotion from the inference to be provided in the next step.

The other error that group members make at this step is to choose an emotion which is really an inference at A. For example, they may say that they felt rejected, let down or insulted. The best way to deal with this situation is to explain briefly why rejection, for example, is an inference and not an emotion and then ask 'What did you feel about being rejected?', orienting the person, if necessary to the emotions listed in the instruction outlined in step 3.

There are two other situations that you need to be aware of with respect to step 3, although strictly speaking neither is an error. First, some clients have idiosyncratic words for specific emotions and you need to be aware of unhealthy negative emotion they are referring to when they use the idiosyncratic term. Thus, one group member used 'gutted' for hurt. Once I had learned this, I could proceed to step 4. It is useful to make a note of which group members use which idiosyncratic words for which emotions and produce for yourself, and perhaps the group as a whole, a kind of glossary of affect terms.

Second, some group members identify what seem to be healthy negative emotions rather than unhealthy negative emotions at this step. This may be due to one of two factors: (i) they use a healthy negative emotion term when they really experienced an unhealthy negative emotion in the episode under consideration or (ii) they have not chosen an example where they experienced self-depreciation, but one where they actually did react healthily to the activating event. If the former is the case, some form of translation is needed. Either the client can be encouraged to use the term denoting the unhealthy negative emotion or you can make that translation in your own mind while continuing to use the client's term. If the latter is the case, then the client should be encouraged to select an episode in which he or she did experience self-depreciation.

Finally, a group member may resist choosing an unhealthy negative emotion because he (in this case) believes that he must not not experience such an emotion. If this reflects self-depreciation (as it often does), then it is worth identifying and tackling. Otherwise, the member concerned will spend much of his time in an ego-defensive mode which will benefit neither him nor the rest of the group. The best way to respond to this situation is to ask the group member if he would depreciate himself if he did experience an unhealthy negative emotion, and if this is the case then you can put this into the ABC framework as the following example from a group member from a different group shows:

A = Experiencing an unhealthy negative emotion (e.g. depression).
B = (i) I must not experience being depressed.
      (ii) If I am depressed then I am a defective person.
C = Shame.

STEP 4: *Ask yourself the following question: What was I most* _____ *about? (where the line indicates the unhealthy negative emotion you listed under C). Write this next to A = .*

Step 4 asks group members to identify the aspect of A about which they were most disturbed in the self-depreciation episode. In REBT this aspect is known as the critical A. Not all group members find it easy to identify their critical As when they are instructed to do so. While there are several methods available to help therapists identify their clients' critical As (Dryden, 1995), most of these are generally too complex to teach clients within the tightly organised curriculum of a self-acceptance group.

However, there is one method that you can teach group members who experience difficulty in identifying their critical As. This involves the following steps:

1. Help the group member concerned (a male client in this case) to discover the major inferential themes involved in his self-depreciation problems. Examples of inferential themes that are frequently implicated in self-depreciation include disapproval, failure, rejection, breaking moral or social codes, criticism, to name but a few.
You can do this specifically by (i) asking him to give you a list of everything that he depreciates himself for, (ii) inspecting this list and (iii) abstracting recurring themes in collaboration with the group member.
2. Ask the group member concerned if what he was most disturbed about in the concrete episode under consideration (i.e. the critical A) was a specific example of one of the themes that you have just identified.
3. If the critical A (as yet unspecified) was a specific example of an identified theme, you can ask the group member to use that theme to come up with the specific critical A. Thus, if rejection was the identified theme, the critical A could have been, 'predicted that I might be rejected by Marie if I asked her out'.
4. However, if the person claims that the critical A (as yet unspecified) was not a specific example of an identified theme, you can ask him to consider ways in which the specific critical A differed from the themes identified earlier. You can then use this discussion to identify the critical A under consideration. When you have done so, ask the group member to consider adding the thematic aspect of the critical A to his theme list. Thus, if the group member's critical A was 'being ridiculed in front if my friends', ask him to consider adding 'ridicule' to his theme list.
5. Encourage the group member to add to his theme list and to use it as an *aide-memoire* when identifying elusive critical As in future ABC assessments.

While you are particularly advised to use this thematic approach when group members are struggling to identify elusive critical As, you can also use it as a more general way of identifying critical As. Clients find it especially helpful to have a list of themes that are implicated in their self-depreciation problems. They often use this list not only to identify past critical As, but to prepare to face possible future critical As. So you may wish to teach this thematic method at some opportune point of the curriculum.

STEP 5: *Identify the demand you were making about A (expressed in the form of a must, absolute should, have to or got to) and write this under B = (i).*

The main error that group members make at this step is failing to identify a 'should' that is absolute. Thus, an unspecified 'should' may be an ideal 'should' or a preferable 'should' rather than one that is absolute. Recall from Chapter 1, that at the heart of emotional disturbance are demands which are essentially rigid in nature. Thus, the only 'should' that is rigid in nature is an absolute 'should' and therefore you should (ideally!) suggest to group members that they look for their absolute 'shoulds' and specify them as such under B = (i).

STEP 6: *Identify the self-depreciating statement you made and write this under B = (ii).*

As I have stressed throughout this book, self-depreciation beliefs are unhealthy because they involve giving the 'self' a single global negative rating. The main error that group members make at this final step is to negatively rate an aspect of themselves rather than their whole 'self'. Thus, they may negatively rate a role that they perform (e.g. 'I am a bad father') or a trait that they have (e.g. 'I am a selfish person'). It may well be that in making such a rating, the group member concerned is also making an implicit self-rating (e.g. 'I am a bad person because I am a bad father', 'I am less worthy because I am selfish'). In which case you are advised to investigate this possibility and help the person concerned to make any implicit self-ratings explicit. In doing so, you should also help the group member concerned and the rest of the group to understand the distinction between self-rating on the one hand and role-rating and trait-rating on the other.

Having reviewed each group member's homework and given relevant feedback, you can proceed to teach them how to dispute their demands and self-depreciation beliefs.

TEACHING GROUP MEMBERS HOW TO QUESTION THEIR DEMANDS AND RELATED SELF-DEPRECIATION BELIEFS

One of the most important tasks that you have to perform in a self-acceptance group is to teach group members how to question (or dispute) their demands and related self-depreciation beliefs, and you should ideally devote the bulk of this third session to this task. When I do this I use part of the structure recommended by Raymond DiGiuseppe (1991), which I discussed more fully in Chapter 1. In that chapter, if you recall, I showed that you can direct three major arguments (empirical, logical and pragmatic) to a number of belief targets (in this context: demands and self-depreciation beliefs).

As you will see from the following dialogue and illustrative excerpts, questioning involves two major tasks: (i) helping group members to see that their demands and self-depreciation beliefs are inconsistent with reality, illogical and yield poor emotional and behavioural results, and (ii) helping group members to construct healthy alternatives to these beliefs (i.e. full preferences and self-acceptance beliefs) and helping them to see that these healthy beliefs are consistent with reality, sensible and yield healthy emotional and behavioural results.

Introducing the Concept of Questioning and Providing a Rationale for its Use

Before teaching group members how to question their demands and self-depreciation beliefs, you will need to introduce the concept of questioning and provide a healthy reason for its use. Here is an example of how I do this.

WINDY: We have now covered the important task of how to assess specific episodes where you have depreciated yourself in some way. Now what is at the heart of your self-depreciation problems?

LIONEL: The beliefs at B.

WINDY: Excellent, Lionel. It is your demands and your self-depreciation beliefs that are the problem. So, if you want to overcome your self-depreciation problems and begin the journey towards self-acceptance, what do you need to change?

FIONA: Our beliefs at B.

WINDY: That's right. What I am going to do today, then, is to teach you the skills of questioning your demands and their healthy alternatives and doing the same with your self-depreciation beliefs. Let's start with demands. Who would like to volunteer to use one of their ABC assessments so I can show the group how to do this?

BETTY: I will.

WINDY: Thank you, Betty. Which ABC do you want to use?

BETTY: The one I did last week.

WINDY: Why don't you remind us of it and I will write it up on the flipchart.

Questioning Demands and Preferences

You will now know that the two major beliefs that are involved in self-depreciation problems are demands and self-depreciation beliefs. My practice is to take these beliefs separately when I teach group members the relevant questioning skills. In this book I am covering demands first because I covered them first in the ABC assessment process (see Chapter 6). Here, if you will recall, B(i) was a demand and B(ii) was a self-depreciation belief. However, it is perfectly permissible to reverse this order and deal with self-depreciation beliefs before demands. Let me now continue with the dialogue.

BETTY: The ABC is as follows:

   A = Imagining singing poorly in public.
   B = (i) I must not sing badly in public.
         (ii) If I do it will prove that I am a complete fool.
   C = Shame.

WINDY: Right. let's first take the belief that is listed under B = (i) 'I must not sing badly in public'. Now in order for you to change this belief, Betty, you first have to question it. But, first it is helpful for you to have a clear idea of what the healthy alternative to this belief is. Do you have any idea what that might be?

BETTY: That it doesn't matter if I sing badly in public?

[This is a common response and needs addressing. You will recall from Chapter 1 that the healthy alternative to a rigid demand is a full preference. It is not indifference.]

WINDY: That's a common response, Betty, but it's not correct. Do you know why?

BETTY: No.

WINDY: Does anyone else know why indifference is not the healthy alternative to Betty's demand?

BRIAN: Because it does matter to Betty if she sings badly in public.

WINDY: Correct, Brian. So the healthy alternative to Betty's demand is?

[No response from group members.]

   Well, have a look at the the handout I gave you in the first week outlining the eleven principles of self-acceptance and see if you can see the answer in one of the principles.

CAROL: Here it is. It's principle number 5: 'Unconditional self-acceptance is closely linked with a flexible, preferential philosophy.'

WINDY: That's exactly right. So, Betty, what do you think your flexible preferential belief is here?

BETTY: I'd prefer not to sing badly in public.

WINDY: That's half of it. What do you think the other half is? The clue is in the term 'flexible'.

BETTY: I'm not sure.

WINDY: Does anyone else know?

[Silence.]

   Well, it negates the 'must'.

SARAH: Is it that Betty would prefer not to sing badly in public, but there's no reason why she must not do so?

WINDY: On the button, Sarah. Do you see that, Betty?

BETTY: Yes.

WINDY: Now, can you put what Sarah said into your own words?

[This step is important. Betty is more likely to commit herself to the healthy belief if she puts it into her own words than if she were to use Sarah's phrasing.]

BETTY: I don't have to sing well in public, but I'd prefer to do so.

WINDY: Right. Now let's put both beliefs side by side.

[I write both beliefs on the flipchart.]

Demand	Full Preference
I must not sing badly in public	I don't have to sing well in public, but I'd prefer to do so.

Now there are three ways of questioning these two beliefs. I'll go over them one at a time and write them on the board. Then, as usual, I'll give you all a handout which will outline a step-by-step guide to questioning your demands and your preferences so that you can see precisely why preferences are healthy and demands are not.

[In this group I have decided to work with Betty's demand and full preference at the same time. I could have chosen to question fully her demand first before questioning her preference. Both strategies are permissible and consistent with REBT theory. Whether one strategy is more effective than the other awaits empirical enquiry. Throughout what follows I write the appropriate information on the flipchart and I also encourage group members to take notes.]

   The first question is: Is my belief true?

   Betty, looking at the two beliefs on the flipchart which belief is true and which is not?

BETTY: The preference belief is true and the must is not.

WINDY: That's right, but do you know why?

[Not only is it important for group members to know THAT their musts are false and their preferences are true, but also WHY this is the case. On this point, we don't take 'yes' for an answer!]

BETTY: Well, it's possible for me to sing badly in public and I won't like it if I do, but it's not true to say that I must not do so.

WINDY: That's correct, Betty. Let me outline a few alternatives to the 'Is it true?' question. (i) Is my belief consistent with reality? (ii) Does my belief follow a law of the universe?

What's the answer to those, Betty?

BETTY: The same as before. My preference is consistent with reality because I have it and it allows for the possibility that I might not sing well, whereas the must precludes me from singing badly. That's not true because I could always do so.

WINDY: That's right. The point here is that if there was a law to say that Betty must not sing badly in public then she couldn't do so. You can't go against a law of the universe.

Right, let's move on to the second question. Is my belief sensible? Now, Betty, which of the two beliefs is sensible or logical and which is not?

BETTY: The preference is sensible and the must is not.

WINDY: Because?

BETTY: When I say that I want to sing well, but I don't demand that I do so, I'm making a perfectly reasonable statement, but when I demand that I must not sing badly, I'm being unreasonable.

WINDY: Why?

BETTY: Well, just because I want to sing well in public doesn't mean that I must do so.

WINDY: That's an excellent point. Your demand doesn't follow logically from your preference. This point becomes clearer if we use your full preference. It doesn't make sense for you to begin by saying 'I'd prefer to sing well in public, but there is no reason why I must do so' and to end up by saying '. . . and therefore I must not sing badly'. Is that clear, group?

[The group members indicate that it is clear.]

WINDY: Fine, let's proceed to the third question, which is: Is your belief helpful or unhelpful and does it lead to healthy or unhealthy results?

Now which of the two beliefs leads to healthy results and which to unhealthy results?

BETTY: The demand leads to worse results than the preference.

WINDY: In what way?

BETTY: My demand leads me to get anxious when I think about singing in public and it leads me to avoid singing in public.

WINDY: Right. Now, what result stems from your preference?

BETTY: Well, I wouldn't be as anxious when I thought about singing in public and I wouldn't necessarily avoid doing so.

WINDY: That's right. Incidentally if you had a strong conviction in your full preference, you wouldn't feel anxious at all, but you would experience healthy concern which, as you say, wouldn't lead you to avoid singing in public. In fact, it would encourage you to do so if that is what you really wanted to do.

[My response to Betty's previous statement is informed by REBT theory which states that healthy negative emotions stem from healthy beliefs and unhealthy negative emotions stem from unhealthy beliefs. Betty's point that she would be less anxious if she held a full preference is really saying that less intense unhealthy emotions stem from healthy beliefs, which is not what I want her to learn.]

BETTY: I see what you mean.

WINDY: Do others see what I mean?

LIONEL: You're saying that concern and anxiety are different emotions and to feel less anxious is not the goal of this therapy, but to feel concerned is.

WINDY: When you are facing a possible threat like singing badly in public, yes that's exactly what I am saying.

Now, let's sum up. Betty. What have you learned from this questioning exercise?

BETTY: That my demand will lead to bad results for me, it isn't sensible and it isn't true . . .

WINDY: Whereas your preference?

BETTY: My preference is healthier for me, it makes sense and it's consistent with reality.

WINDY: So, which belief do you want to commit yourself to strengthening?

BETTY: My preference, of course.

Questioning Self-depreciation and Self-acceptance Beliefs

After I have finished helping Betty to question her demand and full preference, I then turn to helping her to question her related self-depreciation and self-acceptance beliefs (i.e. 'If I sing badly in public it would prove that I am a complete fool' and 'If I sing badly in public it wouldn't prove that I am a complete fool, but a fallible human being who could be said to have acted foolishly'. You will note that I will use the same questions here that I asked in questioning Betty's demand and preference.

WINDY: Now, let's go on to the second belief that is listed under B = (ii): 'If I sing badly it would prove that I am a complete fool.' That's obviously what I call a self-depreciation belief. What would be the healthy alternative to that belief?

BETTY: A self-acceptance belief.

WINDY: Which in this case would be what?

BETTY: If I sing badly in public it wouldn't prove that I am a complete fool, but a fallible human being who could be said to have acted foolishly.

WINDY: Right. Let me put these two beliefs on the flipchart.

Self-depreciation belief	*Self-acceptance belief*
If I sing badly in public it would prove that I am a complete fool.	If I sing badly in public it wouldn't prove that I am a complete fool, but a fallible human being who could be said to have acted foolishly.

Now, let's use the three ways of questioning these two beliefs. Again, I'll go over them one at a time and write on the board. Then, as I said before, I'll give you all a handout which will also outline how to question your self-depreciation beliefs and the self-acceptance belief alternatives so that you can see precisely why the former are unhealthy and the latter are healthy.

The first question again is: Is my belief true?

Betty, looking at the two beliefs on the flipchart which belief is true and which is not?

BETTY: Obviously the self-acceptance belief is true and the self-depreciation belief is false.

WINDY: Correct. What's your proof?

BETTY: Well, I can prove that I am a fallible human being, but I can't prove that I am a complete fool.

WINDY: Right. If you were a complete fool you could only and always do things in what way?

BETTY: Foolishly.

WINDY: And is that true?

BETTY: Obviously not, although that's the way I would feel.

[This is a very common response. When clients make such statements what they tend to mean is that they strongly believe that they are foolish and, thus, they mistakenly believe that this proves that they are fools. This is an example of what Beck *et al.* (1979) have called 'emotional reasoning' where a person judges something to be true because he or she strongly 'feels' that it is true.]

WINDY: But, would that 'feeling' prove that you were a fool?

BETTY: No.

WINDY: Actually, it would only prove that you had a strong conviction that you were a fool. And would this strong conviction be true or false in this instance?

BETTY: It would be false.

WINDY: That's right. Now let's move on to the second question: Is my belief sensible? Now, Betty which of the two beliefs is sensible or logical and which is not?

BETTY: Clearly, the self-acceptance belief is sensible and the self-depreciation belief isn't.

WINDY: And what are your reasons?

BETTY: Well, if I sing badly in public it obviously doesn't prove that I am a complete fool because singing badly in public is one act and being a complete fool is a statement about my whole self.

WINDY: Right. You've identified what is called the part–whole error which occurs when you rate the whole of something on the basis of a part of it. This overgeneralisation is at the heart of your self-depreciation belief. What about the self-acceptance alternative?

BETTY: Well, that's sensible. The conclusion that I am a fallible human being for acting 'foolishly' is perfectly logical.

WINDY: That's right. As a fallible human being you can act foolishly, non-foolishly and in a thousand and one other ways. Thus, as you say, concluding that you are a fallible human being for acting 'foolishly' is perfectly sensible. Is that clear?

BETTY: Quite clear.

WINDY: Does anyone have any questions?

[There are no questions from group members.]

Fine, let's proceed to the third question, which is: Is your belief helpful or unhelpful and does it lead to healthy or unhealthy results? Now, which of the two beliefs leads to healthy consequences and which to unhealthy consequences?

BETTY: The answer's pretty clear. My self-depreciation belief will lead to lousy results. As I see it, it stops me from taking the risk and do what I enjoy doing, singing in public. Also if I did take the risk, I'd be very anxious before the event and ashamed if I did actually sing badly in front of an audience.

WINDY: And the self-acceptance belief?

BETTY: If I believed it, it would encourage me to sing in public and be . . . concerned, is that right?

WINDY: Right, you've remembered well. . . .

BETTY: And be concerned, but not anxious about singing badly. If that eventuality happened, I would feel disappointed, but I wouldn't feel ashamed of myself.

WINDY: That's excellent, Betty. Now, let's sum up again. What have you learned from this questioning exercise, Betty?

BETTY: That my self-depreciation belief has unhealthy consequences, it isn't logical and it's not consistent with reality.

WINDY: And your self-acceptance belief?

BETTY: That obviously has much healthier consequences for me. It's also true and perfectly sensible.

WINDY: So. which belief do you want to commit yourself to strengthening?

BETTY (humorously): My self-depreciation belief, of course.

WINDY (responding with humour): Right, then. I'll help you to put yourself down for England!

[General group laughter.]

Small Group Exercise

Having demonstrated to the group how to question demands and full preferences on the one hand, and self-depreciation and self-acceptance beliefs on the other, you can now suggest a small group exercise. The goal of this exercise is to encourage group members to practise the questioning skills that you have just demonstrated with one of the group members.

First, ask the members to divide into two groups. Second, ask the members to select a specific episode where they depreciated themselves. This may be the situation that they assessed last week in the group or the episode that they assessed for last week's homework task. Third, have them help one another to question the beliefs that were at the core of their self-depreciation (i.e. their demands and self-depreciation beliefs) and their alternative healthy beliefs (i.e. their full preferences and self-acceptance beliefs). Suggest that they focus on one person's beliefs at a time. To help them undertake this task, it is useful to give them all a set of written instructions. The instructions that I give group members are found in Table 7.1. I ask each group to use these instructions as a guide to questioning their demands and full preferences on the one hand, and their self-depreciation and self-acceptance beliefs on the other. Furthermore, I ask them to write their responses in the appropriate spaces on the instruction sheet.

The whole group then divides into two smaller groups and once again I wander from group to group listening to some of the discussion, making suggestions where appropriate and answering questions from group members. I then reconvene the whole group and ask each member to present their written responses. As I go around the group I give feedback, make corrections and help each group member improve his or her questioning skills.

SETTING THE NEXT HOMEWORK TASK

The next homework task again follows logically from the work that you have done in the session. Ask group members to identify and analyse another situation in which they depreciated themselves using the ABC framework. It is helpful if the episode that they select is related to the goal that they set in the second group session. Then ask them to practise questioning the demands and full preferences and the self-depreciation and self-acceptance beliefs that they have identified using the instruction sheet that I have presented in Table 7.1. Again, ask them to make written responses in the spaces provided on the instruction sheet.

Table 7.1: Written Instructions to Help Group Members Question Their Demands/Full Preferences and Self-depreciation Beliefs/Self-acceptance Beliefs

Questioning Demands and Full Preferences

STEP 1: Take your demand and identify the alternative to this belief, which is a full preference. Write them side by side on a sheet of paper under the following appropriate headings:

          Demand   *Full Preference*

STEP 2: Ask yourself the following question: 'Which belief is true and which is false?'

STEP 3: Write down the answer to this question and provide written reasons for your answer.

STEP 4: Ask yourself the following question: 'Which belief is sensible/logical and which doesn't make sense or is illogical?'

STEP 5: Write down the answer to this question and provide written reasons for your answer.

STEP 6: Ask yourself the following question: 'Which belief is helpful/yields healthy results and which is unhelpful/yields unhealthy results?'

STEP 7: Write down the answer to this question and provide written reasons for your answer.

STEP 8: Ask yourself the following question: 'Which of the two beliefs do you want to strengthen and act on?'

STEP 9: Write down the answer to this question and provide written reasons for your answer.

Questioning Self-depreciation Beliefs and Self-acceptance Beliefs

STEP 1: Take your self-depreciation belief and identify the alternative to this belief which is a self-acceptance belief. Write them side by side on a sheet of paper under the following appropriate headings:

        Self-depreciation Belief   *Self-acceptance Belief*

STEP 2: Ask yourself the following question: 'Which belief is true and which is false?'

STEP 3: Write down the answer to this question and provide written reasons for your answer.

STEP 4: Ask yourself the following question: 'Which belief is sensible/logical and which doesn't make sense or is illogical?'

STEP 5: Write down the answer to this question and provide written reasons for your answer.

STEP 6: Ask yourself the following question: 'Which belief is helpful/yields healthy results and which is unhelpful/yields unhealthy results?'

STEP 7: Write down the answer to this question and provide written reasons for your answer.

STEP 8: Ask yourself the following question: 'Which of the two beliefs do you want to strengthen and act on?'

STEP 9: Write down the answer to this question and provide written reasons for your answer.

This brings the third session to a close.

8

SESSION FOUR: THE RATIONAL PORTFOLIO METHOD

In the fourth session of a ten-week self-acceptance group, you should:

- review the previous week's homework task
- teach the rational portfolio technique
- set the next homework task.

REVIEWING THE PREVIOUS WEEK'S HOMEWORK TASK

You will recall from the last chapter that I asked group members to assess another self-depreciation episode relevant to their goal, and to use a structured guide to questioning their demands and full preferences on the one hand and their self-depreciation and self-acceptance beliefs on the other. At the beginning of this session I again ask each member of the group to read out what he or she has written in the relevant spaces of the instruction sheet, and I write these comments on the flipchart. My role in this process is to check the accuracy of group members' responses to the questions asked on the sheet, to correct obvious errors and to encourage the whole group to participate in this checking exercise. I again reinforce what each group member has done.

Let me now consider the most common difficulties that group members have with the questioning task and how these can be addressed.

Common Difficulties with the Questioning Exercise

In this section, I will detail the common difficulties that group members have with following the step-by-step guide to questioning (i) their demands and full preferences, and (ii) their self-depreciation and self-acceptance beliefs. Once again these difficulties become apparent as group members read out what they have written. I will discuss these difficulties as they occur at each of the relevant steps.

Difficulties in Questioning Demands and Full Preferences

STEP 1: *Take your demand and identify the alternative to this belief, which is a full preference. Write them side by side on a sheet of paper under the following appropriate headings:*

Demand   *Full Preference*

The main difficulty that group members experience at this initial step is failing to specify their full preference. Thus, instead of stating that his full preference is 'I would prefer it if my colleagues did not look down on me if I play poorly at golf, but there is no reason why they must not do so', – Lionel wrote: 'I would prefer it if my colleagues did not look down on me if I play poorly at golf.' Lionel's stated belief is known in REBT theory as his partial preference.

A partial preference asserts the person's preference (e.g. 'I would prefer it if my colleagues did not look down on me if I play poorly at golf'), but does not negate his demand ('but there is no reason why they must not do so'). In contrast, a full preference not only asserts the person's preference, but also negates his demand (e.g. 'I would prefer it if my colleagues did not look down on me if I play poorly at golf, but there is no reason why they must not do so').

The reason why it is important for a group member to provide his (in this case) full preference and why his partial preference is not sufficient is that he is quite likely to transform his partial preference into a rigid demand, particularly when this partial preference is strong, whereas this is far less likely to happen when the person provides his full preference. Thus, because Lionel has only provided his partial preference, he is in danger of transforming this into a demand as follows: 'I would prefer it if my colleagues did not look down on me if I play poorly at golf . . . and therefore they must not do so.' However, if he provides his full preference ('I would prefer it if my colleagues did not look down on me if I play poorly at golf, but there is no reason why they must not do so'), he is hardly likely to transform this into a demand since his full preference negates his demand (as when he says: '. . . but there is no reason why they must not do so').

Thus, if a group member provides a partial preference rather than a full preference, help him to see the difference between the two. I find it particularly helpful to remind group members that a full preference has the word 'but' in it. This word usually follows the simple declaration of the preference. In this context, the word 'but' initiates the negation of the demand, as in Lionel's full preference: 'I would prefer it if my colleagues did not look down on me if I play poorly at golf, BUT there is no reason why they must not do so.'

STEP 3: *Write down the answer to the question 'Which belief is true and which is false?' and provide written reasons for your answer.*

While most group members can point out that a demand is false and a full preference, their main difficulty is in elucidating reasons why this is the case. They may something like 'I know that this demand isn't true, but I don't know why', or 'I can see that my full preference is true, but I can't put it into words'. Consequently, your main task here is to help group members to put into words why their demands are false and their full preferences are true.

Thus, when Sarah believes that she must not say something stupid in public, you can show her that this demand is false because there exists no law of the universe which states that she MUST not say something stupid in public. If there was, then she could not say something stupid in front of other people because she could not disobey this universal law.

Along similar lines, you could show Sarah that she is demanding that an empirical law must exist (i.e. that she must not say something stupid in public) in the absence of the existence of such a law (if such a law existed then she would not say anything stupid in public).

Another argument that you could use with Sarah to show her the false nature of her demand is as follows. First, show her that when she or anybody else says something stupid in public, they do so because all the conditions exist for them to do so. Thus, Sarah might say something stupid because she is nervous and, while desperately trying to think of something sensible to say, her desperation interferes with her clarity of thought and leads her to say something stupid. We can say that all the conditions were in place for her to say something stupid. In other words, empirically she should have said something stupid. If this is the case, then when Sarah demands that she must not say something stupid in public, she is saying that these preconditions must not exist. Now if they did exist it is false to demand that they absolutely should not have existed. And if they have not yet occurred, but it is possible for them to occur, it is also false to demand that these preconditions must not exist in the future. The point is that they could always exist.

The final way of showing Sarah that her demand is false is to ascertain whether she thinks such a law exists in the world or in her head. In all probability she will say that it exists in her head. You can then show her that this self-created law does not immediately create a universal law. Indeed, you can also show her that instead of guaranteeing that she will not say anything stupid in public, this self-created demand makes it more likely that she *will* say something stupid in public. Why? Because her self-created law results in anxiety and when you are anxious you increase the chances of saying something stupid in public.

STEP 5: *Write down the answer to the question 'Which belief is sensible/logical and which doesn't make sense or is illogical?' and provide written reasons for your answer.*

Again, the main difficulty that group members demonstrate at this step is providing reasons why demands are illogical and full preferences are sensible, even though they can readily discriminate between the two on this criterion.

When helping a group member to see that his (in this case) demand is not sensible, it is useful to take the following steps, which I will illustrate by showing the work that I did with Brian on this point.

• Take his partial preference and show him how he transforms this into a demand.

Here I showed Brian how he transformed his partial preference, 'I would prefer not to have this weakness' (i.e. unassertiveness), into a demand, 'and therefore I must not have it'.

• Question the logical nature of the conclusion.

Here I questioned the logical nature of Brian's conclusion: 'Does it follow that because you would prefer not to have a weakness that therefore you must not have it?' This helped Brian to see that his demand did not logically follow from his preference.

• Reinforce this by taking the full preference and by showing the person that since this belief is the opposite of a demand, the latter cannot follow logically from the former and is thus not sensible in the present context.

Here, I showed Brian that his full preference 'I'd prefer not to have this weakness, but there's no reason why I must not have it' is the antithesis of his demand 'I must not have this weakness'. Consequently, his demand cannot logically follow from his full preference. It is complete nonsense to say: 'I'd prefer not to have this weakness, but there's no reason why I must not have it and therefore I must not have it.'

STEP 7: *Write down the answer to the question 'Which belief is helpful/yields healthy results and which is unhelpful/yields unhealthy results?' and provide written reasons for your answer.*

In general, group members understand that demands yield healthy results and full preferences yield unhealthy results, and they can usually specify that different emotional and behavioural consequences stem from these different beliefs. There are, of course, exceptions to this general finding and these constitute the difficulties that some group members have with this pragmatic point.

The most commonly encountered problem concerns group members' views of the motivating properties of demands and full preferences. Thus, some clients consider that demands are motivating and without them they would lose the drive to achieve. A related issue concerns full preferences. Here, some clients consider that believing in full preferences would promote resignation or a failure to strive persistently towards one's goals.

REBT theory acknowledges that there can be positive effects from holding demands and there may also be negative effects from holding full preferences. However, for most people, and for most of the time, demands yield far more negative than positive results and the consequences of holding full preferences are far more beneficial than harmful. Thus, when addressing clients' concerns about the resignation aspects of holding full preferences and their reluctance to surrender their demands because of their motivational properties, it is important to acknowledge that there is some merit to their arguments. Having done this you then need to make the following points:

1. While demands can be motivating, they are frequently motivating in unproductive ways. In particular, demands impair objective decision making and thus one's actions are unduly influenced by the disturbed emotions that often stem from rigid demands (see Chapter 1 for a discussion of this point). For example, I often acknowledge that anxiety-related demands can be motivating, but in a frantic, directionless way, like a headless chicken.
2. In contrast, full preferences are motivating because they indicate what the person wants. However, this motivation is far more likely to be

based on careful thought since the person (a male member in this case) acknowledges that he does not have to have his desire met. So the first part of the full preference (e.g. 'I want x . . .') propels the person forward towards getting x and the second part (e.g 'BUT I don't have to get it') ensures that this forward propulsion is not influenced by emotional disturbance.

3. Demands are, in fact, more likely than full preferences to lead to resignation. This is because when your demand is not met you are more likely to conclude that you will never achieve your goal than if your full preference is not met. Holding this latter belief is likely to lead to a realistic appraisal of one's chances of achieving one's goal, and this realistic appraisal is likely to foster persistent striving towards that goal. This is the antithesis of resignation.

In summary, while full preferences may not engender the frantic, mindless type of motivation which is attractive to some because of the short-term energy that it fosters, they often promote a steadier, considered type of motivation which, in the longer term, is likely to produce better results for the person concerned than the frantic, mindless motivation engendered by demands.

A second common difficulty that some group members have with demands and full preferences concerns the relationship that these beliefs have with the standards that people set for themselves. Thus, the reservation is sometimes expressed by group members that if you give up your demands, you are lowering your standards and settling for an average standard or mediocrity. Similarly, I often hear the point made by some clients in a self-acceptance group that if you acknowledge that there is no reason why you have to meet your standards (which is a defining feature of a full preference), then you are in effect settling for second best.

Again these reservations may be true for a minority of people some of the time, but generally they are wrong. It is useful to make the following point to group members when addressing this issue.

Demands and full preferences are beliefs, and are therefore different cognitions to standards. Thus, a person can set high standards for himself or herself and hold either a demand or a full preference about reaching this high standard. Consequently, giving up a demand and retaining a full preference about a high standard does not involve lowering this standard. I often explain that if Mozart had come to consult me because he was anxious about completing his Requiem Mass, I would have helped him by encouraging him to retain his high standard and by urging him to keep his full preference about writing such a challenging work while giving up his demand about doing so. I would not have urged him to give up this difficult project and write a simple sonata instead.

STEP 9: *Write down the answer to the question 'Which of the two beliefs do you want to strengthen and act on?' and provide written reasons for your answer.*

Assuming that you have responded effectively to the concerns that group members have expressed at the previous steps, then they have no hesitation in choosing to strengthen and act on their full preferences.

Difficulties in Questioning Self-depreciation and Self-acceptance Beliefs

STEP 1: *Take your self-depreciation belief and identify the alternative to this belief, which is a self-acceptance belief. Write them side by side on a sheet of paper under the following appropriate headings:*

> *Self-depreciation Belief*   *Self-acceptance Belief*

Group members tend to have two main difficulties with this step. First, they fail to specify a true self-depreciation belief. Instead, they may put forward a statement in which they rate one of their traits (e.g. 'I am selfish') or one of their roles (e.g. 'I am a bad mother').

The way to deal with a trait rating masquerading as a self rating is to help the group member concerned to discriminate between that trait rating ('I am selfish' which really means that I score highly on the trait of selfishness) and a self rating ('I am a less worthy person for being selfish'). Basically you need to help the person to see that a trait is a part of that person's 'self' and not the whole of it.

You can also use this strategy when dealing with a role rating masquerading as a self rating. Thus, when a group member says that she is a bad mother, help her to see that she is rating her overall performance when occupying the role of mother and that this role is only a part of her 'self'.

Having said this, when a person rates negatively one of his or her traits or overall performance when occupying a valued role, that person often makes a self-rating which is implicit and generally outside his or her immediate awareness. Here, your task is to help the person identify and make explicit that implicit self-rating and thence to understand the difference between the two different types of rating.

The second difficulty that group members experience with this step is failing to provide a full self-acceptance belief. For example, let's suppose that Carol says that she is not a bad person for hurting her children's feelings. This statement is what we may call a partial self-acceptance in that Carol states who she is not (in this case she is not a bad person). By contrast, in a full self-acceptance belief Carol would be involved in stating who she is not (e.g. for example, a bad person) and asserting who she is (e.g. a fallible human being who is too complex to give herself a single rating). When a person has included both of these components she has provided a full self-acceptance belief.

It is important for group members to provide a full self-acceptance belief, otherwise they may transform their partial self-acceptance belief into a subtle self-depreciation belief. Thus, if Carol only said 'I am not a bad person for hurting my children's feelings', she could then go on to say '. . . but I would be worthier if I hadn't hurt their feelings'. Self-depreciation beliefs can come in various forms. First, they can be ex-pressed in stark terms as when Carol says 'I am a bad person for hurting my children's feelings'. However, they can also be expressed in a form which demonstrates the variation of human worth. Thus, when Carol says 'I would be more worth while if I did not hurt my children's feelings than if I did', she is adhering to a belief where a person's worth varies along different points of a 'worth continuum'. Carol does not see herself at the 'no worth' end of the continuum (as she does in the statement 'I am bad'); rather she sees herself in the 'less worth' part of the continuum when she hurt her children's feelings.

Consequently, when a group member only provides a partial self-acceptance belief (i.e. by stating who she is not), teach her that a full self-acceptance belief involves her stating both who she is not and who she is and encourage her to use full self-acceptance beliefs whenever possible. Otherwise, the person may well transform her partial self-acceptance belief into a subtle self-depreciation belief.

STEP 3: *Write down the answer to the question 'Which belief is true and which is false?' and provide written reasons for your answer.*

Generally, group members experience little difficulty in seeing that their self-depreciation beliefs are false and the self-acceptance belief alternatives are true. However, they do experience some difficulty in providing reasons to justify this, and in this context they may also refer to what is called the 'head-gut' issue. Carol's response illustrates these two points quite clearly: 'I know that I am not a bad person and that I am fallible, but I find it hard to put into words reasons to back this up. Also, I "feel" that I am a bad person.'

In helping a group member to understand why a self-depreciation belief is false and a self-acceptance belief is true, it is helpful to make the following points which I will illustrate with my work with Carol.

1. If it were true that Carol were a bad person for hurting her children, then everything about her would be bad since 'I am a bad person' means that her essence is bad and thus everything about her is bad. This is obviously false since a moment's objective reflection will help Carol to identify a number of good and neutral things about herself.
2. On the other hand, it is true that Carol is a fallible human being with good, bad and neutral aspects as that moment's objective reflection mentioned above will reveal. The fact that she considers hurting her children's feelings as bad is evidence that she is a fallible human being.

STEP 5: *Write down the answer to the question 'Which belief is sensible/logical and which doesn't make sense or is illogical?' and provide written reasons for your answer.*

Most group members can readily see that self-depreciation beliefs are illogical and self-acceptance beliefs are logical and explain why this is the case. The few who cannot can quickly be shown that self-depreciation beliefs are nonsensical overgeneralizations from negative activating events while self-acceptance beliefs are sensible conclusions from those events. This is best explained by putting the A (i.e. activating event) statement first in your explanation, assuming temporarily that the A is true and acknowledging that the person is rating this event as bad.

Thus, in showing Carol why her self-depreciation belief is illogical, I would have said the following:

WINDY: You said that you have hurt your children's feelings. Is that right?

CAROL: Yes.

WINDY: Let's assume that you did that and it is bad that you did that. OK?

CAROL: OK.

WINDY: So the event you are focusing on is this: 'I hurt my children's feelings and that was bad.' Now, is the following a logical conclusion? 'It therefore follows that I am a bad person through and through.'

CAROL: No, of course not.

WINDY: Why not?

CAROL: Because doing something bad is judging one aspect of myself, while saying that I am a bad person is judging my whole self.

WINDY: Does that second judgement follow logically from the first?

CAROL: No, it's what you called in one of the previous sessions the 'part–whole' error where you judge the whole of something on the basis of one or more of its parts.

WINDY: Now, let's take the first part of the statement again: 'I hurt my children's feelings and that was bad.' Now, is the following a logical conclusion? 'It therefore follows that I am a fallible human being with good, bad and neutral aspects.'

CAROL: Yes, that's perfectly logical.

In short, show group members that self-depreciation beliefs are subject to the part–whole error, whereas self-acceptance beliefs are not.

STEP 7: *Write down the answer to the question 'Which belief is helpful/yields healthy results and which is unhelpful/yields unhealthy results?' and provide written reasons for your answer.*

In general, group members can understand that self-depreciation beliefs yield healthy results and self-acceptance beliefs yield unhealthy results, and they can usually specify that different emotional and behavioural consequences stem from these different beliefs. As with demands and full preferences, there are exceptions to this general finding and these constitute the difficulties that some group members have with this pragmatic point. These difficulties are similar to those that people experience with demands and preferences.

Thus, some group members think that self-depreciation beliefs encourage productive action whereas self-acceptance beliefs promote resignation. The rebuttals to these mistaken ideas are similar to those used to correct similar misconceptions of the motivating properties of demands and full preferences. For example, it is helpful to explain to a group member who thinks that self-depreciation beliefs stimulate productive change that once she (in this case) rates herself as a failure, for example, she decreases her chances of taking productive action. For if she thinks she is a failure then what does a failure tend to do other than fail? Since she predicts that she will fail at an important task when she evaluates herself as a failure, she will be less rather than more likely to persist at that task. On the other hand, it is helpful to explain that if she accepts herself as a fallible human being who can succeed as well as fail, she is more likely to persist at an important task than when she considers herself a failure. This is because she thinks that she has as much chance succeeding at that task than of failing at it.

STEP 9: *Write down the answer to the question 'Which of the two beliefs do you want to strengthen and act on?' and provide written reasons for your answer.*

Assuming that you have responded effectively to the concerns that group members have expressed at the previous steps, then they have no hesitation in choosing to strengthen and act on their self-acceptance beliefs.

Since it takes quite a long time to check the previous week's homework assignment and to deal constructively with the difficulties that group members have encountered in completing it, you will probably only have time to introduce group members to one new and fairly uncomplicated technique. This technique is known as the 'Rational Portfolio'.

TEACHING THE RATIONAL PORTFOLIO TECHNIQUE

The previous techniques that I have introduced and discussed so far are intended to help group members to identify and challenge their demands and self-depreciation beliefs. They also are designed to help group members to understand that these demands and self-depreciation beliefs are false, illogical and unhelpful and that the alternative full preferences and self-acceptance beliefs are true, logical and helpful. At this point you can only expect that the understanding that group members have achieved on these points is intellectual in nature. This means that they understand these points 'in their head', but not 'in their gut'. 'Intellectual insight' is not sufficient for group members to incorporate their full preferences and self-acceptance beliefs into their belief system because they don't have a strong conviction in these healthy beliefs and therefore these new beliefs are too weak to have an impact on their emotions and behaviour.

In order to help group members to strengthen their conviction in their full preferences and self-acceptance beliefs so that they do have a productive impact on their emotions and behaviour (in other words, to help them to develop 'emotional insight'), you need to teach them a further set of cognitive, emotive and behavioural techniques. I will introduce and discuss these techniques in the remaining chapters. The first technique designed to help group members develop emotional insight into their full preferences and self-acceptance beliefs is called 'the rational portfolio'.

The Nature of the Rational Portfolio Technique

In developing a rational portfolio, group members construct as many arguments as they can think of to remind themselves why their full

preferences and self-acceptance beliefs are healthy and why their demands and self-depreciation beliefs are unhealthy. In order to help a
group member develop this portfolio, I suggest that you take the following steps which I will illustrate with my work with Fiona. What I generally do at this stage is to demonstrate the technique in front of the group
with one member's beliefs. I structure the work so that all group members
can participate in the process.

Demonstrating the Rational Portfolio Technique

1. Ask the group member to take one of her (in this case) unhealthy
   beliefs and the healthy alternative to this belief. This pairing could be a
   demand versus a full preference or a self-depreciation belief versus a
   self-acceptance belief. However, at this stage I find it helpful to bring
   the respective beliefs together and compare the group member's
   demand/self-depreciation belief with her (in this case) full preference/
   self-acceptance belief.
2. Have the group member write each belief on a separate piece of paper.
   Fiona's beliefs were as follows:

   UNHEALTHY BELIEF: The woman at the party must like me. If she
       doesn't then I'm worthless.

   HEALTHY BELIEF: I'd like the woman at the party to like me, but she
       doesn't have to do so. If she doesn't like me then I am not worthless.
       Rather I am a fallible human being who is not liked by the woman in
       question.

   Write each belief on a flipchart so that everyone can see the arguments
   that the group will develop.

3. Have the group member take her unhealthy belief and ask her and the
   rest of the group to suggest persuasive arguments against the member's unhealthy belief. Ask the group member concerned to keep a
   note of the arguments and write these up on the flipchart.
4. If any of the arguments are incorrect, explain why to the group and
   help them to refine such arguments.
5. Next, have the group member take her healthy belief and ask her and
   the rest of the group to suggest persuasive arguments in favour of the
   member's healthy belief. Ask the group member concerned to keep a
   note of the arguments and write these up on the flipchart. Don't be
   concerned if some of the arguments that members develop here repeat

arguments that they developed in step 3. Write all relevant and correct arguments down.

6. If any of the arguments are incorrect, again explain why to the group and help them to refine such arguments.

Table 8.1 presents Fiona's rational portfolio. This was partly constructed with the group's help and was completed by Fiona as a homework task.

Table 8.1:   Fiona's Rational Portfolio

Unhealthy Belief

'The woman at the party must like me. If she doesn't then I'm worthless.'

Reasons why this belief is unhealthy:

1. There is no law of the universe which states that the woman at the party must like me. If there was such a law, she would have to like me.

2. When I demand that the woman at the party must like me, I deprive her of her free will. As she is a person, she has the freedom to dislike me if that's how she feels.

3. Demanding that the woman at the party must like me is illogical because this demand does not logically follow from what I want – which is for her to like me. A demand does not logically follow from a preference.

4. If the woman does not like me, this is a fact and therefore it is just not sensible for me to demand that she likes me.

5. If the woman at the party dislikes me, then again this is a fact and when I demand that she must like me, I am insisting that reality must not be reality, which is crazy.

6. Demanding that the woman at the party must like me will lead me to be anxious before I conclude that she doesn't like me, and depressed when I make that conclusion.

7. When I demand that the woman must like me, this demand will result in my trying desperately to get her to like me. When I act desperately, I probably increase the chances that she won't like me or, if she does, she won't be liking *me*, but the false image that I portray.

8. Even if the woman at the party likes me for myself, demanding that she must like me will render me anxious in case she dislikes me later.

9. When I demand that the woman at the party must like me, I will tend to assume that she doesn't like me unless she shows clear evidence that she likes me. Thus, if she likes me a little or is neutral towards me, then the absence of clear evidence that she likes me will lead me to conclude wrongly that she dislikes me.

10. When I conclude that I am worthless if the woman at the party dislikes me, then I am making a false statement. For as a person I cannot be rated. Rather I am a fallible human being who is unrateable. Even if I have worth, this worth

(*continues over*)

cannot be taken away by her dislike of me. I am worth while because I am human, unique and alive and not because the woman at the party likes me.

11. If the woman at the party dislikes me and this is due to my having a dislike-able trait, then this trait only proves that I am a fallible human being with a dislikeable trait. It doesn't mean that I am worthless.

12. If the woman at the party dislikes me, she may well be saying more about her preferences than about my worth. My worth can never be based on another person's preferences.

13. When I evaluate myself as worthless because the woman at the party dislikes me, then this is an arrant overgeneralization. In doing so, I am making the part–whole error even if I have a dislikeable trait. It is not sensible for me to rate my whole self on the basis of a part of me or on the basis of one of my experiences.

14. When I say that I am worthless if the woman at the party dislikes me, then I will be anxious when I am around her.

15. When I say that I am worthless when the woman at the party dislikes me, then I will be depressed for days afterwards.

16. When I conclude that I am worthless if the woman at the party dislikes me, then I will tend to think that it is a fact that she dislikes me in the absence of any evidence.

17. When I conclude that I am worthless if the woman at the party dislikes me, then I will be sceptical of her friendliness towards me. I will tend to conclude that she is only being friendly towards me because she feels sorry for me or that she has an ulterior motive for being friendly.

18. When I say that I am worthless if and when the woman at the party dislikes me, then I will tend to think that most other people will dislike me. How can anybody like a worthless person?

19. If I consider myself worthless if the woman at the party dislikes me, I will tend to avoid other social gatherings and will deprive myself of much pleasure.

20. If the woman at the party clearly shows that she likes me, I may well wrongly tend to conclude that I am a worthwhile person. In doing so, I will reinforce my unhealthy belief that my worth is dependent on people liking me.

Healthy Belief

'I'd like the woman at the party to like me, but she doesn't have to do so. If she doesn't like me then I am not worthless. Rather I am a fallible human being who is not liked by the woman in question.'

Reasons why this belief is healthy:

1. My full preference is true because I am indicating the truth of my desire, i.e. I want the woman at the party to like me.

2. My full preference is also true because I am recognizing that there is no law of the universe which states that the woman at the party must like me.

3. By wanting the woman at the party to like me, but not demanding that she must do so, I am recognizing that she has free will. I am acknowledging that as a person she has the freedom to dislike me if that's how she feels.

4. My acknowledgement that the woman at the party does not have to like me follows logically from my desire that I would like her to do so.

5. If the woman does not like me, this is a fact and therefore it is sensible for me to indicate that she does not have to like me.

6. If the woman at the party dislikes me, then again this is a fact and when I state that I want her to like me, but she doesn't have to do so, I am acknowledging that reality does not have to be different from the way that it is, although I would like it to be so.

7. Preferring, but not demanding, that the woman at the party has to like me will lead me to be concerned, but not anxious before I conclude that she doesn't like me, and sad, but not depressed, after I have made this conclusion. Concern and sadness are healthy negative emotions because they help me to face up to a negative life event without disturbing myself about it.

8. When I prefer the woman to like me, but do not demand that she must do so, this full preference will not result in my trying desperately to get her to like me. I might try to get her to like me, but I will not do so in a desperate manner. My lack of desperation will increase the chances that she will like me and that she will like me for myself and not for any false act that I may put on.

9. If the woman at the party likes me, my full preference will lead me to be concerned, but not anxious, in case she dislikes me later.

10. When I want the woman at the party to like me, but do not demand that she has to do so, I will not automatically assume that she doesn't like me unless she shows clear evidence to that effect. I will allow for the fact that she may like me a little or is neutral towards me.

11. When I conclude that I am not worthless if the woman at the party dislikes me, but that I am a fallible human being, then I am making a true statement.

12. If the woman at the party dislikes me, and this is due to me having a dislikeable trait, then this trait only proves that I am a fallible human being with a dislikeable trait. It doesn't mean that I am worthless.

13. If the woman at the party dislikes me, she may well be saying more about her preferences than about me as a person. The fact that I am a fallible human being is true, no matter what her preferences are.

14. When I accept myself as a fallible human being in the face of the woman at the party disliking me, then this is a logical conclusion.

15. When I say that I am a fallible human being if the woman at the party dislikes me, then I will be concerned, but not anxious, when I am around her, particularly as I want her to like me.

16. When I say that I am a fallible human being, worthless when the woman at the party dislikes me, then I will be sad, but not depressed, since I would like her to like me.

(continues over)

17. When I conclude that I am a fallible human being if the woman at the party dislikes me, then I will tend not to conclude that she dislikes me in the absence of any evidence. I will accept that she may have a range of responses towards me and will decide on her attitude towards me on the basis of evidence.

18. When I conclude that I am a fallible human being if the woman at the party dislikes me, then I will accept her friendliness towards me at face value. I will not think that she is bound to have an ulterior motive or that she feels sorry for me.

19. When I say that I am a fallible human being if and when the woman at the party dislikes me, then I will not generalize from this event and think that most other people will also dislike me. I will judge each person's reaction towards me on evidence.

20. If I accept myself as a fallible human being if the woman at the party dislikes me, I will still attend other social gatherings and will experience the pleasure of doing so.

21. If the woman at the party clearly shows that she likes me, I will still consider myself to be the same fallible human being as I would be if she disliked me. I will not change my opinion of my 'self' on the basis of people's attitude towards me.

At the end of this demonstration, if sufficient time remains, I suggest that you ask the group to divide into two smaller groups and develop rational portfolios for each member, doing so one at a time, with all members suggesting relevant persuasive arguments against the unhealthy beliefs and in favour of the healthy beliefs. It is important that the group spends some time on each member's portfolio rather than all the time on one member's. Explain to the group that they will have an opportunity to complete unfinished portfolios for homework. To this end, recommend that they divide their time accordingly and have one member act as timekeeper.

Have the group write down the arguments on a flipchart or on a very large piece of paper so that you can see which arguments they have developed. Visit each small group periodically and at an opportune time, interrupt the small group and correct any arguments that warrant such correction, explaining your reasons carefully so that each group member can understand the reasoning behind your intervention. Take care to reinforce the correct arguments that the small group has developed so that they can build on their successes.

If you have spent a lot of time reviewing the previous week's homework task, it is unlikely that there will be sufficient time for this small group exercise. If this is the case, proceed to the homework assignment described below.

SETTING THE NEXT HOMEWORK TASK

The next homework task again follows logically from the work that you have done with the group on the rational portfolio technique. This homework assignment is the same whether or not the group has had the time to do the small group exercise mentioned above. Simply, it involves the completion of a single rational portfolio. Each group member may complete a portfolio that was started in the small group exercise (see above) or if there wasn't time for this exercise each member will have to start (and complete) a new portfolio. It is helpful to give each member the instructions presented in Table 8.2 for developing a rational portfolio.

Table 8.2: Instructions to Group Members on How to Construct a Rational Portfolio

1. Take one of your unhealthy beliefs and the healthy alternative to this belief. For your unhealthy belief include both the demand and the self-depreciation statement, and for your healthy belief include both the full preference and the self-acceptance statement.

2. Write each belief on a separate piece of paper under the appropriate heading as follows:

    Unhealthy Belief   *Healthy Belief*

3. Take your unhealthy belief and write down as many persuasive arguments as you can think of against this unhealthy belief. If you get stuck remember that such beliefs are false, illogical and yield poor results.

4. Next, take your healthy belief and write down as many persuasive arguments as you can think of in support of this healthy belief. If you get stuck remember that such beliefs are true, logical and yield good results.

This marks the end of the fourth group session.

9

SESSION FIVE:
THE ZIG-ZAG TECHNIQUE
AND EXPLAINING THE
NATURE OF BELIEF
CHANGE

In the fifth session of a ten-week self-acceptance group, you should:

- review the previous week's homework task
- teach the zig-zag technique
- explain the nature of belief change
- set the next homework task
- conduct a mid-group review

REVIEWING THE PREVIOUS WEEK'S HOMEWORK TASK

The previous week's homework task involved group members completing a rational portfolio. You will probably not have the time to review each group member's portfolio in full, but it is important to review each portfolio in part. Then, you can check the remainder of their portfolios as a homework task for yourself. My practice is to ask group members to come in an hour earlier the next session so that you can give them individual feedback before the next group session. You can, of course, do this with all group members present if you can book the group room for an extra hour.

In my experience there are three types of difficulties that group members encounter when completing a rational portfolio. These are: (i) making incorrect arguments, (ii) making irrelevant arguments and (iii) making arguments that are not persuasive. It is important that you deal with each of these difficulties when they become manifest.

Dealing with Incorrect Arguments

In reviewing group members' portfolios, I ask each member to read out part of their portfolio, ensuring that they provide a sample of arguments in favour of their healthy belief and against their unhealthy belief. As they read out their arguments, I make sure that I reinforce their accurate arguments and that I correct their errors. In correcting their errors, I first ask other group members to state what they think is wrong with particular arguments before correcting the errors myself if nobody in the group identifies them.

Group members tend to make three types of incorrect arguments in their rational portfolios: (i) errors of fact; (ii) errors of logic and (iii) errors of helpfulness. In illustrating how I deal with these errors, I will present the work that I did with Liam whose unhealthy and healthy beliefs were as follows:

UNHEALTHY BELIEF: My girlfriend must only be interested in me. If she is interested in another man it means that I am not good enough as a person.

HEALTHY BELIEF: I want my girlfriend to be only interested in me, but she doesn't have to be. If she is not, it doesn't mean that I am not good enough as a person. I am a worthwhile person because I am human, alive and unique.

Errors of Fact

Errors of fact in rational portfolios relate to group members wrongly identifying beliefs as true when they are false, or wrongly identifying beliefs as false when they are in fact true.

LIAM (*in responding to his unhealthy belief*):   My girlfriend doesn't have to be only interested in me because I don't have to be only interested in her.

WINDY: OK, group, what do you think of that argument?

SARAH: It's not accurate.

WINDY: Why not?

SARAH: Because Liam is implying that if he doesn't allow himself to be interested in another woman, his girlfriend then must not be interested in another man.

LIAM: Oh, I see. So I should have said that even if I am only interested in my girlfriend there is still no reason why she must only be interested in me.

WINDY: Correct. So is your demand true or not?

LIAM: It's not true.

WINDY: Even if you only have eyes for her?

LIAM: Even then.

Errors of Logic

Errors of logic in rational portfolios relate to group members wrongly identifying beliefs as logical when they are illogical, or wrongly identifying beliefs as illogical when they are logical.

LIAM (*in responding to his unhealthy belief*): I know that I am good enough as a person because other women find me attractive.

WINDY: What do you think of that argument, group?

LIONEL: It's not logical.

WINDY: Why not?

LIONEL: Because, Liam has shifted the goal posts. He hasn't dealt with the conclusion that he isn't good enough when his girlfriend is interested in other men. So he is still implying that if that bad event happens his worth goes down.

WINDY: Very good, Lionel. Do you see that, Liam?

LIAM: Right.

WINDY: So what would you conclude about yourself if your girlfriend was interested in another man?

LIAM: That I was still good enough.

WINDY: Because?

LIAM: Because if she was interested in another man, that would be very bad, but it would not be logical to say that my worth would go down because of that bad event. My worth is fixed as long as I am alive, human and unique.

Errors of Helpfulness

Errors of helpfulness in rational portfolios relate to group members wrongly identifying unhealthy beliefs as helpful when they are unhelpful, or wrongly identifying healthy beliefs as unhelpful when they are, in fact, helpful.

LIAM (*in responding to his healthy belief*):   Because I am worth while for being human, alive and unique, it doesn't matter if my girlfriend is interested in someone else.

WINDY (*giving Liam individual feedback*):   Can you see the problem with this argument, Liam?

LIAM: No.

WINDY: Well, you're saying that if your girlfriend is interested in someone else, it is healthy to feel indifferent about this. But, your healthy belief states that you would prefer it if your girlfriend was only interested in you, even though you acknowledge that she doesn't have to be. Now, with that belief you would feel healthily disappointed or concerned if your girlfriend was interested in another man. To feel indifferent in these circumstances would be unhealthy.

LIAM: Because I would be lying to myself?

WINDY: Correct.

Dealing with Irrelevant Arguments

Arguments that are irrelevant are usually not directed to the group member's healthy or unhealthy belief, but to something else. Commonly, they are directed towards inferences. For example:

LIAM (*in responding to his unhealthy belief*):   I have no evidence that my girlfriend is interested in anyone else, so it's a good bet that she is only interested in me.

WINDY: Group, what do you think of this argument?

CAROL: I'm not sure which belief Liam has in mind here.

WINDY: Liam, which belief are you addressing here?

LIAM: The belief that my girlfriend is interested in someone else . . . Oh, I see. I'm supposed to be providing arguments against my unhealthy belief and that's not a belief is it?

WINDY: That's right, you're challenging your inference that your girlfriend is interested in someone else. That's valid, but isn't relevant here.

Dealing with the Situation when Group Members are Not Persuaded by Their Arguments

One of the reasons why I ask group members to read out their arguments is to enable me to listen to their tone of voice, which provides a good clue to their level of conviction in the arguments. When, I sense that a group member isn't persuaded by an argument, I test out my hunch and, if I am correct, I invite the rest of the group to help the group member concerned to make the argument more persuasive.

Although there is no research evidence on this point, my hunch (based on clinical experience) is that group members find helpfulness arguments most persuasive and logical arguments least persuasive. If I am correct on this point, it does not follow that you can encourage group members to omit logical arguments and to a lesser extent empirical arguments since all arguments add something to their portfolio. However, it is useful to explain that most people find helpfulness arguments the most convincing.

TEACHING THE ZIG-ZAG TECHNIQUE

The zig-zag technique is another cognitive method which helps group members to weaken their conviction in their unhealthy beliefs and strengthen their conviction in their healthy beliefs, thus helping them to move from intellectual insight to emotional insight into the latter. The zig-zag technique is based on the observation that people often respond to their healthy arguments with a further set of arguments that cast doubt on their full preferences and self-acceptance beliefs and which advocate a return to their demands and self-depreciation beliefs. The zig-zag technique formalizes this debate between the parts of the person representing healthy beliefs and unhealthy beliefs and gives group members practice at defending their healthy beliefs against a variety of attacks. As such, this method helps group members integrate their healthy beliefs into their belief system.

When using the zig-zag technique, group members are asked to use the zig-zag form that I have devised (see Figure 9.1). In brief, a group member begins by writing down her (in this case) healthy belief and rating her degree of conviction in this belief. Then, she responds to this healthy belief with an attack which encapsulates the person's reservation, doubt or objection to this belief. After she has formulated this attack the person responds vigorously to it. The attacks and responses continue in this vein

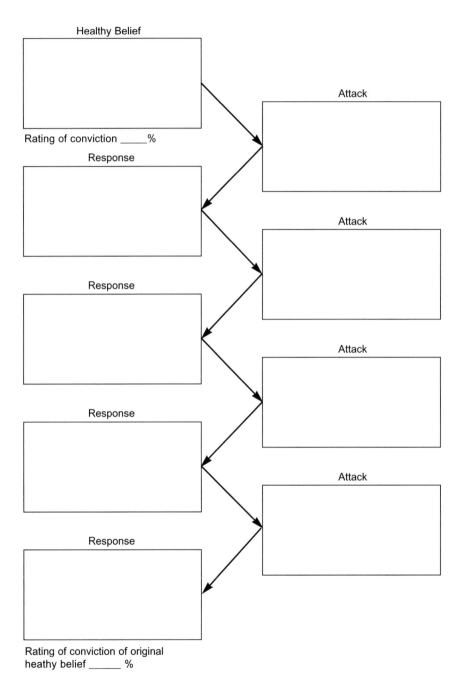

Figure 9.1: The zig-zag form

until the group member has responded fully to all of her attacks. The person then re-rates her degree of conviction in her originally stated healthy belief, which is usually increased if the person has used the technique properly.

Let me demonstrate how I used the zig-zag technique with Brian. Note that I write Brian's responses on the flipchart so that all the group members can see his attacks and responses. Also note that I strive to involve the other group members whenever possible during this demonstration.

WINDY: OK, let me demonstrate the zig-zag technique. Who would like to volunteer?

BRIAN: I will.

WINDY: OK, Brian, the first step is for you to state the healthy belief that you want to strengthen.

BRIAN: I regard my lack of assertiveness as a weakness which I'd rather not have, but there is no reason why I must not have it. I am not a weak, defective person for being unassertive. Rather I am a worthwhile person who is worth while because I am human, alive and unique.

WINDY: Now, at this moment, how much do you believe that on a scale from 0 to 100%?

BRIAN: 55%.

WINDY: Good, now the next step is for you to attack this healthy belief. This attack might be a doubt you may have about the belief, a reservation about it or an objection to it.

BRIAN: But a real man would be able to assert himself whenever he wanted and you can't. You're a wimp.

WINDY: Now how would you respond to this attack?

BRIAN: I'd say: 'No I'm not.'

WINDY: What do you think about that response, group?

LIAM: Brian isn't giving any reasons.

WINDY: Right, Liam. Brian, in this technique it's really important that you spell out your reasons in full. Really try to rip up the attack.

BRIAN: OK. I'm not a wimp for not being able to assert myself at times. I'm a worthwhile person who has flaws and this is one of them.

WINDY: Good. Now attack the healthy belief again.

BRIAN: Yeah, but if you could assert yourself when you want to, you'd be more worth while than if you can't.

WINDY: Response?

BRIAN: That's not true. My worth doesn't go up and down like a yo-yo. It's fixed. It's sensible for me to rate my assertiveness as good and my lack of assertiveness as bad, but nothing can detract from my worth. That's fixed as long as I'm alive, human and unique.

WINDY: Good, what's the next attack?

BRIAN: But, most people would think you a wimp if you can't assert yourself.

WINDY: Response?

BRIAN: That may be true, but who cares what they think.

WINDY: What do you make of that, group?

BETTY: That's probably a lie.

WINDY: Right and it also doesn't respond to the attack. Brian, have another go.

BRIAN: OK. Well, if other people think I'm a wimp, I do care obviously, but that doesn't make them right. In fact, they're overgeneralizing from one part of me, which might be wimpish, to a wimp through and through. That's illogical. I'm far too complex to be rated on the basis of one part of me.

WINDY: Good. Let's go on.

BRIAN: But in this day and age, you have to be able to assert yourself, otherwise people will walk all over you.

WINDY: Response?

BRIAN: I don't think people would do that.

WINDY: Group?

FIONA: That's not responding to the attack.

BRIAN: Oh, yes. Let me have another go. They might walk over me and that would be undesirable, but that still doesn't mean that I have to assert myself. Musts like that don't exist in the world. I'd like to assert myself and I'm going to deal with my anxiety about doing so, but if there was a law of the universe stating that I have to, I would do so.

WINDY: Another attack.

BRIAN: I think I've answered them all.

WINDY: Right, now let's go back to your original belief. Here it is on the flipchart. Study it and tell how much you believe it now on the same 0 to 100% scale.

BRIAN: You mean at this minute?

WINDY: Yes.

BRIAN: 85%. But I'm sure it will go down again.

WINDY: That's why it's important to do this technique quite often so that you get used to responding to your attacks. Otherwise, if you allow your attacks to go unchallenged, you will rehearse your unhealthy beliefs and strengthen them.

Dyad Exercise

After you have demonstrated the zig-zag technique, I suggest that you ask the group to divide into pairs and help one another to complete a zig-zag. To help them to do this, I suggest that you give each member a handout containing detailed written instructions on how to fill out this form (see Table 9.1 for the instructions that I distribute). Your task during this exercise is to go from dyad to dyad and make sure that each group member adheres to these instructions. In particular, I suggest that you encourage group members to respond to each element of their attacks. There are other versions of the zig-zag technique and if you ever decide to run longer self-acceptance groups, you may want to teach them to group members. In which case I refer you to Dryden (1995) for a discussion of these other versions.

EXPLAINING THE PROCESS OF BELIEF CHANGE

At this point, group members have had some experience of weakening their unhealthy beliefs and strengthening their healthy beliefs. This would therefore be a good time for you to explain to group members the process of belief change from an REBT perspective. My practice is to outline the following points:

1. Belief change involves weakening unhealthy beliefs and strengthening healthy beliefs. I point out that group members have begun to do this when using the healthy portfolio and zig-zag techniques.
2. As they strengthen their healthy beliefs and weaken their unhealthy beliefs, group members will experience a strong sense of discomfort. This discomfort is due to the fact group members are used to their unhealthy beliefs and unused to their healthy beliefs. In order to

Table 9.1: Instructions on How to Complete a Zig-zag Form

1. Write down your healthy belief in the top left-hand oblong of Figure 9.1.
2. Rate your present level of conviction in this belief on a 100-point scale with 0% = no conviction and 100% = total conviction and write down this rating in the space provided on the form.
3. Respond to this healthy belief with an attack that is directed at the healthy belief. This may take the form of a doubt, reservation or objection to the healthy belief. Make this attacking statement as genuinely as you can. The more it reflects what you actually believe, the better. Write down this attack in the oblong on the right of Figure 9.1.
4. Respond to this attack as fully as you can. It is really important that you respond to each element of the attack. Do so as persuasively as possible and write down this response in the second oblong on the left of Figure 9.1.
5. Continue in this vein until you have answered all your attacks and cannot think of any others.
   If you find this exercise difficult, you might find it easier to make your attacks gently at first. Then, when you find that you can respond to these attacks quite easily, begin to make the attacks more biting. Work in this way until you are making really strong attacks. When you make an attack, do so as if you really want to believe it. And when you respond, really throw yourself into it with the intention of demolishing the attack and raising your level of conviction in your healthy belief.
   Don't forget that the purpose of this exercise is to strengthen your healthy belief, so it is important that you stop when you have answered all your attacks. Use as many forms as you need and clip them together when you have finished.
   If you make an attack that you cannot answer, stop the exercise and we will discuss, as a group, how you can best respond to it.
6. When you have answered all your attacks, re-rate your level of conviction in the healthy belief as before. If you have been successful at responding to your attacks, then this rating will have gone up. If it has not increased or has only done so a little, we'll discuss the reasons for this in the group.

---

consolidate their belief change group members need to tolerate this discomfort while continuing this weakening–strengthening process.

3. As they do so, it is very important that group members begin to act in accord with their healthy beliefs and refrain from acting in accord with their unhealthy beliefs. If they change their thinking in the direction of their healthy beliefs, but keep acting in accord with their unhealthy beliefs, they will undermine the belief change process.
4. Group members will facilitate the belief change process if they *frequently* practise thinking and acting in accord with their healthy beliefs.
5. Group members will facilitate the belief change process if they add force, energy and passion to this process. This means strongly rehearsing their healthy beliefs rather than doing so in a weak, wimpish manner. It also means acting in accord with their healthy beliefs in a whole-hearted manner rather than doing so tentatively.

6. If group members stop acting and thinking in accord with their healthy beliefs they will increase the chances of returning to their unhealthy beliefs.

SETTING THE NEXT HOMEWORK TASK

The next homework task involves group members finishing the zig-zag form if they have not had the time to complete it in the dyad exercise, or to fill out a fresh zig-zag form. Again I suggest that you ask them to follow the instructions outlined in Table 9.1.

CONDUCTING A MID-GROUP REVIEW

You have now reached the mid-point of the group, a timely moment to review the group's progress with its members. I conduct this review very informally and ask the members for their general impressions. If any problems are expressed by individual members, I listen respectfully to their account and ask other members if they share these views. If you have selected group members carefully, explained the nature of a self-acceptance group and have taken care to involve all group members in the various ideas and tasks that you have introduced, it is unlikely that these problems will concern the basic nature and structure of the group. Rather, they will usually reflect group members' concerns about the pace of the group and whether the material will be covered in time. In addition, group members use this opportunity to express their concerns about what will happen when the group finishes.

When responding to concerns about the pace of the group (and I have received comments that a group is proceeding too slowly or too quickly!), it is important that you remind all group members that the purpose of a self-acceptance group is to equip its members with the necessary skills to begin and to continue the journey towards self-acceptance. To this end it is useful to reassure them that by the end of the group sessions you will have covered the material necessary for them to do this.

When responding to concerns about what will happen after the group sessions end, I have found it useful to suggest to group members that there is nothing to stop them from becoming a self-help, self-acceptance group after the formal group sessions end. This idea is usually taken up with enthusiasm and, indeed, several self-help, self-acceptance groups that started life as brief, therapist-led, self-acceptance groups still continue to meet periodically. I discuss this more fully in Chapter 14.

This marks the end of the fifth group session.

10

SESSION SIX: THREE EMOTIVE TECHNIQUES TO FACILITATE CHANGE

In the sixth session of a ten-week self-acceptance group, you should:

- review the previous week's homework assignment
- teach the group a number of techniques – the tape-recorded version of the zig-zag technique, the use of forceful self-statements, and rational-emotive imagery (REI) – designed to help them further weaken their conviction in their unhealthy beliefs and strengthen their conviction in their healthy beliefs
- set the next homework tasks.

REVIEWING THE PREVIOUS WEEK'S HOMEWORK TASK

You will recall that the previous week's homework task involved group members completing a written zig-zag form. When you review the forms with group members, it is important that you detect and correct the errors they have made. As usual, such feedback is best received when you also reinforce accurate responses. Here is a list of (i) common errors that group members make in completing zig-zag forms and (ii) brief suggestions on how you need to intervene when you discover them, which I will illustrate from my work with some of the group members. Note how I strive to involve other group members when I am working with one of their number.

Error 1: *Failing to Attack the Healthy Belief*

When this happens, it is likely that the person will respond to this irrelevant attack, thus sending the zig-zag off track.

INTERVENTION: Point this out to the group member concerned and help her (in this case) to understand why her attack was off beam. Then, help her to formulate an accurate attack.

Illustration

SARAH'S HEALTHY BELIEF: I'd prefer not to say something stupid and for people not to laugh at me, but there is no reason why either of these must not happen. If they do, I'm not a jerk. I'm human, alive and unique.

SARAH'S ATTACK: But if people laugh at you, it means they think you are a jerk.

WINDY'S QUESTION TO THE GROUP: Is this a good attack, group?

FIONA: No, because it just states that if people laugh at Sarah this means that they think she is a jerk. This doesn't attack Sarah's healthy idea that she doesn't think she is a jerk if other people think she is.

WINDY: Do you see Fiona's point, Sarah?

SARAH: Now that she has made it, yes.

WINDY: So what would be a more direct attack on your healthy belief?

SARAH: Something like, 'If people laugh at you and think you are a jerk, they all can't be wrong. You are a jerk if they think you are.'

WINDY (*addressing the group again*):   Is that a better attack?

BRIAN: That's spot on.

WINDY: Right. I suggest, Sarah, that you continue your zig-zag from this point.

Error 2: *Failing to Respond to the Attack*

INTERVENTION: Point this out to the group member concerned and help her (in this case) to understand why her response was off beam. Then, help her to formulate an accurate response to the attack.

Illustration

CAROL'S HEALTHY BELIEF: I'd much rather I didn't hurt my children's feelings, but very unfortunately there's no reason why this absolutely should not have happened. I'm not a rotten person for hurting their feelings. I'm a fallible human being who did something I wish hadn't happened.

CAROL'S ATTACK: Of course you're a bad person. If you weren't, you wouldn't have hurt their feelings.

CAROL'S RESPONSE: But I didn't mean to hurt their feelings. I love them really.

WINDY (to the group):   What do you make of Carol's response to her attack?

BETTY: It's not a good response.

WINDY: Why not?

BETTY: Because it doesn't respond to the idea that Carol is a rotten person for hurting her children's feelings. It just makes the point that she didn't mean to hurt them.

WINDY: Carol, do you see what Betty means?

CAROL: Yes I do.

WINDY: So what would be a more accurate response?

CAROL: I'm not a bad person whether or not I hurt my children's feelings. If I was a bad person, I could only do bad things and that's obviously ridiculous. No, even though I hurt their feelings, I'm not bad; I'm fallible and unrateable even though it is bad that my children's feelings may be hurt.

Error 3:   *Failing to Respond to all Elements of the Attack*

INTERVENTION: Reinforce the person for responding accurately to some elements of his (in this case) attack, then explain those elements of the attack which he did not respond to at all or did so inaccurately. Building on the accurate aspects of his previous response, help him to formulate a response which deals accurately with all elements of the attack.

Illustration

LIONEL'S HEALTHY BELIEF: I'd rather not play poorly in front of my golfing colleagues, but there's no law preventing me from doing so. If I play poorly, I'm not an insignificant person, but a fallible human being who can play well, poorly and averagely.

LIONEL'S ATTACK: But you're not supposed to play poorly. If you do it must prove that you are less worthy than if you play well.

LIONEL'S RESPONSE: My worth doesn't depend on how I play. My ability to play golf is just one aspect of me, not the whole of me. I am a complex, unrateable person. I can rate my golfing play, but not my 'self'.

WINDY: That's a really good response, Lionel. But you've missed one thing, Have another look at your response and see if you can spot the missing bit.

LIONEL: Oh, the bit about me being supposed to play well?

WINDY: That's it. How could you respond to that bit?

LIONEL: I could say, 'There is no law which decrees that I'm supposed to play well. I'm not a golfing machine. I'm a human being. Even Nick Faldo has his off days.'

WINDY: Excellent. Now if you put both of those statements together, that would be a powerful response.

Error 4: *Failing to Develop Persuasive Responses to the Attacks*

INTERVENTION: Test out your hunch that the person does not find her (in this case) response persuasive. If you are correct, help the person to make her response more persuasive. You can do this by helping the person change the wording of the response (e.g. by using more forceful language) or by modifying the argument.

Illustration

BETTY'S HEALTHY BELIEF: I prefer to sing well in public, but I don't have to do so. If I do sing poorly in public, I'm not a fool. I'm fallible.

BETTY'S ATTACK: But you have had all that training, you must be able to sing well in public.

BETTY'S RESPONSE (*weakly*):   There is no such law. If there was, I could not sing poorly.

WINDY: You don't sound too convinced by your response. Am I right?

BETTY: Yes.

WINDY: How could you make that response more persuasive?

BETTY: I like Lionel's concept of not being a golfing machine. So I could say something like: 'If there was a law which said that I must be able to sing well in public, I'd be a singing machine.' That's stupid. I'm a fallible human being and as such there is always the possibility that I might not sing well when I give a public recital. I don't like that, but I do admit that that possibility exists.

WINDY: Do you find that response more persuasive than your original one?

BETTY: Much more persuasive.

TEACHING THE TAPE-RECORDED VERSION OF THE ZIG-ZAG TECHNIQUE

The tape-recorded version of the written zig-zag technique involves group members verbalizing their attacks on their healthy beliefs and their responses to these attacks. It enables them to inject force and energy into the process by varying the tone and intensity of their voice. In this way it becomes very apparent which responses to their attacks they find persuasive, and which not. Because it is much harder for group members to keep focused on attacking their healthy beliefs and on their responses to these attacks when doing so verbally rather then in writing, it is important that group members do not move on to this version of the zig-zag technique until they have become proficient at the written version. Indeed, it may well be a good idea to encourage group members initially to do a written zig-zag and then to record this dialogue on tape before putting future dialogues directly on to tape.

Table 10.1 shows the steps that group members are advised to take while doing the tape-recorded version of the zig-zag. Once again this can be presented as a written handout. I find it useful to model this technique for group members, thus showing how to put these steps into practice before suggesting that they take it as a homework task.

TEACHING THE USE OF FORCEFUL SELF-STATEMENTS

I have already discussed the role of force and energy in helping group members to integrate their healthy beliefs into their belief system. The use of forceful self-statements is particularly powerful in promoting such integration. In teaching group members to use forceful self-statements, I suggest that you do the following:

Table 10.1: Instructions on How to Use the Tape-recorded Version of the Zig-zag Technique

1. You will need to use a hand-held, good-quality tape recorder with a good-quality tape for this exercise. A good micro- or mini-cassette recorder will suffice.
2. Find a time and space when you won't be interrupted and cannot be overheard. Put your answer machine on or take the phone off the hook. You will need to set aside about 20 to 30 minutes for this task.
3. Begin the recording process by stating your healthy belief on tape, noting verbally your level of conviction in it, using a 0–100% scale.
4. Try to get yourself to return to your unhealthy belief by attacking your healthy belief.
5. Respond to this attack in a forceful and persuasive manner making sure that you answer all elements of the attack.
6. Go back and forth in this matter (making sure that your responses are more forceful and persuasive than your attacks) until you can think of no more attacks.
7. Re-rate your level of conviction in your originally stated healthy belief.
8. Listen to the recording and note the following:
   (i)   Instances when you went off the point. Formulate an alternative response at this point that would have enabled you to keep to the point.
   (ii) Instances when you failed to respond to an element (or elements) of an attack. Formulate a response to that unanswered element.
   (iii) Instances when you sounded unpersuaded by your response to an attack. Formulate more persuasive ways of responding to this attack in both tone of voice and content of argument.

---

1. Describe forceful self-statements and provide a healthy belief for their use.
2. Take a healthy belief (preferably not one that any of the group members wish to strengthen) and write it on the flipchart (e.g. 'I want to do well in my driving test but I don't have to do so. If I fail, I can accept myself. I am not a failure').
3. Read out this belief to the group, once in a powerful forceful manner and once in a weak, wimpish manner.
4. Ask the group to identify which of the two 'versions' is the most presuasive. In my experience, virtually all group members are able to identify the forceful 'version' as the most convincing.
5. Have each group member identify a healthy belief that he or she wishes to strengthen.
6. Ask the members to verbalize this belief once in a loud and forceful manner and once in a weak manner and ask them to determine which of the 'versions' they find most persuasive. Again, in my experience, virtually all group members say that the forceful 'version' is the most persuasive.
7. Then, ask the group members to whisper their healthy beliefs, retaining the same level of force and energy as they used in the forceful

'version' in step 6. You may want to model this if any group members are unsure of how to do this.

8. Finally, ask the group members to rehearse their healthy beliefs silently, retaining the same level of force and energy as before.

Here is a list of the forceful self-statements that the group members decided to practice:

RONALD: If my colleagues think I'm a has-been, they're wrong. I'm a fallible person who has been made redundant; I'm not redundant as a person.

BETTY: If I sing poorly in public, I'm not a fool. I'm fallible.

SARAH: If I say something stupid and people laugh at me, I'm not a jerk. I'm human, alive and unique.

LIONEL: I'm not an insignificant person if I play poorly in front of my golfing colleagues. I can accept myself as an FHB no matter how I play.

CAROL: I don't want to hurt my children's feelings, but if I do it's bad, but I'm fallible.

BRIAN: I'm worth while whether or not I assert myself.

FIONA: I'd like people to like me, but they don't have to.

LIAM: I'm worth while even if my girlfriend is interested in other men.

TEACHING RATIONAL-EMOTIVE IMAGERY (REI)

Rational-emotive imagery (REI) is a cognitive-emotive technique designed to encourage clients to practise changing their unhealthy beliefs to healthy beliefs while vividly imagining a negative activating event. There are two versions of REI, one devised by Albert Ellis and one by Maxie C. Maultsby Jr. My practice is to teach the Ellis version first and to teach the Maultsby version if and when a group member cannot use the Ellis version. This is best determined when you review the homework task at the beginning of the next group session. While teaching group members rational-emotive imagery, it is useful to take the following steps.

1. Describe rational-emotive imagery and give a healthy belief for its use. Explain that the technique utilizes the capacity of group members to use their imagination for better or for worse. Thus, you can explain that we frequently use our imagination to disturb ourselves. Thus, we may imagine a negative activating event and bring our

unhealthy beliefs at B to this imagined A, thus creating our emotional disturbance at C. In this way, you can stress to group members that we practise disturbing ourselves. Then, you can emphasize that if we can use our imagination for worse we can also use it for better. Thus, while imagining the same negative event at A, we can gain practise at changing our emotional response at C, by implicitly changing our beliefs at B.

2. Ask for a volunteer with whom you can demonstrate REI.
3. Ask the volunteer to identify a specific negative, activating at A, about which he (in this case) depreciated himself.
4. Ask the person to identify how he felt about this negative activating event. Agree on an emotion which is clearly an unhealthy negative emotion (see Chapter 1 for a discussion of unhealthy and healthy negative emotions).
5. Ask the person to close his eyes and to vividly imagine the selected negative activating event.
6. Then, ask him to really experience his unhealthy negative emotion at C, while still imagining the same A and to signal when he feels this emotion.
7. Next, ask the person to change his unhealthy negative emotional response to a healthy negative emotion while still vividly imagining the same A. Stress that it is important that, as he changes his feeling, he keeps the intensity of the feeling the same. Ask him to signal when he feels this healthy negative emotion.
8. Ask the person how he changed his emotional response at C.
9. Ensure that the person changed his emotional response by changing his unhealthy belief to a healthy belief. If not, correct his error and reiterate the importance of changing C by changing B. If you had to do this, go back to step 3 and repeat steps 3 to 8.

A Demonstration of REI

Here is the demonstration that I did with Ronald. You might find it helpful to refer to the above steps as you read this demonstration.

WINDY: OK, Ronald, what is your selected negative activating event, an event where you put yourself down?

[See step 3 above.]

RONALD: It's an event that hasn't happened yet, but something that I fear happening.

WINDY: That's fine. What is this event?

RONALD: It's where my business colleagues think I'm a has-been when I tell them that I have been made redundant.

WINDY: And how do you feel about this happening?

[See step 4 above.]

RONALD: Anxious.

WINDY: OK, close your eyes and vividly imagine that you are about to tell your business colleagues that you have been made redundant and that they may think of you as a has-been. Can you imagine that?

[See step 5 above.]

RONALD: Easily.

WINDY: Now really make yourself anxious as you think that they may consider you are a has-been when you tell them that you have been made redundant. When you feel anxious, signal to me by raising your right-hand index finger.

[See step 6 above.]

[Ronald raises his finger after about 15 seconds.]

WINDY: Now keep vividly imagining that your colleagues may think of you as a has-been when you tell them that you have been made redundant. As you do so, change your feeling of anxiety to one of concern, making sure that you keep the same level of intensity as you do so. When you feel concerned, signal to me by raising your index finger again.

[See step 7 above.]

[Ronald raises his finger after about 30 seconds.]

WINDY: How did you change your feeling?

[See step 8 above.]

RONALD: I told myself that I'm not a has-been. I'm a fallible human being who has been made redundant, but is not redundant as a person.

You can then ask group members to practise REI on their own. In this context it is helpful to give them written instructions to remind them of the steps they need to follow (see Table 10.2). They can also use these instructions when they are practising REI as a homework task. Before they begin to practise REI, tell the group members to signal to you if they get stuck. If they do so, offer the appropriate help.

Table 10.2:   Instructions on How to Practise Rational-emotive Imagery (REI) –
Ellis Version

1. Identify a specific negative, activating at A, about which you depreciated yourself. Make sure that you have selected an event about which you disturbed
   yourself.
2. Close your eyes and vividly imagine this negative activating event.
3. Allow yourself to really experience the unhealthy negative emotion that you
   felt at C while still imagining the same negative activating event. Ensure that
   your unhealthy emotion is one of the following: anxiety, depression, guilt, hurt,
   shame, jealousy, unhealthy envy or unhealthy anger.
4. Feel that emotion for a moment or two and then change your emotional response to a healthy negative emotion, while still vividly imagining the same
   activating event. Don't change the intensity of the emotion, just change the
   emotion.
   Thus, if your original emotion was anxiety, change it to concern; if it was
   depression, change it to sadness. Change guilt to remorse, hurt to sorrow,
   shame to disappointment, jealousy to concern for your relationship, unhealthy
   envy to healthy envy, and unhealthy anger to healthy anger.
   Again, change the emotion, but keep the level of intensity the same for each
   different emotion.
   Keep with this new emotion for about five minutes, all the time imagining the
   same event at A. If you go back to the former emotion, bring the new one back.
5. At the end of the five-minutes period ask yourself how you changed your
   emotion.
6. Make sure that you changed your emotional response by changing your unhealthy belief to a healthy belief. If you did not do so (e.g. you changed your
   feeling by changing some aspect of the A), carry out the exercise again and
   keep doing so until you have changed your emotion only by changing your
   unhealthy belief to its healthy alternative.
7. If you still cannot do this, bring your difficulty to the group and we will discuss
   it.

SETTING THE NEXT HOMEWORK TASKS

In this group session, you have taught the group how to use three techniques that will help them to deepen their conviction in their healthy
belief and thereby to integrate it into their belief system. It therefore
follows that the homework tasks you will want group members to undertake will involve practising these techniques. I recommend that you ask
group members to undertake the following:

- one tape-recorded version of the zig-zag
- ten minutes' daily practice using forceful self-statements based on
  selected healthy beliefs
- two six-minute REIs per day.

I also suggest that you ask group members to read and note any objections to chapter 4 of Hauck's (1991) book entitled *Hold Your Head Up High*. This chapter considers the importance of behavioural methods in the development of self-acceptance, a topic which will be a major focus of the next two group sessions.

This marks the end of the sixth group session.

11

SESSION SEVEN: THE CONJOINT USE OF COGNITIVE AND BEHAVIOURAL TECHNIQUES

In the seventh session of a ten-week self-acceptance group, you should:

- review the previous week's homework tasks
- provide a rationale for the conjoint use of behavioural and cognitive techniques
- set the next homework task (this involves the conjoint use of behavioural and cognitive techniques)
- teach mental rehearsal of behavioural-cognitive tasks
- identify and overcome obstacles to carrying out behavioural-cognitive tasks.

REVIEWING THE PREVIOUS WEEK'S HOMEWORK TASKS

At the end of the previous group session, I recommended that you set the group four homework tasks. Since you do not have the time to check every group member's homework in this group session, I suggest that you check a sample of each set of tasks and give feedback to members on any unchecked homework after the end of this session or before the next session begins. I will now review the common issues that you will encounter when you check each of the four homework tasks and possible responses to these issues.

One Tape-recorded Version of the Zig-zag

The issues that you will encounter here are the same as those you met when checking group members' written zig-zags (see Chapter 10). In brief, these involve dealing with the following four client errors or difficulties:

- failing to attack the healthy belief
- failing to respond to the attack
- failing to respond to all elements of the attack
- failing to develop persuasive responses to the attacks.

You should deal with these issues using exactly the same methods that you used to deal with them when group members reported them on their written zig-zags (see pp. 156–159 in Chapter 10). When listening to members' tape-recorded zig-zags, you will find it quite easy to spot when a group member is relatively unconvinced by his or her response to one of his or her attacks. When addressing this issue it is not only important to help members to increase the persuasiveness of their responses, it is also important to encourage them to respond to their attacks with force and energy. Tape-recorded zig-zags are most effective when the person's responses are both more persuasive in content and more forcefully expressed than his or her attacks.

Ten Minutes' Daily Practice Using Forceful Self-statements Based on Selected Healthy Beliefs

In checking a group member's use of forceful self-statements, it is important to check both the content of the statement and the level of force that the person used when rehearsing it. With respect to the content of the self-statement, sometimes a group member may modify the statement that she (in this case) specified in the previous group session. This is acceptable as long as the modified statement accurately reflects the healthy belief that the person has targeted for strengthening. If it does not accurately reflect this healthy belief then it is important that you help the person understand why it does not do so and suggest that she return to using the original statement. The errors that group members make in modifying their self-statements include the following:

1. *Changing a full preference to a partial preference* (e.g. changing 'I want to be liked, but I don't have to be liked' to 'I want to be liked'). If this happens help the person to see that a partial preference is too easily

transformed into a demand. Once you have done this, encourage her (in this case) to use the full preference.

2. *Introducing an element of indifference into the self-statement* (e.g. changing 'I want to be liked, but I don't have to be liked' to 'I want to be liked but, if I'm not, it doesn't matter'. If this happens, help the person to see that trying to convince himself (in this case) that it doesn't matter if he is disliked when he really wants to be liked is tantamount to lying to himself. Then, encourage him to revert to his originally devised accurate self-statement.

3. *Asserting who one is not, rather than affirming who one is as well as who one is not* (e.g. changing 'I can accept myself as a person who has failed. I am not a failure' to 'I am not a failure for having failed'. When a group member changes her (in this case) self-statement in this way, stress that it is important that she use the negating *and* the affirming statement rather than just the negating one. Using both statements increases the chances that the person will develop self-acceptance in the longer term.

4. *Changing a self-acceptance statement to a trait statement* (e.g. changing 'I am a fallible human being who unfortunately acted unkindly to my wife the other day' to 'Although I acted unkindly to my wife the other day, I am basically a kind person'). If a group member makes this error, it is important that you explain to him (in this case) the difference between a self-acceptance statement and a trait statement. The former involves the person forgoing rating the 'self' and focuses instead on acknowledging that the essence of the 'self' is fallibility, while the latter by-passes this level and involves rating one of the person's traits which actually takes the form of a self-rating. After you have explained this to the person, encourage him to develop and practise a forceful *self*-acceptance statement.

In addition to correcting the above errors, it is important that you ask group members to let you hear the level of force with which they practised their self-statements. If you consider that their self-statements lacked force, encourage them to practise the statement in the group with an increased level of force. Help them to see the difference between this increased level and the level they used and to experience the effect of these two levels. Then, suggest that they practise the self-statement with the increased level of force during the coming week.

Practising REI for Six Minutes Twice per Day

You also asked group members to practise REI for six minutes twice daily. When you check this homework task, it is helpful to ask them to refer to the written instructions that you gave them in the previous session (see Table 10.2) as a framework for identifying any problems they experienced in using this method. Let me consider the most common difficulties that group members experience with REI at each step and show how you can respond when these are revealed.

STEP 1: *Identify a specific negative, activating at A, about which you depreciated yourself. Make sure that you have selected an event about which you disturbed yourself.*

The first difficulty that group members experience at this step involves the person identifying a general event rather than a specific one. This is a problem because group members are less likely to be able to form a vivid image of a general event than that of a specific event. If they form a vague image, they will be unlikely to experience a strong unhealthy negative emotion, which is important if they are to access and subsequently change their unhealthy beliefs. If this happens, you need to explain to the person the importance of choosing a specific negative activating event and then help the person to do this.

The second difficulty that group members experience at this step involves the person choosing an event about which he (in this case) did not depreciate himself and did not experience an unhealthy negative emotion. This is a problem because in such an instance the person has no unhealthy belief to modify. If this occurs, reiterate that the purpose of REI is to change unhealthy beliefs to healthy beliefs, then help the person to select a specific negative event about which he did depreciate and disturb himself.

STEP 2: *Close your eyes and vividly imagine this negative activating event.*

The main difficulty that group members experience at this step is failing to imagine the activating event with sufficient vividness. There may be three reasons for this. First, the person may have selected an event about which in reality she (in this case) only experienced a mild level of disturbance. In which case, help her to select an event about which she experienced a much stronger level of disturbance.

Second, the person may edit out the aspects of the event that she found most disturbing. If this is the case, reassure the person that it is natural for people to do this, but that if she is to get the most out of REI, she needs to do the somewhat unnatural thing and deliberately imagine those elements.

Finally, some people do not have the capacity to imagine events very vividly. If this is the case, encourage them to imagine the selected event as vividly as they can and not to worry if their image is not clear. It is worth noting in this context that no tests have been conducted on the the hypothesis that people who do have the capacity to imagine events with great vividness will benefit more from REI than those who do not have this capacity.

STEP 3: *Allow yourself to really experience the unhealthy negative emotion that you felt at C while still imagining the same negative activating event. Ensure that your unhealthy emotion is one of the following: anxiety, depression, guilt, hurt, shame, jealousy, unhealthy envy or unhealthy anger.*

Group members experience a number of difficulties at this step. First, on enquiry, they may report a vague emotion like feeling 'upset' or 'bad' rather than a specific unhealthy negative emotion such as anxiety or shame. The problem with vague emotions such as 'upset' or 'bad' is threefold. First, it is unclear if they refer to an unhealthy or a healthy negative emotion. Second, their vagueness tends to interfere with the person's ability to create and sustain a vivid representation of the specific activating event. Finally, if such vaguely expressed emotions are based on healthy beliefs the whole purpose of REI (which is to practise changing unhealthy beliefs to their healthy equivalents) is nullified.

Thus, when a group member indicates that he experienced a vaguely expressed negative emotion, first explain why this is problematic for the practice of REI, then refer her (in this case) to the list of emotions found in step 3 of the client instructions to REI and encourage her to select one specific unhealthy negative emotion when she practises REI on subsequent occasions.

Second, a group member may report experiencing a healthy rather than an unhealthy negative emotion (e.g. concern rather than anxiety). As noted above, since the purpose of REI is to help the person practise changing his (in this case) unhealthy beliefs to healthy beliefs, it is important that he selects an event in which he experienced an unhealthy negative emotion. Otherwise he will not have the opportunity to practise changing his unhealthy belief (which underpins his unhealthy negative emotion) to a healthy belief. So, if a group member reports a healthy negative emotion, explain to him why such an emotion is problematic for REI and encourage him to choose an unhealthy negative emotion from the list shown in step 3 whenever he practises REI in the future.

The third problem that some group members have with this step in the REI process is that they find it difficult to sustain their vivid image of the activating event at the same time as they focus on their unhealthy negative emotion. This problem is usually overcome when the person gains more experience at using the Ellis version of REI. However, if no improvement is shown on this point, then the group member concerned may derive more benefit from a different version of REI; for example, the Maultsby version. (See Table 11.1 for client instructions on how to practise this version of REI.)

Step 4: *Feel that emotion for a moment or two and then change your emotional response to a healthy negative emotion while still vividly imagining the same activating event. Don't change the intensity of the emotion, just change the emotion.*

Thus, if your original emotion was anxiety, change it to concern; if it was depression, change it to sadness. Change guilt to remorse, hurt to sorrow, shame to disappointment, jealousy to concern for your relationship, unhealthy envy to healthy envy, and unhealthy anger to healthy anger.

Again, change the emotion, but keep the level of intensity the same for each different emotion.

Keep with this new emotion for about five minutes, all the time imagining the same event at A. If you go back to the former emotion, bring the new one back.

Group members experience two types of difficulties at this step. First, they may not change their unhealthy negative emotion to a healthy emotion. Thus, they may change their unhealthy emotion (e.g. anxiety) to (i) another unhealthy negative emotion (e.g. shame) – if they do this they

Table 11.1: Instructions on How to Practise Rational-emotive Imagery (REI) –
Maultsby Version

Step 1: Identify a specific negative, activating at A, about which you depreciated yourself. Make sure that you have selected an event about which you disturbed yourself.

Step 2: Close your eyes and vividly imagine this negative activating event.

Step 3: Deliberately rehearse the unhealthy belief that you held about this event.

Step 4: Allow yourself to really experience the unhealthy negative emotion that you felt at C while still imagining the same negative activating event. Ensure that your unhealthy emotion is one of the following: anxiety, depression, guilt, hurt, shame, unhealthy anger, jealousy or unhealthy envy.

Step 5: While still imagining the same activating event, change your unhealthy belief to its healthy alternative and stay with this new belief until you experience a healthy negative emotion at the same level of intensity as your unhealthy negative emotion. Your healthy negative emotion will be one of the following: concern, sadness, remorse, sorrow, disappointment, healthy anger, concern for one's relationship, or healthy envy.
Keep with this healthy belief and emotion for about five minutes, all the time imagining the same event at A. If you go back to the former unhealthy belief, bring the new one back.

---

will be changing one unhealthy belief to another unhealthy belief; (ii) a less intense version of the same unhealthy negative emotion (e.g. less anxious) – if they do this they will only be lessening the intensity of their unhealthy belief; or (iii) a neutral emotion (e.g. calmness) – if they do this they will be changing their unhealthy belief to an inappropriate indifference belief.

If a group member makes one of the above errors, explain to her (in this case) the nature of the error and then encourage her to select an appropriate healthy negative emotion in future REIs. It is only when group members do this will they gain practice at changing their unhealthy beliefs to healthy beliefs.

The second difficulty that group members may experience at this step is that they may lose the actual image of their selected activating event or the vividness of this image when they change their unhealthy negative emotion to its healthy equivalent. In this case, encourage them to keep the image of the activating event as vividly in their mind as possible when they change the healthiness of their emotion. If after sufficient practice they are still unable to do this, teach them the Maultsby version of REI (see above).

STEP 5: *At the end of the five-minute period, ask yourself how you changed your emotion.*

This is an important step because otherwise group members will not be able to check whether or not they have changed their emotion by appropriately changing their belief. The most common error that group members commit here is to omit this step. If this happens, encourage them to reinstate it in future practice of REI.

STEP 6: *Make sure that you changed your emotional response by changing your unhealthy belief to a healthy belief. If you did not do so (e.g. you changed your feeling by changing some aspect of the A), carry out the exercise again and keep doing so until you have changed your emotion only by changing your unhealthy belief to its healthy alternative.*

This is the step with which group members have most difficulty. They usually make one of three errors. The most common error made here involves group members failing to change their unhealthy beliefs to healthy beliefs. Rather they replace their unhealthy belief with another cognition. A common example of this occurs when a group member changes her (in this case) inference of the situation (e.g. a group member pictures being rejected at A and replaces her unhealthy belief, 'I must not be rejected,' with a different inference, 'They misunderstood me, but like me really'. The problem with doing this is that the person changes her emotions by changing an aspect of the A (in the above example, changing 'They rejected me' to 'They understood me, but like me really'). In doing so the person is not gaining experience at changing her emotions by changing her unhealthy beliefs to healthy beliefs.

When a group member commits this error, first help her to understand what she has done and why it is problematic. Then give her an accurate example of what you are advocating (by role playing an REI and verbalizing the important sixth step of modifying one's emotions by changing one's beliefs) before suggesting more REI practice.

The second common error committed by group members at this stage occurs when they change their unhealthy demands to partial preferences. As I have already discussed (see pp. 128–129), when a person holds a partial preference (e.g. 'I want to be accepted') she (in this case) explicitly asserts what she wants, but does not explicitly state that she does not have to get what she wants (e.g. '. . . but I don't have to be accepted'). In not making this last statement explicit the person runs the risk of converting her partial preference back to a demand (e.g. 'I want to be accepted . . . and therefore it is essential that I am accepted'). Thus, when a group member indicates that she has changed her unhealthy negative emotion to a healthy equivalent by changing her demand to a partial preference, explain the danger of doing so and urge her in future to ensure that she changes her demand to a full preference.

The final error committed by group members at this step is similar to the one just discussed. Here the person indicates that she has changed her unhealthy negative emotion to a healthy equivalent by changing her self-depreciation belief to a partial self-acceptance belief. (See pp. 133–134 for a discussion of partial and full self-acceptance beliefs.)

When a person holds a partial self-acceptance belief (e.g. 'I am not a fool') he (in this case) explicitly states who he is not, but does not explicitly state who he is (e.g. 'I am a rateable fallible human being who has acted foolishly'). In not making this last statement explicit the person runs the risk of converting his partial self-acceptance belief back into a self-depreciation belief (e.g. 'I am not a fool for acting foolishly, but I would be more worthy if I acted sensibly'). Thus, when a group member indicates that he has changed his unhealthy negative emotion to a healthy equivalent by changing his self-depreciation belief to a partial self-acceptance belief, explain the dangers of doing so and urge him in future to ensure that he changes his self-depreciation belief to a full self-acceptance belief.

Finally, as I have already noted, some group members do not find the Ellis version of REI helpful and others are not able to implement it. My practice in such cases is to teach these clients a different version of REI that was pioneered by Maxie C. Maultsby Jr (see Table 11.1).

Chapter 4 of Paul Hauck's (1991) Book

Hauck's chapter distinguishes between self-confidence and performance confidence. In it, he makes the important point that self-confidence implies self-rating and impedes the person from developing new skills and is thus to be avoided. Instead the person is urged to develop performance confidence which involves her (in this case) practising new behaviour and accepting herself along the way. Hauck stresses that when the person begins to practise new skills, she is unlikely to be very good at it. Accepting herself under these conditions increases the chances that the person will continue to practise the desired behaviour until she develops performance confidence.

Having made the case for the concept of performance confidence as opposed to self-confidence, Hauck argues that if the person wishes to develop performance confidence then she is advised to (i) refrain from procrastinating; (ii) settle for less than perfection; (iii) take small behavioural steps; (iv) learn from one's errors; (v) risk failure, and (vi) apply sensible rewards and penalties. Throughout, Hauck encourages his readers to accept themselves when the going gets tough and to realize that once they have become competent at the desired behaviour this does not mean that they are more worthy than if they fail to do so.

The main query that group members have about this chapter concerns the issue of perfectionism and high standards. Here is how I dealt with this issue in the group.

WINDY: OK, what questions do you have about the chapter I asked you to read from Paul Hauck's book?

CAROL: He urges people to settle for less than perfection, but in doing so isn't he advocating that we lower our standards?

WINDY: That's a good question and one that is frequently asked. Let me clarify this point. When you are perfectionistic you are intolerant of yourself when you achieve less than perfection. However, when you set high standards for yourself, this by itself is no problem. However, when you demand that you must achieve this high standard and that you are less worthwhile when you don't, you make yourself emotionally disturbed before and after failing to reach your standard. Indeed, this belief will make it quite likely that you will stop striving to reach your standard. However, if you believe that you want to reach your high standard, but don't *demand* that you must do so, and if you accept yourself as an unrateable, fallible human being if and when you fail to achieve your standard, then you will tend to learn from your performance so that you might improve it. You will do this without disturbing yourself and you will tend to persist until you have reached your goal. If you develop a non-demanding and self-accepting philosophy as you strive towards your high standard, then there will be no need for you to lower this standard. You will, however, give yourself credit for what you have done well, and focus on how you can improve. Is that clear?

CAROL: That's very clear.

WINDY: Let me just make one more point. I make a distinction between high achievable standards and perfectionistic unachievable standards. Let me illustrate. If Torvill and Dean, the former Olympic ice dance champions, set, as a standard, scoring maximum points in the Olympic finals, then although this is a very high standard it is achievable. Indeed, they did achieve this standard. Theirs is an example of a very high, but achievable standard. However, if they had said that they wanted to achieve a maximum score whenever they skated no matter how prepared they were or how tired they were, this would be an example of a perfectionistic, unachieveble standard. Can you see the difference?

CAROL: Yes, I can. In order to achieve the last standard they would have to be robots.

WINDY: That's right. Perfectionistic standards are inhuman. So, I urge people to set high achievable standards, but to ensure that they adhere to a non-demanding, self-acceptance philosophy as they pursue these standards.

PROVIDING A RATIONALE FOR THE CONJOINT USE OF BEHAVIOURAL AND COGNITIVE TECHNIQUES

Hauck's chapter provides a useful introduction to the idea that group members need to take action if they are to internalize their non-demanding, self-acceptance beliefs. Before you agree such a homework task with each member, it is important that you provide the group with a plausible rationale for the conjoint use of behavioural and cognitive techniques. Here is such an example.

WINDY: So far you have learned a number of techniques that will help you to weaken your conviction in your unhealthy beliefs and strengthen your conviction in your healthy beliefs to enable you to incorporate them into your belief system. However, unless you learn to act in a way that is consistent with your healthy beliefs and inconsistent with your unhealthy beliefs you will not truly internalize your healthy beliefs and your conviction in those beliefs will be light and theoretical.

The best thing that you can do to facilitate this internalization process is to act on your healthy beliefs while at the same time deliberately rehearsing them. In this way you line up your thinking and behaviour together. What's your reaction to what I have just said?

RONALD: That makes a lot of sense. It's a question of acting on what you know so that you know it more fully.

WINDY: That's a very eloquent way of putting it.

BETTY: I'm not quite sure that I've followed what you've said. Can you give me a concrete example?

WINDY: Good point, Betty. I'll be glad to. Let's take the goal that you set in the second group session.

BETTY (*looks through her notes*):   OK, here it is. 'To sing in public on two occasions and accept myself as a fallible human being if I sing poorly, and if this happens to feel disappointed about it.'

WINDY: OK! Between now and next week can you arrange to sing once in public?

BETTY: Yes, I can. There's a small choral group that meets once a week for whom I have an open invitation to sing.

WINDY: Excellent. Now, let's suppose that you have contacted them. At which point will you feel most anxious?

BETTY: They usually meet at 7.30 p.m. Let me think . . . I'll get there at about 6.45 p.m., so I'll be most anxious then.

WINDY: Right, at this point I suggest that you forcefully rehearse your rational belief. How will that sound?

BETTY: If I sing poorly I won't like it, but I can accept me.

WINDY: So start rehearsing that belief at 6.45 p.m., or earlier if you need to, until the time you sing, and after that if in fact you do sing poorly. Is that clear?

BETTY: Very clear.

SETTING THE NEXT HOMEWORK TASK

By our above discussion I have just helped Betty to set her behavioural-cognitive homework task. I then help the rest of the group members to set their behavioural-cognitive tasks. These relate very closely to the goals they set in the second group session and usually involve the person in doing something that would significantly aid her (in this case) in achieving these goals, but fall short of actually achieving them. In doing so I check explicitly that it is feasible for the person to undertake the task before the next session. Table 11.2 lists each group member's behavioural-cognitive homework task. You will note that each task involves the person in doing something and conjointly rehearsing a healthy belief.

TEACHING MENTAL REHEARSAL OF BEHAVIOURAL-COGNITIVE TASKS

After you have helped group members to set homework tasks it is useful to help them to mentally rehearse these tasks before they do them *in vivo*.

Table 11.2: Group Members' Behavioural-cognitive Tasks

LIAM:	To watch my girlfriend talk to another man over coffee at a seminar that we are attending, and tell myself: 'If she does find him attractive I really wouldn't like it, but I am still worth while because I'm unique, alive and fallible.'
LIONEL:	I will play 9 holes of golf and tell myself: 'If I play badly in front of others, that would be very unfortunate, but I will only be revealing my human fallibility.'
CAROL:	I am going to tell my daughter that I plan to get married again, and if she disapproves of me I will practise telling myself: 'I am not a bad person for hurting her feelings. Rather, I am a fallible human being for doing so.'
BRIAN:	To assert myself with one person and to practise telling myself: 'I don't like being rejected, but I still have worth if this happens.'
SARAH:	To speak up at two seminars that I attend and practise showing myself: 'I am not a stupid person if I say something stupid. I am an unratable person who screwed up on this occasion.'
FIONA:	To talk to two people who I think don't like me and tell myself: 'I prefer to be liked, but being liked isn't essential. I can accept myself in the face of being disliked, although it is unpleasant.'
BETTY:	To sing in public at the local choral group and practise telling myself: 'If I sing poorly I won't like it, but I can accept me.'
RONALD:	To telephone at least two of my business contacts, tell them that I have been made redundant and ask them to help me get another job. In doing so I will practise the following idea: If they look down on me, I don't have to look down on me. I am a fallible person who has been made redundant. I am not a redundant person.

I generally encourage members to practice imagining carrying out their behaviour (i) where they encounter their negative activating event and (ii) where they encounter a positive activating event. Thus, I want them to prepare themselves for the worst and to envisage that a favourable environment is also possible. Let me illustrate this with my work with Sarah.

WINDY: Now before you do your homework task it is helpful for you to rehearse it first in your mind's eye. Let me show you what I mean. Who would like to volunteer?

SARAH: I will.

WINDY: Fine. Now close you eyes, Sarah, and imagine that you are in your seminar group and see yourself say something stupid. When you realize that you have done so, rehearse in your mind the statement 'I am not a stupid person for saying something stupid. I am an unrateable person who screwed up on this occasion.' Can you see yourself doing this?

SARAH (*after 30 seconds*):   Yes I can.

WINDY: Now how do you feel when you say this to yourself?

SARAH: Disappointed that I have said something stupid.

WINDY: But not ashamed?

SARAH: No.

WINDY: Good. Now the next step is for you to practise seeing yourself speaking and not saying anything stupid. This is important, because it is also possible that what you say will make sense. So it's important that you prepare yourself for both a bad outcome and a good outcome. Is that clear?

SARAH: Yes.

WINDY: So close your eyes and imagine that you are speaking in your seminar group and what you say is quite sensible. Can you see yourself doing this?

SARAH (*after 35 seconds*):   Yes, I can.

WINDY: And how do you feel, seeing yourself doing this?

SARAH: Pleased.

WINDY: Excellent. Now I suggest that you practise these imaginary exercises two or three times a day. Start off imagining the worst, and then practise seeing a favourable outcome. OK?

SARAH: OK.

[I then go round the group helping each person to practise rehearsing a bad outcome with the appropriate healthy belief and a good outcome and I suggest that they practise each scenario two or three times a day.]

IDENTIFYING AND OVERCOMING OBSTACLES TO CARRYING OUT BEHAVIOURAL-COGNITIVE TASKS

I mentioned in Chapter 6 that group members do not always carry out their homework tasks, and when this happens it is important to investigate this closely and help them to identify and overcome these obstacles to homework task completion. Because the completion of these behavioural-cognitive tasks is so important, I suggest that you help each group member to identify and overcome the likely obstacles to the completion of this important homework assignment. Let me illustrate how I generally do this by referring to my work with Brian.

WINDY: Now everyone knows what their homework task is. However, because it's very likely that you will find this task difficult to do you may well be tempted not to do it. So what I want to do now is to go round the group and help each of you to identify and overcome the likely obstacles that you may encounter which may prevent you from doing this task. Let's start with Brian. What's your homework task, Brian?

BRIAN: To assert myself with one person and to practise telling myself: 'I don't like being rejected, but I still have worth if this happens.'

WINDY: OK. Now how might you stop yourself from doing this?

BRIAN: Well, when it comes to it, I might get so uncomfortable that I might decide to back down.

WINDY: What do you think you might be telling yourself about this discomfort that would lead you to back down?

BRIAN: I can't stand this discomfort.

WINDY: Right, now let me put this into the ABC framework that we used earlier in the group.

A = Strong discomfort.
B = I can't stand this discomfort.
C = Backing down.

Is that accurate?

BRIAN: Yes.

WINDY: Right, so let me help you to challenge the belief that leads you to back down. Which is true: you can't stand this strong discomfort or it's difficult to stand, but it is tolerable?

BRIAN: That it's uncomfortable, but I can stand it.

WINDY: Right. Now is it worth tolerating this discomfort?

BRIAN: Yes.

WINDY: Why?

BRIAN: Because it will help me to assert myself and eventually get me over my problem.

WINDY: Right. Finally, we know that the strong discomfort that you are likely to feel is difficult to tolerate, but does it follow that it's intolerable?

BRIAN: No, if it's difficult to tolerate at least I'm standing it.

WINDY: Right. Now, when you come to assert yourself and begin to experience that strong discomfort, what can you tell yourself to still assert yourself?

BRIAN: That I can stand this discomfort and that it's worth tolerating because doing so will help me to solve my assertion problem.

WINDY: And it will help you to gain the practice of accepting yourself in the face of any rejection you might encounter.

BRIAN: Right.

WINDY: Now, do you think that if you practise this healthy belief about tolerating the strong discomfort you may well experience before you decide to assert yourself, then you will do the homework task?

BRIAN: Yes, that will work.

WINDY: Any other obstacles?

BRIAN: Not that I can think of.

I then go round the rest of the group helping them to identify and over-come their obstacles to homework task completion. Wherever possible I help each group member to put his or her obstacle into the ABC frame-work that I used with Brian. In particular, I help each person to challenge and change his or her relevant unhealthy belief and see if practising a new healthy belief will dissolve the obstacle, which it usually does. Once again I refer you to Appendix 2, which lists the most common obstacles to homework task completion.

This marks the end of session seven.

12

SESSION EIGHT: MORE COGNITIVE-BEHAVIOURAL TASKS AND SHAME-ATTACKING EXERCISES

In the eighth session of a ten-week self-acceptance group, you should:

- review the previous week's homework task
- set other behavioural-cognitive tasks as a homework assignment
- give a rationale for the use of shame-attacking exercises and suggest that group members carry out one such task as an additional homework assignment.

REVIEWING THE PREVIOUS WEEK'S HOMEWORK TASK

You will recall that the previous week's homework assignment involved group members in undertaking a behavioural-cognitive task – in this case, in doing something that was in line with their previously agreed goals and, at the same time, in rehearsing a healthy belief. Since behavioural-cognitive tasks play such an important role in internalizing self-acceptance beliefs, it is worth checking this homework assignment very carefully with all group members. When you do so, I suggest that you check the following two points and issues arising from these points. In discussing these points, I will refer to the work that I did with Sarah. Let me first remind you of Sarah's agreed behavioural-cognitive task: 'To speak up at two seminars that I attend and practise showing myself: I am not a stupid person if I say something stupid. I am an unrateable person who screwed up on this occasion.'

1. *Did the person undertake the behavioural part of the agreed homework task in all of its aspects?*

Here, a group member may have changed the task in some way. If this is the case it is important to investigate what prompted him (in this case) to make this modification. It is likely that any such alteration was prompted by the person adhering to an unhealthy belief and your task is to test out this hunch and, if correct, to help the person challenge and change this belief.

2. *Did the person rehearse the healthy belief? If so, did the person do this accurately?*

If a group member did not rehearse his healthy belief, help him to determine the reason for this omission. If the person did attempt to rehearse the belief, but did not do so accurately, help him to understand why his attempt was incorrect and what would have been an accurate attempt.

WINDY: OK, Sarah. What did you do for homework?

SARAH: I did half of the homework. I spoke up at one of the seminars, but not at the other.

WINDY: OK, tell me what happened at the seminar you did speak at.

SARAH: Well, before the seminar I told myself that it didn't really matter if I said something stupid or not as long as I spoke up.

WINDY: I see. But did you truly believe that it didn't really matter if what you said was stupid?

SARAH: I guess not.

WINDY: That's right, because it does really matter. You see, you have a healthy desire which is: 'I would much prefer not to say something stupid.' This is a healthy belief as long as you add '. . . but there's no reason why I must not do so'. Acknowledging this will help you to believe the healthy self-acceptance idea that you agreed to practise as part of the homework task. If you recall, this was: 'I am not a stupid person if I say something stupid. I am an unrateable person who screwed up on this occasion.'

SARAH: So I tried to convince myself that it really didn't matter if I said something stupid when it really does?

WINDY: That's right. And because you tried to convince yourself of this lie, you didn't rehearse the self-acceptance belief.

SARAH: I see that now.

WINDY: Now, how did you stop yourself from speaking at the second seminar as agreed?

SARAH: Well, when I said something stupid, I guess I thought I was a stupid person because I said something and I didn't want to risk the disapproval of my fellow students if I said something stupid again.

WINDY: So, I'm hearing two things. Correct me if I'm wrong. First, you thought you would be a stupid person if you said something stupid again. Second, you predicted that your fellow students would disapprove of you if you said something stupid for the second time, and you believed that this mustn't happen. Am I right?

SARAH: That's spot on.

WINDY: Are you a stupid person if you say two stupid things in consecutive seminars?

SARAH: No.

WINDY: How about three things?

SARAH (*laughs*): I get your point. I'm not a stupid person because I am a complex person. I may say stupid things at seminars, but I say sensible things most of the time.

WINDY: Right, now why must your fellow students not disapprove of you?

SARAH: Because it would mean that they think I'm stupid.

WINDY: And if they think you are stupid?

SARAH: Oh, I see. If they think I'm stupid, then that proves that I am stupid. But I'm really not, for the reason I spelt out before.

WINDY: So, it's important for you to accept yourself as a fallible, complex human being who is not a stupid person (i) if you say something stupid in future seminars and (ii) if your fellow students think you are stupid. I suggest that you rehearse these healthy beliefs the next time you speak at a seminar.

SETTING OTHER BEHAVIOURAL-COGNITIVE HOMEWORK TASKS

This homework assignment builds on what the person has achieved and learned from the previous week's behavioural-cognitive task. If all has gone well, the person may well be ready to carry out an assignment which, if done successfully, would signal the achievement (or near achievement) of her (in this case) goal set in the second group session. If all has not gone well with the previous task, the person may still be ready to undertake a task that signals goal achievement, but this will depend on what went wrong with the previous task and what she learned from this experience. Broadly speaking, the more difficult a group member found the previous task, the less likely it is that she is ready to undertake a task that signals goal achievement. In which case, help her to select a homework task based on a more gradual movement towards her goal.

Table 12.1 lists the second set of homework tasks that group members agreed to do for homework. If you compare these tasks with the goals they set for themselves in Session Two (see Chapter 6, p. 104), you will note that most members' tasks, if successfully carried out, would signal goal achievement. This is, in fact, quite a common finding. You will recall from Chapter 6 that the goals which I suggested that group members should set for themselves should be realistic and, if reached, constitute a sign that they had begun the journey towards self-acceptance rather than

Table 12.1:   Group Members' Second Set of Behavioural-cognitive Tasks

LIAM: To watch my girlfriend talk to another man at a party we are at and tell myself: 'If she does find him attractive, I really wouldn't like it, but I am still worth while because I'm unique, alive and fallible.'

LIONEL: I will play a round of golf and tell myself: 'If I play badly in front of others that would be very unfortunate, but I will only be revealing my human fallibility.'

CAROL: To tell my son that I plan to get married again and if he disapproves of me I will practise telling myself: 'I am not a bad person for hurting his feelings. Rather I am a fallible human being for doing so.'

BRIAN: To assert myself with three people and tell myself: 'I don't like being rejected, but I still have worth if this happens.'

SARAH: To speak up at every seminar that I attend and practise showing myself: 'I am not a stupid person if I say something stupid or if my fellow students think that I am stupid. I am an unrateable person if either of these things happens.'

FIONA: To talk to six people who I think don't like me and tell myself: 'I prefer to be liked, but being liked isn't essential. I can accept myself in the face of being disliked, although it is unpleasant.'

BETTY: To sing in public on two occasions and practise telling myself: 'If I sing poorly I won't like it, but I can accept me.'

RONALD: To telephone at least five more of my business contacts, tell them that I have been made redundant and ask them to help me get another job. In doing so I will practise the following idea: 'If they look down on me I don't have to look down on me. I am a fallible person who has been made redundant. I am not a redundant person.'

its ultimate achievement. The fact that most group members are ready to undertake a task that signals goal achievement indicates that (i) they had indeed, with your help as group leader, set realistic goals and (ii) they have made good progress in the self-acceptance group.

When you agree this second behavioural-task with group members, you need to consider a number of points, some of which are similar to the points you considered when you helped them to set the first set of tasks. Let me outline these points:

1. Ensure that you assist group members to build on what they learned from their previous behavioural-cognitive tasks and encourage them to set tasks which help them to actually or nearly achieve their goals. However, if some group members are not ready for this, agree tasks that are challenging, but not overwhelming (Dryden, 1987).
2. Help group members to set tasks that are feasible, which means that they actually have (or can create) the opportunity to carry out the task before the next group session.
3. Help group members to develop a healthy belief which they can re-hearse when they carry out the agreed behavioural task. This healthy belief should be the same or similar to that rehearsed with the first behavioural task. You may help the person to modify or add to the belief on the basis of his or her experience with the first task.
   For example, Sarah's initial healthy belief statement was: 'I am not a stupid person if I say something stupid. I am an unrateable person who screwed up on this occasion.' However, on discussing her expe-riences with carrying out her first behavioural-cognitive task it trans-pired that she hadn't included a statement in her healthy belief to deal with what her fellow students thought of her. Consequently, I suggested that Sarah incorporate such a statement into her belief which she could rehearse when carrying out her second behavioural-cognitive task. Thus, her new healthy belief statement was: 'I am not a stupid person if I say something stupid or if my fellow students think that I am stupid. I am an unrateable person if either of these things happens.'
4. Help group members to mentally rehearse the behavioural-cognitive task so that they are prepared for the worst, but can also see that a good outcome is possible. If you recall, you did this when helping them to prepare for their first behavioural-cognitive task (see pp. 178–179 for a full discussion of this point).
5. Finally, help group members to identify and overcome possible ob-stacles to task completion in the same way that you did in the previous group session (see pp. 179–180).

PROVIDING A RATIONALE FOR THE USE OF SHAME-ATTACKING EXERCISES AND SUGGESTING THAT GROUP MEMBERS CARRY OUT SUCH EXERCISES AS ADDITIONAL HOMEWORK ASSIGNMENTS

Up to this point in self-acceptance groups, the tasks that you have set group members, and which they have agreed to do, have been serious in both content and objective. Now is the time to have a bit of fun, but fun with a serious purpose as you will see, for it is at this point that I introduce the concept of 'shame-attacking' exercises. These exercises involve group members acting publicly in a 'shameful' manner and practising their healthy self-acceptance beliefs as they do so.

When explaining the nature of such exercises to group members and providing a rationale for their use, it is important to stress the following points.

- *Shame involves self-depreciation*

  At the heart of shame and some forms of embarrassment are self-depreciation beliefs. These emotions are experienced largely (although not exclusively) in public situations and thus in order to 'attack' your feelings of shame it is important to practise acting 'shamefully' in a public situation while rehearsing a self-acceptance belief.

- *You often significantly limit yourself because you are scared of what others think of you*

  Shame and the philosophy of self-depreciation that underpins it is a frequent inhibitor of healthy risk-taking. This philosophy leads you to become scared of what others would think of you if you do not succeed in your risky endeavour and, thus, you back away from taking this risk. Consequently, if you wish to take healthy risks you need to do so without shame, which means that you need to accept yourself whether or not your risky behaviour pays off and whether or not people think poorly of you.

- *It is important to overcome such fears by encouraging others to think poorly of you*

  When you take risks you frequently achieve a favourable environmental outcome and there is no reason why people should think poorly of you. The problem with this situation is that you are not provided with an opportunity to accept yourself in difficult circumstances, i.e. when people do think poorly of you. When you eventually devise a shame-attacking exercise, and resolve to practise a self-acceptance belief at the same time, it is important that you experience social disapproval of some kind, otherwise you will not 'attack' your shame under optimal conditions.

- *In devising shame-attacking exercises it is important to plan doing something that will attract the attention and disapproval of others*

  Since it is important to 'attack' your shame in the face of social disapproval, it is important that you plan to do something that will attract others' attention and their disapproval. Here are some examples of shame-attacking exercises which illustrate these features:

  (i) Wearing different coloured shoes.
  (ii) Asking to buy a three-piece suite in a sweet shop.
  (iii) Singing off-key in public.
  (iv) Asking for directions to a town one is already in.
  (v) Shouting out the stops on a train.
  (vi) Shouting out the time in a department store.

- *Remain in the situation and maintain eye contact*

  Immediately after you have done a shame-attacking exercise, you may experience a strong tendency either to leave the situation immediately or to avoid eye contact with others. These tendencies are sure signs that you are experiencing shame. Thus, in order to overcome your feelings of shame through rehearsing self-acceptance beliefs in the face of social disapproval, you need to remain in the relevant situation and maintain eye contact with those present.

- *Take appropriate steps to protect yourself and others*

  While devising shame-attacking exercises that will incur social disapproval, it is important to take appropriate steps to protect yourself and other people. Thus, do not do anything that will:

  (i) alarm others
  (ii) offend your or others' moral code
  (iii) break the law
  (iv) jeopardize your job or your friendships.

- *Develop healthy self-acceptance and HFT belief statements*

  Once you have decided upon a shame-attacking exercise, you need to develop two belief statements which you will practise while carrying out the exercise. In your first healthy belief statement, you need to accept yourself both for acting foolishly and in the face of social disapproval, while in your second belief you need to tolerate the discomfort you will undoubtedly experience when you carry out your shame-attacking exercise.

- *Use rational-emotive imagery before you carry out your shame-attacking exercise*

Before you carry out your shame-attacking exercise *in vivo*, I suggest that you use mental rehearsal. Picture yourself carrying out the exercise and incurring social disapproval and, as you do so, see yourself practising your two healthy belief statements. In this image, see yourself feeling disappointed (rather than ashamed) and acknowledge that you feel uncomfortable, but tolerably so. See yourself remaining in the situation and maintaining eye contact with those present. Practise this mental rehearsal technique several times before you carry out the shame-attacking exercise *in vivo*.

- *Identify and overcome obstacles to carrying out your shame-attacking exercise*

Finally, ask yourself how you might prevent yourself from carrying out your shame-attacking exercise *in vivo*. Identify and overcome these obstacles in the same way that you did before carrying out your first behavioural-cognitive task in the last group session and when deciding on your second behavioural-cognitive task earlier in the present session.

Rather than ask group members to specify which shame-attacking exercise they will carry out in this session, my practice is to suggest that they each choose such an exercise for themselves without telling their fellow group members. This adds to the level of anticipation when they report on their experiences in the following group session.

This marks the end of session eight.

13

SESSION NINE: DISTORTED INFERENCES – HOW TO CHALLENGE THESE PRODUCTS OF IRRATIONAL BELIEFS

In the ninth session of a ten-week self-acceptance group, you should:

- review the previous week's homework tasks
- teach the group the effect of beliefs on the way they think
- teach the group how to challenge distorted inferences
- set the next homework task.

REVIEWING THE PREVIOUS WEEK'S HOMEWORK TASKS

You will recall that you set group members the following two tasks: (i) a second behavioural-cognitive task, and (ii) one shame-attacking exercise. As usual, I suggest that you begin the group sessions by checking these two tasks.

The Second Behavioural-cognitive Task

The second behavioural-cognitive task involved group members building on what they achieved from their first task and doing something which in most cases represented what they set as their goal in the second group session. This task again involved them carrying out a behavioural assignment, while rehearsing a healthy belief statement.

Once again I suggest that you check this assignment very carefully given the central role that behavioural-cognitive tasks play in helping group members to internalise self-acceptance beliefs. I explained how to do this in the previous chapter (see pp. 181–183) so I will just emphasise here that when you check this task, it is important that you assure yourself that:

- The person undertook the behavioural part of the homework task, as agreed, in all of its aspects.
- The person rehearsed the healthy belief and did so accurately.

One Shame-attacking Exercise

The purpose of shame-attacking exercises is for group members to act 'shamefully' and to accept themselves for their actions in the face of social disapproval. You will remember that I suggested that you did not ask group members to specify what they would do for a shame-attacking exercise. This generally heightens the sense of anticipation that group members experience when you come to check this assignment.

When you do check each group member's shame-attacking exercise, it is important that you do the following:

1. Ask the group member to tell the group what he (in this case) did.
2. Find out the response of others who witnessed the shame-attacking exercise.
3. Discover which healthy beliefs the person practised before, during and after carrying out the exercise.
4. Evaluate the effect of these beliefs on the person's feelings and behaviour.
5. Encourage the group member to summarize what he has learned from doing the exercise that he can use in the future.

Let me illustrate these points with the work that I did with Ronald.

WINDY: OK, Ronald. What did you do for your shame-attacking exercise?

RONALD: I went into a department store and rode one of those children's horses that you put money in.

[Group laughter.]

WINDY: What was other people's response to you doing that?

RONALD: Well, that was interesting. I remembered what you said about not avoiding the gaze of others, so I deliberately looked at people, but they wouldn't look at me. You know how people don't look at you, but you know they know what you are doing. They are too intent at not looking at you. So I'm assuming that they didn't approve of me, but no one overtly showed any disapproval.

LIAM: This is England after all!

RONALD: But one or two children said loudly, as only children do, 'Look at that funny man, mummy', but mummy just hurried them away.

WINDY: That's an interesting observation. People may well show their disapproval by turning away from you when you do something like that, rather than by turning to you and saying something offensive. But you need to look at them to see that. If you didn't look at them you may have assumed wrongly that they were actively glaring at you in a hostile fashion, for example.

Now which beliefs did you practise? Let's start by looking at what you told yourself before you carried out the assignment.

RONALD: Beforehand, I was very much aware of feeling nervous so I told myself that these feelings were understandable and bearable and that they wouldn't stop me from doing the shame-attacking exercise.

WINDY: Excellent. What effect did rehearsing that statement have on you?

RONALD: It helped me to do the exercise first and foremost, but it helped keep the nervous feelings within manageable bounds.

WINDY: Good. Now what did you tell yourself while you were on the horse?

RONALD: I told myself that even though I looked a prat, I am not a prat. I'm just a human being acting unconventionally.

WINDY: What effect did that have?

RONALD: That statement definitely helped me to stay on the horse and got me to look at people rather than avert my gaze.

WINDY: And how did you feel in response to that statement?

RONALD: I felt awkward, but not ashamed.

WINDY: And what did you tell yourself afterwards?

RONALD: After I got off the horse, I stayed in the department store and saw some of the people who made a point of not looking at me while I was on the horse. They didn't seem to recognize me.

WINDY: Without your horse!

[General laughter.]

RONALD: Right, so I wasn't aware of telling myself anything afterwards.

WINDY: How did you feel afterwards?

RONALD: I felt good, pleased that I had done it. I also thought that it wasn't as bad as I had thought.

WINDY: In what way?

RONALD: In that I thought that people would have been more overtly hostile to me, but as Liam said, this is England.

WINDY: But, as I'll show you later, when we hold a self-depreciation belief, we often predict that what we encounter will be more aversive than it turns out to be in reality. Apart from that, what did you learn from doing the exercise that you can use in the future?

RONALD: I learned that I can take risks more easily than I thought and that putting myself down has stopped me from doing so in the past. If I can practise this stuff, I can stop limiting myself as much as I have done in the past.

Having checked Ronald's shame-attacking exercise, I go round the group and do likewise with each member.

Dealing with Group Members' Difficulties with Shame-attacking Exercises

While group members generally find doing shame-attacking valuable and instructive, some experience difficulties in doing them and, in what follows, I will review these difficulties and suggest ways of dealing with them.

Failing to Do the Exercise

When a group member has not completed a shame-attacking exercise, this should be carefully investigated. Wherever possible, put this situation into an ABC framework so that you can help the person concerned to identify, challenge and change his (in this case) beliefs that prevented him from doing the assignment. Then, once the person has gained practice at over-coming this obstacle, suggest that the person do the assignment again.

Partially Completing the Task

Sometimes a group member reports that she (in this instance) only par-tially completed the task. Thus, she may have set out to do something strange in a shop and wait to see people's reactions to her behaviour, but in reality left the shop as soon as she acted strangely so that she did not experience the responses of the other people present. Such examples are usually a sign that the person disturbed herself about what she did and about the possible disapproval that she might encounter as soon as she acted stupidly. In such cases, it is important that you help the person to formulate this avoidant response in ABC terms and, in particular, help the person to identify, challenge and change the unhealthy beliefs which prompted her rapid withdrawal from the situation in question. Then, you can suggest that she does the shame-attacking exercise again and this time stay in the situation afterwards while rehearsing the relevant healthy belief(s).

Changing the Nature of the Task

Here the person has made up her (in this case) mind what to do as a shame-attacking exercise, but at the last minute changes the nature of the task so that it is far less shameful. For example, Betty decided to shout out the time in a department store, but she changed the task and deliberately dropped the contents of her handbag on to the floor. I responded by helping her to focus on the moment that she decided to change the task and helped her to put this into the ABC framework. I then helped her to challenge and change the unhealthy beliefs that we identified and suggested that she do the original assignment while rehearsing her newly developed healthy beliefs.

Of course, a group member may not spontaneously disclose that she changed the nature of the task at the last minute, but if you suspect that the person has completed a task that was minimally risky, be ready to explore the possibility that the person initiated such a change. If you are correct, proceed in the manner described above.

Failing to Rehearse Healthy Beliefs

On close questioning you may discover that the person did not do the cognitive part of the task, i.e. he (in this case) omitted rehearsing a relevant healthy belief while behaving 'shamefully' or he practised rehearsing a new inference instead of a healthy belief. If the former is the case, find out why the person omitted this important step and take appropriate action. If, as is usually the case, the person claims to have forgotten this part of the task, ask him to practise mental rehearsal of the shame-attacking exercise paying particular attention to the cognitive component of the task before he does it *in vivo*.

This situation is quite common and is worthy of further discussion. You will recall from Chapter 1 that REBT theory argues that the A in the ABC framework stands for activating event. Such events frequently represent the person's inference about an event. As I mentioned in Chapter 1, inferences are hunches about reality and need to be tested before they can be accepted as factual. Instead of rehearsing a healthy belief, a group member may 'attack' his shame by changing an inference rather than a belief. For example, Fiona helped herself to overcome her feelings of shame about buying black-ribbed condoms in a pharmacy by telling herself that the salesperson would be accustomed to such requests instead of inferring that the salesperson would regard her as a slut. For Fiona to have overcome her shame by the preferred method of rehearsing a healthy belief, she would have had to tell herself something like, 'Even if the salesperson does regard me as a slut, I am not and I don't need that person's approval to accept myself as a fallible human being with certain sexual tastes. I can do that even in the face of such disapproval.' Consequently, if the person has rehearsed a new inference instead of a healthy belief, explain why this is not the best way of overcoming shame and suggest that she do the assignment again while this time rehearsing a healthy belief statement.

Failing to Incur Social Disapproval

In reality, it is not as easy to incur social disapproval as you might think. Thus, it often happens that group members do not incur the disapproval of others who were present when they carried out their shame-attacking exercises. If this happens the member can still derive some benefit from carrying out the exercise in that (i) she (in this case) has done something 'shameful' and has been able to practise accepting herself for doing so; (ii) she has practised accepting herself in the eventuality that others did disapprove of her, and (iii) she has had the experience of tolerating the discomfort that she experienced before, during and after undertaking the shame-attacking exercise. However, she has not had the experience of attacking her shame in the face of actual disapproval from others.

If it transpires that a group member has done a shame-attacking exercise and did not encounter actual disapproval from others, first help the person to see what benefits she did derive from the experience. Then, help her to see why it is important for her to have the experience of accepting herself in the face of social disapproval and encourage her to select another exercise which would, in all probability, serve to elicit such social disapproval. Then, suggest that she carries out this new exercise and that she practise rehearsing her healthy belief when she encounters actual disapproval from those present.

Failing to Relate to Shame-attacking Exercises

Some group members just do not relate to shame-attacking exercises and think of them as trivial or silly. One reason for this response is defensiveness. If such people were to take these exercises seriously either they would significantly depreciate themselves for acting stupidly and would not use this as an opportunity to practise self-acceptance or they would disturb themselves about the discomfort they predict they would experience if they undertook the exercise. If you suspect that a group member's sceptical attitude towards shame-attacking exercises is based on defensiveness, then explore it briefly with the person. Ask him (in this case) how he would genuinely feel about doing such an exercise if he did take it seriously. If, in response to this line of enquiry, the person can acknowledge that he is defending himself through his scepticism, you can ask him to experiment and carry out a shame-attacking exercise *as if* he took it seriously. If the person cannot engage with this line of enquiry then I suggest that you drop it.

It is important to note that failing to relate to the concept of shame-attacking exercises may be a genuine response. Some people think of shame-attacking exercises as silly and trivial, and that is the end of it. If this is the case, it is futile to try to encourage them to carry out such an exercise even on the 'as-if' basis mentioned above. Rather, such group members may be more likely to carry out a risk-taking exercise where they agree to do something that they have always wanted to do, but where they have in the past held themselves back for self-depreciation reasons. If they agree to do a risk-taking exercise then the procedure is the same as for the execution of shame-attacking exercises: i.e. carrying out the desired action and rehearsing of a healthy self-acceptance belief before, during and after the act with appropriate use of mental rehearsal as preparation. Indeed, some REBT therapists prefer to use risk-taking exercises at this point in a self-acceptance group instead of shame-attacking exercises.

Whichever type of exercise you favour at this point it is important to convey to group members that they will gain most from such activities when they practise them regularly. I often say to group members that if they committed themselves to undertake to do one shame-attacking exercise or one risk-taking exercise a week for two years, then they would be amazed at the progress they would make at the end of this period.

TEACHING THE GROUP THE EFFECT OF BELIEFS ON THE WAY THEY THINK

In Chapter 1, I pointed out that there are three major types of consequences of holding irrational beliefs: emotional, behavioural and cognitive. In this section, I will discuss this latter influence, i.e. the effect of holding healthy and unhealthy beliefs on the way we think as human beings.

Let me first deal with a potentially confusing point. In the ABC model, cognitive factors can occur at A, B or C. As, if you recall, stand for activating events and these can be actual events or inferences. Inferences are clearly cognitive in nature as they are hunches about reality which go beyond the data at hand and thus need to be tested. As such, inferences can be accurate or inaccurate. Bs are clearly cognitive in that they are either flexible healthy beliefs or rigid unhealthy beliefs, and evaluate the actual events or the inferences that people make about these events at A. Cs can also be cognitive and are again largely inferential in nature. These C inferences are the consequences of the beliefs that people hold about the A.

Let me demonstrate the omnipresence of cognitive factors in the ABC framework as follows:

A = Inferences about the actual event.
B = Beliefs.
C = Cognitive consequences of the belief in the form of inferences.

As an illustration, consider Brian's ABC:

A = My unassertiveness is a weakness.
B = (i) I must not have this weakness.
    (ii) I am a weak, defective person for being unassertive.
C = People will look down on me and take advantage of me.

Brian's ABC clearly shows how his unhealthy beliefs lead him to form the inference (as a cognitive consequence) that people will look down on him and take advantage of him. Now let's see what happens when Brian's beliefs are healthy.

A = My unassertiveness is a weakness.
B = (i) I'd prefer not to have this weakness, but it's not essential that I do not have it.
    (ii) I am not a weak, defective person for being unassertive. Rather I am a worthwhile person because I am alive, unique and human with weaknesses and strengths.
C = People will have a range of responses towards me. Some may look down on me and take advantage of me, but others will show compassion towards me and be on my side.

Beliefs then clearly influence the type of cognitions a person develops at C (Bond & Dryden, 1996). However, beliefs also influence the type of inferences the person makes at A. Thus, Brian brings his unhealthy belief 'I must not be unassertive and if I am it means that I am a weak, defective person' to instances of his failure to assert himself and leads him to infer that being unassertive is a weakness. Once Brian has changed his unhealthy belief to the healthy belief 'I'd prefer not to be unassertive, but it's not essential that I assert myself. I am not a weak, defective person for being unassertive. Rather I am a worthwhile person because I am alive, unique and human with weaknesses and strengths', he is less likely to regard unassertiveness as a weakness. Thus, he is more likely to consider it as a skill deficit, for example. If his healthy belief still leads him to think of unassertiveness as a weakness, he will probably regard it as a minor weakness, whereas his unhealthy belief will lead him to think of his unassertive behaviour as a major weakness.

Your task at this point is to explain to group members the influence of beliefs on both cognitive consequences at C and on inferences at A. Here is how I did this specifically with Brian after making the general point that beliefs affect inferences both at C and at A.

WINDY: I've made the general point that beliefs influence the type of inferences that you make at C and at A. Let's see how this works in a specific case. Who would like to volunteer for demonstration purposes?

BRIAN: I will.

WINDY: Let's take one of your ABCs, Brian.

BRIAN (*looking through his notes*):   What about the first one we considered?

WINDY: Fine. Read it out and I'll put it on the board.

BRIAN: Here it is.

A = My unassertiveness is a weakness.
B = (i) I must not have this weakness.
      (ii) I am a weak, defective person for being unassertive.
C = Shame.

WINDY: Good. Now, from this ABC do you clearly understand the effect of your belief on your feelings at C?

BRIAN: Yes. I'm going to feel ashamed, as long as I believe that I must not be unassertive and I am weak and defective if I am.

WINDY: That's exactly right. But from what I said a bit earlier today, beliefs also affect the way you act at C *and* the way you think at C. Let's focus on the effect of your beliefs on the way you subsequently think at C.

I want you to imagine that you first hold an unhealthy belief and then that you hold a healthy belief. The unhealthy belief is 'I must not act in an assertive manner and if I do this proves that I am a weak, defective person for being unassertive', and the healthy belief is 'I'd prefer not to have this weakness, but it's not essential that I do not have it. I am a not weak, defective person for being unassertive. Rather I am a worthwhile person because I am alive, unique and human with weaknesses and strengths.' Now, which belief will lead you to think that people will look down on you and take advantage of you and which belief will lead you to conclude that people will have a range of responses towards you with some looking down on you and taking advantage of you, but with others showing you compassion and being on your side?

BRIAN: When I hold the belief that I must not be unassertive, and I am weak and defective when I act that way, then I will tend to think that others will look down on me and take advantage of me.

WINDY: And when you hold the alternative healthy belief?

BRIAN: When I think that I am a worthwhile person, even though I don't assert myself, and when I prefer but don't *demand* that I must be assertive, I will tend to think that others will have a range of responses towards me.

WINDY: And you will gauge their reactions towards you by how they actually treat you. So, group, can you all see how your unhealthy beliefs will skew your subsequent thinking at C very much towards the negative while your healthy beliefs will lead you to be more realistic in your thinking at C?

[Group members all indicate that this point is clear.]

Now, the second point that I want you to consider, Brian, is how beliefs can affect the inferences that you make about your unassertive behaviour at A. First, I want you to imagine that you bring the following unhealthy belief to your unassertive behaviour at A: 'I must not act in an assertive manner and, if I do, this proves that I am a weak, defective person for being unassertive.' Then, I want you to imagine that you bring the following healthy belief to this same situation: 'I prefer to act unassertively, but it's not essential that I do so. I am not a weak, defective person for being unassertive. Rather I am a worthwhile person because I am alive, unique and human with positive aspects, negative aspects and neutral aspects.' Can you do that?

BRIAN (*after about 30 seconds*):   OK.

WINDY: Now when you bring your unhealthy belief to your unassertiveness, how do you tend to think about it?

BRIAN: As a weakness.

WINDY: A minor weakness, a moderate weakness or a major weakness?

BRIAN: Definitely a major weakness.

WINDY: And how do you tend to think about your unassertiveness
when you bring your healthy belief to this situation?

BRIAN: I see it as a consequence of my fear of confronting people.

WINDY: Do you still see it as a weakness?

BRIAN: Not really. I see it more as a sign that I need to address my
original fear.

[Here Brian demonstrates an important point. When he accepts himself
for his unassertive behaviour, he can think more objectively about it and
see that it stems from a prior fear which needs addressing. However,
when he depreciates himself for his unassertiveness he is not able to
adopt such an objective standpoint and is thus far less able to address his
original problem.]

WINDY: But if you did view it as a weakness, would you see it as a
minor weakness, a moderate weakness or a major weakness?

BRIAN: If I still saw it as a weakness, I would see it as a minor weakness.

WINDY: Right, so can you all see what different effects bringing unhealthy and healthy beliefs to your thinking at A have on this thinking?

CAROL: Unhealthy beliefs lead you to make more negative inferences
about A than healthy beliefs do.

WINDY: Very accurately and succinctly put, Carol.

TEACHING THE GROUP HOW TO CHALLENGE
DISTORTED INFERENCES

One of the distinctive features of the practice of REBT therapists is that
after we have helped clients to assess a self-depreciation episode using
the ABC framework, we focus on helping them to change their unhealthy
beliefs before we help them to question their distorted inferences at A.
Thus, we often urge clients to assume temporarily that their inferences
are true at A so that we can then help them to identify, examine, challenge
and change their unhealthy beliefs at B. If we successfully helped them

first to challenge their distorted inferences at A, then they would be less motivated to change their unhealthy beliefs because they would have gained the immediate relief of thinking more accurately at A. However, if we do this we leave them vulnerable to future self-depreciation because their unhealthy beliefs (which, as I have argued in this book, are at the core of self-depreciation) remain unchanged.

Conversely, the best time to help group members to challenge their distorted inferences at A is when they have modified their unhealthy beliefs at B. This is because of the effect that the presence of unhealthy beliefs has on one's ability to be objective about the inferences one has made at A. As I discussed earlier in this chapter, a group member is more likely to be objective about the accuracy of his (in this case) inference at A when his beliefs at B are healthy than when these beliefs are unhealthy. Having made this point, let me outline the steps that you need to take in helping group members to investigate their inferences at A. In doing so, I will illustrate this process with the work I did with Liam.

1. *Make sure that the person has made some progress at changing his unhealthy belief to its healthy alternative at B so that he can adopt an objective standpoint when checking the validity of his inference at A.*

Liam's original ABC was as follows:

> A = Thinking that when my girlfriend spoke to another man yesterday, it meant that she was interested in having a relationship with him.
> B = (i) She must only be interested in me.
>   (ii) If she is interested in another man it means that I am not good enough as a person.
> C = Jealousy.

Liam had achieved a fair measure of belief change so that his new ABC was as follows:

> A = Thinking that when my girlfriend spoke to another man yesterday, it meant that she was interested in having a relationship with him.
> B = (i) I'd prefer it if she was only interested in me, but this isn't essential.
>   (ii) If she is interested in another man it does not mean that I am not good enough as a person. Rather I am a worthwhile person whether or not she is interested in another man.
> C = Concern for my relationship.

2. *Write down the inference you are checking with the group member.*

When you do this, I suggest that you reiterate for the benefit of all group members that an inference is a hunch about reality that may or may not be correct, but that needs testing out against the available evidence.

Liam's inference is: Thinking that when my girlfriend spoke to another man yesterday, it meant that she was interested in having a relationship with him.

3. *Help the person to see the distorting effect of his unhealthy belief on his inference at A.*

Liam readily understood that his unhealthy belief, 'My girlfriend must only be interested in me and if she is interested in another man it means that I am not good enough as a person', influenced his inference that because his girlfriend spoke to another man yesterday she is interested in having a relationship with him.

4. *Help the person to look for evidence that supports and contradicts his inference and have him write this down under separate headings.*

It is a good idea to ensure that group members keep these two tasks separate.

(i) Evidence that supports the inference that when my girlfriend spoke to another man yesterday it meant that she was interested in having a relationship with him:

- The fact that I was jealous meant that she was interested in having a relationship with the man.
- She was laughing and joking with him.
- I thought that she was interested in having a relationship with him.

(ii) Evidence that contradicts the inference that when my girlfriend spoke to another man yesterday, it meant that she was interested in having a relationship with him:

- She is naturally friendly and she was just being friendly with him.
- I've thought that she was interested in having a relationship with men that she has spoken to before, but as far as I am aware she never has.
- She may have found the man attractive, but that does not mean that she is interested in having a relationship with him. I find a lot of women attractive, but I'm not interested in having a relationship with any of them.
- She assures me that she is only interested in me.

5. *Help the person to evaluate this evidence.*

Liam's evaluation of his evidence was as follows:

(i) Evaluating the supportive evidence:

- The fact that I was jealous meant that she was interested in having a relationship with the man.

   This is emotional reasoning. My jealousy only proves that I was jealous and does not say anything about my girlfriend's interest or lack of interest in the man.

- She was laughing and joking with him.

   This could mean that she was interested in having a relationship with him, but it could also mean that she was being friendly. My girlfriend is a friendly person and laughs and jokes with all kinds of people including old men, women and children. This obviously doesn't mean that she wants to have a sexual or emotional relationship with them.

- I thought that she was interested in having a relationship with him.

   This is an example of cognitive reasoning – because I think something, it must be so. My thoughts are hunches about reality and may not be a good guide to reality.

   This evidence is also an example of mind reading. I obviously don't know what my girlfriend is thinking, but I do know that I have a tendency to project my thinking into her and infer that she actually thinks in the way that I fear she does.

(ii) Evaluating the contradictory evidence:

- She is naturally friendly and she was just being friendly with him.

   This is probably the case, but I don't know for certain. This is quite revealing since I tend to think that not being certain that she isn't interested in having a relationship with someone means that she is interested. I find it difficult to accept probability.

- I've thought that she was interested in having a relationship with men that she has spoken to before, but as far as I am aware she never has.

   Again I can't stand uncertainty and think that not knowing for sure that she hasn't had a relationship with someone means that she has. This just shows that I need to go with probability and give up my need for certainty.

- She may have found the man attractive, but that does not mean that she is interested in having a relationship with him. I find a lot of women attractive, but I'm not interested in having a relationship with any of them.

  This is true although I also demand that she must only find me attractive. This is a double standard since I don't have this rule for myself.

- She assures me that she is only interested in me.

  My girlfriend is very honest and I'm pretty sure that if she was interested in the man she would tell me. She wouldn't lie, although I can't be 100% sure of this. There I go again demanding certainty.

6. *Encourage the person to stand back and evaluate all the available information and select the most accurate inference.*

Here it is useful to recommend that group members ask themselves what conclusion an objective jury would come to when faced with all the available evidence. Then encourage them to accept or reject their original inference. If they reject it, encourage them to choose the alternative inference that best fits the information available to them.

Liam's conclusion was as follows:

From what I have written it is clear to me that I am bringing my unhealthy beliefs to this situation and situations like it. My girlfriend is friendly and when she talks to people she laughs and jokes with people. She is also honest. I tend to be jealous and think that what I think and feel is a good indication of what is real when objectively it isn't. I also see now that I demand certainty that my girlfriend isn't interested in men and think that lack of such certainty means that she definitely is interested in them.

Given all this information I conclude that my girlfriend wasn't interested in having a relationship with that man. She was just being friendly with him.

Before leaving this subject it is useful to give group members a handout explaining how to check the validity of their inferences (see Table 13.1).

SETTING THE NEXT HOMEWORK TASK

Therapists who believe in the value of helping people to raise their self-esteem (as opposed to develop self-acceptance) think that it is a good idea

Table 13.1:   Guidelines for Checking the Validity of Inferences

1. Make sure that you have made some progress in changing your unhealthy belief to its healthy alternative at B so that you can adopt an objective standpoint when checking the validity of your inference at A.
2. Write down the inference you are checking on a piece of paper.
3. Understand the possible distorting effect of your unhealthy belief on your inference at A.
4. Look for evidence that supports and contradicts your inference and write this down under separate headings.
5. Evaluate this evidence.
6. Stand back and evaluate all the available information and select the most accurate inference.

to encourage such people to formulate a list of their strengths and weaknesses. While as an REBT therapist I would not disagree with this strategy, I would encourage group members to do this at the end of a self-acceptance group, whereas other therapists would be more likely to do this towards the beginning of their self-esteem therapy.

The main reason I would ask group members to do the 'strengths–weaknesses' exercise at the end of a self-acceptance group is closely related to the effect that beliefs have on the way people think. If I asked group members to develop a list of their strengths and weaknesses at any other time in the group process, then they would bring their unhealthy demands and self-depreciation beliefs to this task and their responses would be very much coloured by such beliefs and show a distinct skewing to the negative. Thus, their list would show a decided focus on their weaknesses and would contain very few strengths. Developing such a biased list too early in the group process is likely to have a demoralizing effect on group members and would interfere with the adoption and development of the healthy preferences and self-acceptance beliefs which is the objective of these groups.

On the other hand, when group members develop such a list as a homework task between the penultimate and the final group session, they are more likely to do so while adhering to healthy full preferences and self-acceptance beliefs. Indeed, doing this is an integral part of the homework assignment. Consequently, the list of strengths and weaknesses that they develop is more accurate than it would have been if it were developed earlier in the life of the group, particularly at the beginning.

When you suggest developing the list of strengths and weaknesses as a homework task, it is important to stress that the goal of the exercise is twofold. First, the intention is for group members to see that they have both strengths and weaknesses and that their job is to maximize the former and work on the latter. The second purpose of the task is to encourage group members to use the list to remind themselves that they are complex human beings with a myriad of different aspects. Consequently, urge them to develop a long list – the longer the better.

The most important point that you should stress when explaining this task is that they should do it after they have worked for about twenty minutes on accepting themselves and acknowledging that they may have desires about the way they want to be, but that these desires should not be transformed into demands. Sometimes, with certain groups, I suggest that they develop two lists, one when they are in a self-accepting frame of mind and one when they are in a self-depreciating frame of mind. I do this because I want them to see the effect that different beliefs have on their view of their strengths and weaknesses.

Finally, group members sometimes say that they could not think of many strengths or weaknesses. To pre-empt this situation, suggest that, if they get stuck, they can go through the dictionary and focus on words that stand for personal characteristics, skills, abilities, talents and the like. If they do this then they will have a wealth of information on which to draw.

As the next group session is the last, I suggest that group members also organize their thoughts and prepare to talk about the progress they have made since beginning the group, and to present their evaluation of the group at the final session.

This marks the end of the ninth and penultimate group session.

$$\boxed{14}$$

SESSION TEN: ENDING, EVALUATION AND BEYOND

In the last session of a ten-week self-acceptance group, you should:

- review the previous week's homework task
- evaluate the progress made by group members
- give group members the self-acceptance quiz
- elicit feedback from group members on the group
- help group members to maintain and extend their gains.

REVIEWING THE PREVIOUS WEEK'S HOMEWORK TASK

If you recall, the previous week's homework task was the strengths–weaknesses exercise where group members were asked to provide a list of their strengths and weaknesses while holding a self-acceptance belief. In checking these lists it is important to ask each person what he or she learned from the exercise. In my experience, most group members express surprise about the large number of strengths they put in their list and can see clearly the role that holding a self-acceptance belief has played here.

When a group member provides a list that contains many more weaknesses than strengths, this is usually due to three factors. First, she (in this case) did the exercise while implicitly holding a self-depreciating belief. If this occurs, urge the person to do the task again, but this time while strongly holding a self-acceptance belief. Second, the person may think that in order for something to count as a strength, she has to excel in it. In this case, help the person to see that strengths can include something that she is good at as well as what she excels in. Then, suggest that the person does the exercise again using this more liberal criterion as she does so. Finally, the person may think that it is arrogant or boastful to acknowledge that one has strengths. If this is the case, it is useful to ask other group members for their views on this position. It normally transpires that other group members disagree quite strongly with this view and explain why. After this exchange of views, suggest that the person does the exercise again while challenging the idea that it is arrogant or boastful to acknowledge strengths.

EVALUATING THE PROGRESS MADE BY GROUP MEMBERS

When asking group members to evaluate the progress they have made during the group, it is very useful to refer them to the goals that they set in Session Two (see Table 6.1, p. 104). These goals pointed to what members thought that they could realistically achieve by the end of the group.

In my experience most group members manage to achieve their goals and some have gone beyond what they thought they would achieve. When a group member has not achieved his (in this case) goal, you need to assess the reasons for this very carefully. Common reasons are as follows:

1. The person has consistently not carried out the homework tasks. You ideally should have picked this up earlier, although very occasionally the person claims that he has completed homework tasks when in fact, as he later admits, he hasn't.
2. The person's self-depreciation problems turned out to be more serious than they appeared when you assessed the person for inclusion in the group.
3. The person's problems turned out to be more representative of discomfort disturbance than ego disturbance.
4. The person admits that he did not get on with REBT and would have preferred a different therapeutic approach.

If the person's lack of expected progress can be attributed to one of the first three reasons, then recommend that he seeks longer-term individual REBT. If the latter reason explains his lack of progress, discover which therapeutic approach he may benefit from and effect a suitable referral.

Unfortunately, I have no empirical data to attest to the effectiveness of REBT-oriented self-acceptance groups. The main reason for this is that whenever I have run such groups, group members have at the same time been attending other therapy groups or have been in individual therapy.

Thus, as I explained in Chapter 4, I have most frequently run self-acceptance groups in the context of a private psychiatric hospital where patients attend a variety of different groups. Consequently, it would be impossible to attribute any progress that group members might have made to their participation in the self-acceptance group. The second reason why I have not formally evaluated the effectiveness of self-acceptance groups is that an adequate measure of self-acceptance consistent with REBT theory does not exist. Many measures of self-esteem exist, but, as you will appreciate by now, self-esteem and self-acceptance are very different concepts.

It is my hope that this book will inspire others (i) to run self-acceptance groups in settings where their effectiveness can be adequately investigated and (ii) to devise an adequate measure of the REBT concept of unconditional self-acceptance. Why have I not done so myself? The reason is that I have been involved with other research, clinical and writing projects and have not had the time to do so. I recognize that this situation casts doubt on the effectiveness of self-acceptance groups, and while I regret this and take responsibility for this lacuna, I do not depreciate myself for it!

GIVING GROUP MEMBERS THE SELF-ACCEPTANCE QUIZ

In the spirit of fun and as a way of assessing what members have learned from the group, I ask them to complete a short written quiz (see Table 14.1). Why not try the quiz yourself and see what you have learned from the book? You can find the answers at the end of the chapter.

I sometimes find that group members answer question 4 correctly, but answer question 5 incorrectly. If you study these two questions carefully, you will see that if a person's answer was that the statement listed in question 4 is false, then that person logically has to say that the statement listed in question 5 is false since this latter statement is a specific case of the general statement in question 4. Thus, if you say that you cannot give a human being a single global rating which completely accounts for that person, then you cannot say that someone who rapes a small child is wicked through and through since the person who carried out the rape is a human being and 'wicked through and through' is a single global rating which attempts to completely account for that person.

When I go through group members' answers and she (in this case) gets one of them wrong, I invite the other members to discuss the person's

Table 14.1:   The Self-acceptance Quiz

Answer all questions and give reasons for each of your answers.

1. Having the love of a significant other makes you a more worthwhile person.
   True or False?

2. If someone you admire is better than you at an important activity, he or she is a better person than you.
   True or False?

3. If you fail at something really important, you are not a failure but a fallible human being.
   True or False?

4. You can give a human being a single global rating which completely accounts for them.
   True or False?

5. Someone who rapes a child is wicked through and through.
   True or False?

6. Mother Theresa and Adolf Hitler are of equal worth as humans.
   True or False?

response with her rather than correcting her answer myself. However, if after such a discussion the person is still convinced that her answer is correct, then I will intervene.

Here is what happened when Carol gave an incorrect answer to question 5.

WINDY: So, Carol, you think that someone who rapes a small child is wicked through and through?

CAROL: That's right.

WINDY: What do others think?

BETTY: Well, my immediate strong reaction to that question was that anyone who rapes a small child is wicked through and through, but then I thought that if I believed that then I would also have to believe that you can give a human being a single global rating that completely accounts for them, which I most definitely don't.

LIONEL: I had the same reaction, but I thought that if the answer to question 4 was false the answer to question 5 would also have to be false.

CAROL: But what if it were your child who was raped?

FIONA: I thought about that and I concluded that I would probably think that the person who raped her was wicked through and through, but I'd be wrong.

CAROL: I see.

BRIAN: Do you think that if you said that such a person wasn't wicked through and through then you would be condoning the crime in some way?

CAROL: Not condoning it, but not condemning it as much as I should.

LIAM: Aha! But why can't you condemn the crime as an act of great wickedness without condemning the person as wicked through and through?

CAROL: I guess you can.

WINDY: So what's the answer to question 5?

CAROL: False, but it will take some getting used to.

HELPING GROUP MEMBERS TO MAINTAIN AND EXTEND THEIR GAINS

You will recall that the purpose of self-acceptance groups is to help group members to take the first few steps on the path towards self-acceptance and to equip them with the knowledge and skills they will need as they continue along this path.

At this juncture, my practice is to remind group members of this point and to review with them the skills they have developed and the written instructions they have been given about how to implement these skills. I also stress that they can refer to Paul Hauck's (1991) book if they need to be reminded of any of the theoretical ideas concerning self-acceptance. In this way they can maintain and extend the gains that they have achieved over the past ten weeks.

In the past, a number of groups have decided to meet after the formal group sessions have ended to continue working towards greater self-acceptance in a self-help capacity. These self-help groups have generally met once a month and I have allowed them to consult with me on an *ad hoc* basis if they disagree on any issue. This has proved to be a particularly useful way of helping group members to maintain and extend their gains.

I mentioned this latter point to the present group and they enthusiastically decided to meet once every six weeks to carry on their self-acceptance work.

ELICITING FEEDBACK FROM GROUP MEMBERS ON THE GROUP

Your final task is to elicit feedback from group members concerning their reactions to the group as a therapeutic and educational experience. In doing so I suggest that you ask them the following questions:

1. What did you learn from the group?
2. What did you hope to learn from the group but didn't?
3. In what ways was the group helpful to you?
4. In what ways was the group not helpful to you?
5. How do you think the group can be improved?

Over the years that I have run self-acceptance groups, I have made a number of modifications to the group on the basis of group members' feedback. Thus, in response to such feedback, I have extended the group from eight weeks to ten weeks and have provided group members with written instructions to help them practice at home the skills that I have taught them in the group. The curriculum that I have presented in this group is the latest version, but in the spirit of being open to consumer views, I will probably refine it even further. Thus, as a result of the present group's feedback I am planning to write my own self-acceptance self-help book which I will integrate into the curriculum. My work in running self-acceptance groups is, like the self itself, an organic process.

This marks the end of both the group sessions and the book. I hope you have found it valuable. I would be grateful for any feedback you have to give me c/o the publisher. Thank you for your interest.

Answers to the Self-acceptance Quiz

1. False   2. False   3. True   4. False   5. False   6. True

If you gave any incorrect answers, re-read Chapters 2 and 5, or read Chapter 3 in Paul Hauck's (1991) book.

Appendix 1

THREE TECHNIQUES FOR TEACHING THE REBT CONCEPT OF UNCONDITIONAL SELF-ACCEPTANCE

There are many techniques that you can use to teach group members the REBT concept of unconditional self-acceptance (see Palmer, 1997, for a review). The three techniques that I most commonly use are (i) the Big I – little i technique (Lazarus, 1977); (ii) the three-circles technique and (iii) the two-scales technique.

THE BIG I – LITTLE i TECHNIQUE

When I use this technique (Figure A1.1) I teach group members that the Big I represents their 'self' and the little i's, which are inside the Big I, represent the myriad of different aspects of their 'self'. As I discussed in Chapter 5, I show them that it is perfectly sensible for a person to rate his or her aspects (or little i's), but it is illegitimate to rate his or her 'self' (or Big I) because it is too complex to merit such a rating.

THE THREE-CIRCLES TECHNIQUE

In Figure A1.2 a tick represents a good aspect of a person, a cross represents a bad aspect of a person and a circle represents a neutral aspect of a person. I first ask group members what they would call a person with only good aspects (represented by the circle with ticks). They reply: 'a saint', 'perfect' or 'a good person'. I then ask them what they would call a

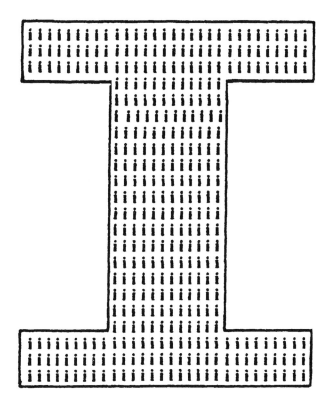

Figure A1.1: The big I – little i

person with only bad aspects (represented by the circle with crosses). They reply: 'a bad person', 'evil' or 'the devil'. Finally, I ask them what they would call a person with a mixture of good, bad and neutral aspects (represented by the circle with ticks, crosses and circles). They reply: 'normal', 'ordinary' or 'fallible'.

I then show them that once they focus on a bad aspect in the fallible circle and demand that they must not have this aspect, they transform themselves from being 'fallible' to being 'bad' because they are demanding that they should be thoroughly good. Then I show them that if they focused on the same bad aspect in the fallible circle and preferred, but not demanded, that they did not have this aspect they would feel badly about that aspect, but would still accept themselves as fallible.

Thus, the three-circle technique is a good method to show how demands lead to self-depreciation.

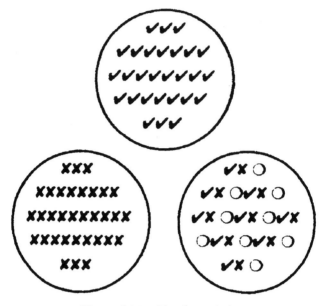

Figure A1.2: The three circles

THE TWO-SCALES TECHNIQUE

When I use this technique, I explain to group members that rating aspects of themselves is fine and will not lead to emotional disturbance as long as they 'weigh' these aspects on the scale that moves (Figure A1.3). If they rate an aspect as good, the scale goes up, and when they rate an aspect as bad, it goes down. To ensure that they do not rate their 'self' as good for having a good aspect and as bad for having a bad aspect, it is important that they put their 'self' on the scale that doesn't move. This scale has a fixed position called 'fallible human being'.

I then explain that emotional problems result when they put their aspects *and* their 'self' on the scale that moves. This may not seem apparent when the scale reads 'That's a good aspect, I am worth while', but this 'read-out' implies that if the aspect was bad then the person would be rated as 'worthless' or 'less worthy'. So it is best to use the scale that moves for aspects and the fixed scale for weighing the 'self'.

Figure A1.3: The two scales

Appendix 2

POSSIBLE REASONS FOR NOT DOING SELF-HELP ASSIGNMENTS

(TO BE COMPLETED BY GROUP MEMBERS)

The following is a list of reasons that previous group members have given for not doing their self-help assignments during the course of the group. Because the speed of improvement depends primarily on the amount of self-help assignments that you are willing to do, it is of great importance to pinpoint any reasons that you may have for not doing this work. It is important to look for these reasons at the time that you feel a reluctance to do your assignment or a desire to put off doing it. Hence, it is best to fill out this questionnaire at that time. If you have any difficulty filling out this form, it might be best to do it together during a group session. (Rate each statement by ringing 'T' (True) 'F' (False). 'T' indicates that you agree with it; 'F' means the statement does not apply at this time.)

1. It seems that nothing can help me so there is no point in trying.   T/F
2. It wasn't clear; I didn't understand what I had to do.   T/F
3. I thought that the particular method the group leader had suggested would not be helpful. I didn't really see the value of it.   T/F
4. It seemed too hard.   T/F
5. I am willing to do self-help assignments, but I keep forgetting.   T/F
6. I did not have enough time. I was too busy.   T/F
7. If I do something the group leader suggests I do it's not as good as if I come up with my own ideas.   T/F
8. I don't really believe I can do anything to help myself.   T/F
9. I have the impression the group leader is trying to boss me around or control me.   T/F

10. I worry about the group leader's disapproval. I believe
    that what I do just won't be good enough for him or her.   T/F
11. I felt too bad, sad, nervous or upset (underline the
    appropriate word(s)) to do it.   T/F
12. I would have found doing the homework assignment too
    upsetting.   T/F
13. It was too much to do.   T/F
14. It's too much like going back to school again.   T/F
15. It seemed to be mainly for the group leader's benefit.   T/F
16. Self-help assignments have no place in a self-acceptance
    group.   T/F
17. Because of the progress I've made these assignments are
    likely to be of no further benefit to me.   T/F
18. Because these assignments have not been helpful in
    the past, I couldn't see the point of doing this one.   T/F
19. I don't agree with this particular approach to develop
    self-acceptance.   T/F
20. OTHER REASONS (please write them).

REFERENCES

Beck, A.T., Rush, A.J., Shaw, B.F. & Emery, G. (1979). *Cognitive Therapy of Depression*. New York: Guilford.

Bond, F.W. & Dryden, W. (1996). Modifying irrational control and certainty beliefs: Clinical recommendations based upon research. In W. Dryden (Ed.), *Research in Counselling and Psychotherapy: Practical Applications*. London: Sage.

Carkhuff, R.R. (1983). *The Art of Helping*, 5th edition. Amherst, MS: Human Resource Development Press.

DiGiuseppe, R. (1991). Comprehensive cognitive disputing in RET. In M.E. Bernard (Ed.), *Using Rational-Emotive Therapy Effectively*. New York: Plenum Press.

Dryden, W. (1985). Cognition without ignition. *Contemporary Psychology*, **30**(10), 788–789.

Dryden, W. (1987). *Current Issues in Rational-Emotive Therapy*. Beckenham: Croom Helm.

Dryden, W. (1994). *Invitation to Rational-Emotive Psychology*. London: Whurr.

Dryden, W. (1995). *Brief Rational Emotive Behaviour Therapy*. Chichester: Wiley.

Dryden, W. (1996). *Inquiries in Rational Emotive Behaviour Therapy*. London: Sage.

Egan, G. (1994). *The Skilled Helper*, 6th edition. Pacific Grove, CA: Brooks/Cole.

Ellis, A. (1959). Requisite conditions for basic personality change. *Journal of Consulting Psychology*, **23**: 538–540.

Ellis, A. (1962). *Reason and Emotion in Psychotherapy*. Secaucus, NJ: Lyle Stuart.

Ellis, A. (1985). *Overcoming Resistance: Rational-Emotive Therapy with Difficult Clients*. New York: Springer.

Ellis, A. (1991). The revised ABCs of rational-emotive therapy. *Journal of Rational-Emotive and Cognitive-Behavior Therapy*, **9**(3), 139–172.

Ellis, A. (1994). *Reason and Emotion in Psychotherapy*. Revised and updated edition. New York: Birch Lane Press.

Gandy, G.L. (1995). *Mental Health Rehabilitation: Disputing Irrational Beliefs*. Springfield, IL: Charles C. Thomas.

Hauck, P. (1991). *Hold your Head up High*. London: Sheldon.

Knaus, W.J. & Haberstroh, N. (1993). A rational-emotive education program to help disruptive mentally retarded clients develop self-control. In W. Dryden & L.K. Hill (Eds), *Innovations in Rational-Emotive Therapy*. Newbury Park, CA: Sage.

Lazarus, A.A. (1977). Toward an egoless state of being. In A. Ellis & R.M. Grieger (Eds), *Handbook of Rational-Emotive Therapy*, Volume 1. New York: Springer.

Maslow, A. (1968). *Toward a Psychology of Being*. New York: Van Nostrand Reinhold.

Maultsby, M.C. Jr. (1984). *Rational Behavior Therapy*. Englewood Cliffs, NJ: Prentice-Hall.

Neenan, M. & Dryden, W. (1996). *Dealing with Difficulties in Rational Emotive Behavior Therapy*. London: Whurr.

Palmer, S. (1997). Self-acceptance: Concept, techniques and interventions. *The Rational Emotive Behaviour Therapist*, **5**(1): 4–30.

Rogers, C.R. (1957). The necessary and sufficient conditions of therapeutic personality change. *Journal of Consulting Psychology*, **21**: 95–103.

Rosenthal, R. & Jacobson, L. (1968). *Pygmalion in the Classroom: Teacher Expectation and Pupils' Intellectual Development*. New York: Holt.

Yalom, I. (1995). *The Theory and Practice of Group Psychotherapy*, 4th edition. New York: Basic Books.

INDEX

Index compiled by Sylvia Potter

Wiley Series in Brief Therapy and Counselling ...

Brief Therapy with Couples
An Integrative Approach
Maria Gilbert and **Diana Shmukler**

A concise, practical guide for couples with relationship problems, that relates therapy to the cultural, racial and religious context of relationships, as well as key issues like parenting and same-sex relationships.

0-471-96206-6 218pp October 1996 pbk

Brief Rational Emotive Behaviour Therapy
Windy Dryden

Provides concepts in the context of a brief therapy process. Practitioners will find useful insights and guidance on applying these methods throughout the process of therapy, including building the working alliance, assessment, formulation, and work in sessions and outside the sessions. The whole process is illustrated by a case study which reflects the problems of real life work with a client.

0-471-95786-0 244pp September 1995 pbk

Brief Therapeutic Consultations
An Approach to Systemic Counselling
Eddy Street and **Jim Downey**

This book provides a practical framework which describes how to construct a client-counsellor relationship which is brief, collaborative and consultative in purpose but therapeutic in form.

0-471-96343-7 174pp August 1996 pbk

Counselling Couples in Relationships
An Introduction to the RELATE Approach
Christopher Butler and **Victoria Joyce**

This book presents the theories and practices which together make up the RELATE approach in an open and approachable way.

0-471-97778-0 252pp December 1997 pbk

Visit the Wiley home page http:\\www.wiley.co.uk